The Truth Is Out There

Christian Faith and the Classics of TV Science Fiction

Thomas Bertonneau
and Kim Paffenroth

BrazosPress
Grand Rapids, Michigan

Published by Brazos Press
a division of Baker Publishing Group
P.O. Box 6287, Grand Rapids, MI 49516-6287
www.brazospress.com

Printed in the United States of America

Library of Congress Cataloging-in-Publication Data
Bertonneau, Thomas.
The truth is out there : Christian faith and the classics of TV science fiction / Thomas Bertonneau and Kim Paffenroth.
p. cm.
Includes bibliographical references and index.
ISBN 10: 1-58743-126-2 (pbk.)
ISBN 978-1-58743-126-5 (pbk.)
1. Science fiction television programs. 2. Television broadcasting—Religious aspects—Christianity. I. Paffenroth, Kim, 1966– II. Title.
PN1992.8.S35B47 2006
791.45′66—dc22 2005037355

Dedicated to
James Doohan (1920–2005)

CONTENTS

Acknowledgments

Thanks are due to our colleagues in the Religious Studies Department at Iona College and in the English Department at the State University of New York at Oswego, and especially to our deans—Alex Eodice at Iona, and Sarah Varhus at SUNY Oswego. Our library staffs also deserve special thanks—particularly Richard Palladino, Kathleen Pascuzzi, Matt McKee, and Ed Helmrich at Ryan Library; and Mary Loe at Penfield Library. Outside of our two institutions, both our academic and nonacademic friends have also provided valuable feedback, especially Richard Cocks, John Doody, Scott Field, Victor Gibbs, David Hill, Marylu Hill, Robert Kennedy, Dan Morehead, Andrew Murphy, Jim Pangborn, and Brian Weimer.

Introduction

Science, Religion, and Storytelling

> The scientific spirit cannot come first. It presupposes the renunciation of a former preference for . . . magical causality. . . .
>
> The invention of science is [thus] not the reason that there are no longer witch-hunts, but the fact that there are no longer witch-hunts is the reason that science has been invented. The scientific spirit, like the spirit of enterprise in an economy, is a by-product of the profound action of the Gospel text.
>
> René Girard, *The Scapegoat*

Science and Religion

Popular discussion at the beginning of the twenty-first century typically sets science and religion at odds, portraying them as incompatible. The idea is that, as soon as one has adopted the scientific point of view—presented as the uniquely valid view—one can no longer legitimately traffic with religion, particularly with biblical religion; or if one were religious, then one could not possibly also be scientific in one's thinking. Never mind that many supposedly scientific theories—such as the notion of the earth as a single living entity, or "Gaia"—give the impression of a lapse into quite primitive conceptual categories. Science, under this argument, operates rationally, religion irrationally. The idea has gained enormous purchase in modern Western society in the last 250 years, especially among those who fervently praise what they call secular civilization and the progress of technology. It is nevertheless a false, vulgar idea, rightfully offensive both to scientists and to believers, and especially to those who are both.

But the complementary counterclaim made by some religious people that science is an enemy of religion is similarly distorted and false. Not only is the systematic, rational investigation of nature—for this is how to define science—not incompatible with religious conviction, but it is essential to making religious beliefs reasonable and persuasive. The French theologian, philosopher, mathematician, and scientist Blaise Pascal (1623–62) put it bluntly: "If we offend the principles of reason our religion will be absurd and ridiculous" (*Pensées,* fr. 273 [173]). And Saint Augustine (354–430 CE) stated it more fully:

> Usually, even a non-Christian knows something about the earth, the heavens, and the other elements of this world, about the motion and orbit of the stars and even their size and relative positions, about the predictable eclipses of the sun and moon, the cycles of the years and the seasons, about the kinds of animals, shrubs, stones, and so forth, and this knowledge he holds to as being certain from reason and experience. Now, it is a disgraceful and dangerous thing for an infidel to hear a Christian, presumably giving the meaning of Holy Scripture, talking nonsense on these topics; and we should take all means to prevent such an embarrassing situation, in which people show up vast ignorance in a Christian

and laugh it to scorn. (Augustine, *The Literal Meaning of Genesis,* ACW 41)

It is not scientific investigation and knowledge that is an enemy of Christian belief; scientific ignorance is the real enemy that Christians are to defeat through reason and study. Rightly understood, increasing our knowledge of creation results in greater understanding and appreciation of the Creator.

Science had two great moments in Western history, and at both of those, it seized hold of the minds of thoughtful people within the framework of a religious, theological orientation. The first took place in the ancient Greek world some 2,500 years ago and is called by historians the Ionian Revolution. The second took place beginning around four hundred years ago, mainly in England and France; it is generally called the Scientific Revolution proper and is bound up with the Protestant Reformation and with the philosophical movement of the Enlightenment. Both moments were characterized by great religious as well as scientific fervor and development, and significantly for our study, it is also at these two junctures that science-fiction literature came into being.

Science Fiction and Religion

The *Timaeus,* one of the dialogues of the Greek philosopher Plato (428–347 BCE) bids fair to be considered the first science-fiction story, and it has exercised a fascination down through the ages. Much of the dialogue is given over—significantly—to a discussion of the idea that the world, which is beautiful, was created by a god—"The World Maker"—who is rational and moral. Those who attune their minds toward an appreciation of the beauty in nature and who contemplate goodness and justice gain an intuition of God. In the course of the dialogue, Socrates listens to the tale, told by the title character, about the fabled ancient kingdom of Atlantis. Nine thousand years before his own time, Timaeus says, the power of Atlantis made itself felt in the world. Zeus rewarded its people for their piety and made them prosperous. When the Atlanteans decided to use their technical prowess and their wealth to conquer other nations, however, Zeus decided to punish them: he sent the earthquakes and waves that engulfed the island-continent and destroyed its people and all their wondrous works. We see the obvious parallelism with the Old Testament story of the Tower of Babel, but Plato develops in detail a theme that is present only in a parabolic way in the biblical episode—the idea that, in awe over their own mechanical and practical achievements, a people can come to think of itself in inflated terms and forget its humility before the heavenly powers to whom it owes its existence. Saint Paul also vividly describes this sinful dynamic in words that could easily have been applied to the arrogant Atlanteans and Zeus's striking down of them:

> For what can be known about God is plain to them, because God has shown it to them. Ever since the creation of the world his invisible nature, namely, his eternal power and deity, has been clearly perceived in the things that have been made. So they are without excuse; for although they knew God they did not honor him as God or give thanks to him, but they became futile in their thinking and their senseless minds were darkened. Claiming to be wise, they became fools. (Rom. 1:19–22)

Greater knowledge of creatures should lead to greater awe and gratitude toward their Creator, as Paul believes God is "clearly perceived in the things that have been made," but it all too often leads only to a worsening of the human creature's own pride, arrogance, and violence. And this salutary lesson was expressed thousands of years ago in the first attempt at science fiction, as well as in the New Testament.

Plato's dialogue inspired a host of later stories in which explorers discover a technological utopia in a remote part of the world. The Sicilian Greek Euhemerus (second century BCE) spun such a yarn, with a serious purpose in mind, setting his island-nation of enlightened philosophers in the Indian Ocean. The wise gymnosophists of Euhemerus's story prove themselves through their knowledge that the myths that the Greeks and other people have inherited from the remote past about the so-called gods are in error. Because of their naiveté, ancient peoples attributed a superhuman status to kings and warriors and other impressive individuals; in the course of many generations of storytelling, this status got lifted up even further into godhood. Thus, Zeus would be the inflated memory of a primordial king and conqueror. There is a real god—typically singular—but he has nothing to do with the false gods of the sagas. We notice that Euhemerus, like Plato, makes a distinction between appearances (the mythic version of the gods) and reality (the philosophical intuition of the true deity). Thus, one outcome of the moral and religious critique begun by the Greeks was the emergence of an important new category: the moral and philosophical idea of *superstition,* of a debased form of religiosity based only on false appearances and outward forms, that is contrasted with true belief in the real God. Plato makes much of the superstition theme in his dialogues—in *Phaedrus,* for example.

But at about the same time that Plato's teacher Socrates (ca. 470–399 BCE) was active, the Greek scientist/philosopher Democritus (ca. 460–375 BCE) arrived at another notion that would have ramifying consequences in later centuries—indeed in later millennia. Like Thales (ca. 625–546 BCE), Democritus *wondered*—the word has a peculiar force in Greek—about the inner nature of matter and of material things. He too believed that whatever exists—all the disparate things of the world—must have a common basis. He proposed as his solution to the problem of the underlying unity of diverse appearances the idea of the *atoms*. Everything that exists, Democritus argued, consists of a combination of tiny, invisible, and indivisible particles, restricted in their species, of which however an infinite number of any given species may be imagined. Each species of atom has a particular shape, so that like tends to hook on to like, although atoms of different species can also combine. Any combination of different kinds of atoms, moreover, is subject to the law of dissolution: as the atoms can join to make the familiar shapes of the natural world, so also can they come disjoined—and so return to the eternally circulating reservoir of underlying atomic material. One finds in Democritus's view an undeniably skeptical element, as Socrates himself noted in his criticism of atomistic speculation. Said Socrates, as recorded by Plato, Democritus's scheme leaves little room, if any, for such topics as God or the soul. Socrates nevertheless appreciated the elegance of atomistic thinking and responded to it. In *Timaeus,* the World Maker fashions the universe from stores of tiny, invisible, and indivisible particles that differ only in their geometric shape—pyramids, hexahedrons, octahedrons, and so forth. It lies in the genius of the World Maker to construct from a limited *range* of basic modules the infinite variety of the sensible universe. We see how, while the hypothesis of the atoms can threaten belief in God or the soul, it can also be turned to bolster such belief. Again, scientific study of the material world is neither inimical nor equivalent to faith. What it does mostly is strengthen the human intellect, and a person who already has a strong faith will find it strengthened by such investigation, and a person who is adamant in their disbelief will also find their disbelief strengthened.

Plato could acknowledge a material world while stipulating that the soul did not find its birth there but descended into its incarnation from the heavenly, immaterial realm. Plato would even argue, following cues from his teacher Socrates, that the soul needed to be redeemed from the material world. Platonism would become a kind of religion in the period of the Roman Empire. It would appeal to people who felt that a world empire based on the will of an all-too-human emperor and the might of his armies—a world subject to rebellion and suppression—offered to the spiritually inclined individual no true home, but only a wicked, inhospitable place foreign to the best in humanity. And when the Roman Empire was Christianized in the fourth century, Platonism became the dominant philosophical influence on developing Christian theology, which itself already had a very similar image of the faithful as sojourners and strangers on this sinful earth:

> These all died in faith, not having received what was promised, but having seen it and greeted it from afar, and having acknowledged that they were strangers and exiles on the earth. For people who speak thus make it clear that they are seeking a homeland. . . . But as it is, they desire a better country, that is, a heavenly one. Therefore God is not ashamed to be called their God, for he has prepared for them a city. (Heb. 11:13–14, 16)

Saint Jerome (ca. 340–420 CE) and especially Augustine saw the compatibility between Platonism and Christianity on this and other points.

This Platonist and Christian intuition, that the soul is an alienated sojourner in the world, informs the exploration narrative in two of Plutarch's dialogues, *On the Decline of Oracles* and *On the Face in the Moon.* Plutarch (46–120 CE), one of the most popular writers and intellectual figures of his day, insists in *The Decline* that the old gods are dead. He has one of his speakers tell how, on a reconnaissance of remote islands north of Britain, he heard a great commotion followed by the shout, "The great god Pan is dead!" *On the Face in the Moon* discusses a thesis first put forward by the atomistic thinker Epicurus (ca. 341–270 BCE) that there is a "plurality of worlds." Where the ancients thought of the stars and other celestial objects as gods, Epicurus explained them simply as other suns attended by other worlds, like the earth, and he supposed that these other worlds must be peopled by intelligences similar in character to human beings. Plutarch presents the argument that the moon is such a world and that, given the plenitude and goodness of *the* god—the World Maker—it must be peopled by an appropriate lunar humanity. As did Epicurus, Plutarch assumes that, as one moves up from the earth toward the heavens, the quality of matter becomes ever more refined. He believes therefore that the lunar humanity will possess organs of sense more keen than our own and that its mental processes, less encumbered by gross matter, will likewise be swifter and surer than ours. Another theme shared by both dialogues is the moral imperfection of earthly life under the Roman Empire, the social and intellectual corruption of which figures in many religious expressions of the first century. Plutarch's *Isis and Osiris* gives vent to his concern for the salvation of the soul from the trammels of matter and his sense that the inherited religious forms no longer answer to such a purpose. A writer of the next generation after Plutarch, Lucian of Samosata (115–200 CE), articulated a similar combination of anxiety and longing in his essay *On the Syrian Goddess*. And it was this same Lucian who first combined the notions of nautical exploration and interplanetary travel in his remarkable *True History*, generally dated around 160 CE.

True History is in every way unexpected. Its narrator and protagonist describes himself as a young man of energy who finds himself utterly bored by the known world; given the sentiments in *The Syrian Goddess*, however, we might also say that his boredom stems from the restlessness and dissatisfaction of his soul, its unexpressed intuition that it is not at home in *this world*. Noticing that sailors have for centuries not dared to venture into the Atlantic main, Lucian's explorer constructs a special ship, stronger than any other and designed to brave the high seas; recruits a complement of hardy souls; and weighs his anchor to attempt the west. Contrary to popular opinion, ancient people never believed that the world was flat and that one might sail off the edge. Lucian, an educated Greek-speaking Syrian under Roman sovereignty, knew, as did Plato, that the world was a globe; but he did not know what lay westward of England. Our narrator, then, in a spirit of enterprise, boldly goes—to borrow a well-known motto—where no man has gone before. After many weeks of voyaging, the ship discovers a beautiful island, and the crew makes a landing; extraordinarily handsome people greet them and invite them to hospitality. Gradually, Lucian reveals that his explorers have made port in the Isles of the Blest, fabled in Greek and Latin lore as the home of the heroes after their earthly passing. Now, however, these isles have become the retirement home, so to speak, of the Homeric gods. One of them, Hermes, explains to the travelers that he and his fellow gods had grown disgusted with the barbarity of human worship and of the way in which people represented the gods in poetry and art—so they quit their Olympian habitation (too close to humanity) for these farther, insular parts, where they need not constantly witness the sad spectacle of human vanity, ferocity, and superstition. We note that the Roman Empire was supposed, according to its own propaganda, to represent a great *Pax* or "Peace." Lucian has cleverly and perhaps at some risk put a round moral criticism of the status quo of political and social affairs into the mouth of a deity. In another episode, reminiscent of the story of Jonah, a gigantic whale swallows the ship. The explorers discover inside the whale several competing civilizations stemming from earlier hapless wanderers into the monstrous maw: the narrator and his shipmates help a community of human beings fight off an attack from horrific lobster-men. The most bizarre sequence is yet to come.

Escaping the whale, the explorers cross paths with a colossal waterspout that whisks them right off the earth, whirls them through space, and deposits them on the moon. The Lunarians (Lucian, writing in Greek, calls them Selenites) are a wise people who run their affairs according to philosophical principles. They are currently at war with the Kingdom of the Sun. The protagonist and his mates agree to help the Lunarians. Lucian describes a great battle in the stellar spaces with outrageous inventions like giant flea-riders, towering garlic-throwers, and similarly scaled poppy-seed shooters. The Lunarians seem to have the upper hand when reinforcements arrive from the star Sirius to help the Solar armies. The combatants conclude an armistice, however, and sign a treaty. The voyagers manage to return to the earth and set down in an unknown sea. There are no referents to tell them where they are. They are lost. The story breaks off. But this is not because the manuscript is fragmentary; it is because Lucian has abruptly ended his tale, the exaggerated and comic elements of which have misled interpreters to regard it as a meaningless fillip, a "tall tale" with no other significance. On the contrary: Lucian gives us in his baroque fantasy an allegory of human existence as the quest of the anxious soul for an obscure goal, which would be its healing or salvation or return home, but whose fulfillment cannot be found in *this world.* Odysseus, in Homer's great poem of geographical wanderings, can come home; Lucian's heirs of Odysseus cannot.

Before addressing—briefly—the status of the "marvelous romance" at the beginning of the modern scientific period, a word should be added about a story written long after Lucian's *True History,* possibly by a writer who knew Lucian's tale (for the Irish monks preserved their Greek). *The Voyage of Saint Brendan* (written down around 600 or 700 CE) concerns the intrepid missionary work of an early Irish Christian, Brendan, who lived in the middle of the sixth century. Like Lucian's uneasy adventurer, Brendan feels a stirring in his soul, but not for inchoate voyaging in search of a goal that remains seen only as through a glass darkly. Rather, Brendan takes heed of an angel who commands him to take the Word of God—the gospel—westward to the unknown and presumably unredeemed Gentiles who live in the ocean lands beyond the misty horizon. He takes with him a handful of companions, and they sail into the horizon for forty days, encountering many strange visions along the way, including an island that turns out actually to be a great whale, into whose maw they narrowly miss falling. After forty days more, they discover a vast land, which the angel refers to as "the promised land." They establish a chapel and deposit the Holy Scriptures and preach the Word. Then, as the angel confirms that they have fulfilled their sacred charge, they find themselves transported miraculously back to Ireland, where they began. The Brendan author might well have drawn on real accounts of brave journeys made in their *cuirraghs* by the Irish missionaries—who were already in Iceland in 700 CE when the Vikings first got there. Certainly, Brendan himself existed. Yet the meaning of the story transcends any empirical details. To sail into the unfamiliar sea befalls Brendan as a moral imperative; the world into which he goes appears in the tale as beautiful—even its moments of terror testify to the greatness of the unseen Creator. If the people who live in foreign distances would strike us as odd or barbarous, nevertheless they would be human too, also sons and daughters of the Creator, who require redemption as much as we. It was in a similar spirit almost a thousand years later that a Dominican friar in the Caribbean, Bartolomé de Las Casas (1484–1566), wrote to the Spanish government in Madrid about the mistreatment of the native peoples. They were souls, too, he reminded his superiors. In the familiar television series *Star Trek,* this takes the name of "the Prime Directive," the protection of vulnerable people from powerful forces that might overwhelm them, sap their morale, or wreck their material culture.

To write of Bartolomé de Las Casas is to bring us into a century, the sixteenth, of great religious ferment in Europe—erupting into violence and war—but also one of scientific revival. The astronomer Johannes Kepler (1571–1630) began as a theology student in Tübingen, a Protestant enclave of the Catholic Hapsburg realm. He switched to mathematics and astronomy and went on to work with Tycho Brahe, in those days the living astronomer of greatest renown. Kepler translated Plutarch's *On the Face in the Moon,* discovered the elliptical character of the planetary orbits, revived the Heraclitean and Pythagorean idea of "the Harmony of the Worlds," and published, in the final year of his life, a sequel to Lucian's *True History,* his *Somnium,* or "Dream." Kepler's mother had once stood accused of witchcraft, and the trial in her case extended, by delay after delay, down through the years; she died, having been shown the instruments of torture, within a year of her acquittal. A Lutheran Christian of mystical inclination, Kepler grasped the difference between superstition, on the one hand, and revealed faith, on the other; he also saw that the discoveries of science served the cause of faith by demonstrating the marvel, the poetic inner workings, of creation.

In *Somnium,* Kepler pretends to have taken possession of the papers of one Duracotas, an Icelander; Duracotas's mother, a witch, imparted to him the secret of attracting certain creatures from an island in the sky, Levania, who in their turn can convey human beings through the stellar spaces to the moon. After studying astronomy in Denmark with Brahe (the motif is again autobiographical), Duracotas returns to Iceland, ascends the slopes of Mount Hekla, calls down the Levanians, and bids them ferry him to the lunar globe. Once there, he reports in scientific detail on what he sees: the harsh conditions of the moon have pressed life into diverse and monstrous forms, although, in the heat-inspired madness of the great hordes on the far side of the moon, one can only see a metaphor for the bloody disruptions, the irrational persecutions of all kinds, the grisliness of life that had overtaken Europe, supposedly civilized, supposedly Christian, in the period of sectarian wars. Kepler's voluminous other writings sport everywhere the names of Democritus, Leucippus, Plutarch, Plato, Pythagoras, yet he never ceased his insistence, even under duress, on the fixity and sincerity of his Christian beliefs.

In giving us a cosmic perspective on ourselves, science and science fiction restore to us a proper humility—a meekness before the awe of creation appropriate to our station. Reginald Scott, an exact contemporary of Kepler, was writing in Edinburgh along exactly these same lines, noting, in his *Discovery of Witchcraft* (1599), that the persecution of so-called witches required of the persecutors a belief in vulgar superstition inconsistent with both the Gospels and the emerging picture of natural causality. If one believed in creation, Scott argued, then one could hardly believe that mere human conjurors could casually reorder God's laws; if witches cannot make magic, then they cannot be guilty of what their accusers charge them. Kepler's arguments about the laws of nature have the same ethical import even as they aim at sharpening the understanding of the physical order of the cosmos. Thus, in inventing the modern genre of science fiction proper, Kepler also infused it with cosmological and theological speculation, uniting themes from ancient Greek *and* from New Testament thinking.

Such a deeply theological vision of science fiction is shown in the works of Plato, Lucian, and Kepler, and it continues in the classics of science fiction literature, which almost invariably exhibit religious themes—from Edgar Allan Poe's pseudo-Platonic dialogues of cosmic catastrophe and the fate of the soul; through H. G. Wells's *War of the Worlds,* which ends with an invocation of deity; to the works of Walter M. Miller, a Roman Catholic; Philip K. Dick, an unaffiliated Platonist Christian who incorporated elements of Coptic Christianity into his strange novels; and Clifford Simak, whose gentle robots and mentally enhanced canines take up the gospel in a far future when humanity has become decadent and has ceased to care about such matters as the soul or salvation. Of course, science fiction is most emphatically present in the last forty years as a television phenomenon—but here, too, the old themes persist—as we shall see.

Considering the degree to which the foregoing part of this introduction has dealt with literary science fiction, it would certainly not be unfair for a perceptive reader to pose the question, at this point, of why we have devoted our study to the classics of television science fiction. As Judaism and Christianity are scriptural religions, it would seem logical to seek their influence on science fiction taken as a purely literary phenomenon. While it is true that an exegesis, say, of Stapledon or Dick might be rich and brilliant in its discovery of particular influences and adaptations, the result would likely appeal mainly to literary critics, religious studies professors, and other scholars of the humanities. Then again Stapledon is a fairly difficult read and there is no particular reason why any given individual ought to have read him; so, too, with Dick, who, despite the devotion of his fans, remains a rather esoteric interest. While we might eagerly recommend either Stapledon or Dick or both to inquiring parties, we would never, therefore, take it for granted that busy people, no matter how thoughtful, ought to stop what they are doing to dedicate themselves to a specialist's time-consuming chore. We seek a wider, more general audience.

Let us propose a parallel. We suppose that most college graduates have read a half a dozen Shakespeare plays, a few poems by William Wordsworth and John Keats, and maybe a novel by Joseph Conrad or F. Scott Fitzgerald; but we do not suppose, for there is no reason to do so, that most college graduates have read—or even *should have* read—*The Golden Bowl* by Henry James or *The Egyptian* by Mika Waltari. Meritorious James and Waltari certainly are, but tough propositions both, whose works lie beyond the reasonable demands of a sound, basic education. On the other hand, we might remind people of a sound, basic education that a lavishly mounted 1972 BBC production of *The Golden Bowl* does impressive justice to James's ethical vision, and that, given the production's availability in the new viewable formats, such people might both enjoy and be edified by a serious encounter with it. Similarly, Waltari's novel, long out of print, assumes a good deal of specialized historical and theological knowledge on the part of its readers; but director Michael Curtiz's 1954 film, while maintaining faith with Waltari's word, makes Waltari's basic insights dramatically clear in an immediately understandable way. Enough people will remember the BBC *Golden Bowl* from its broadcast in America as part of PBS's "Masterpiece Theater," or will have caught *The Egyptian* on Turner Classic Movies, that a discussion of one or the other would be plausible, given a few reminders. An intelligent viewer, reminded of the BBC *Golden Bowl,* might readily be persuaded to see in it, as James meant, an illustration of marriage as a manifestation of faith. The same intelligent viewer, reminded of Curtiz's film of *The Egyptian,* might readily be persuaded to see in it, as Waltari meant, an illustration of the way in which prebiblical religion often anticipates Hebrew prophecy or the Gospels. This affording of a view into important but esoteric matters has always been one of the values of popular culture in a Western, Judeo-Christian context.

Jesus spoke in parables—stories of a popular type and with characters personifying moral ideas—readily graspable by unlettered people. He did not present metaphysical treatises. The writing down of the Gospels in common rather than literary Greek had the same aim of making an important message as readily available as possible to the largest number of people. In the Middle Ages, when literacy belonged only to an elite, monks and priests occasionally turned thespian to act out the Mystery Plays according to a regular calendar to familiarize the many with a scripture that they themselves could not directly access because they could not read the written word. By a wonderful irony, the Mystery Plays became literature. The classic Mystery Play, *Everyman,* figured until recently in the high-school English curriculum; today, most college graduates will have met up with it in their English literature survey. In this way high culture has always culled and relied on popular culture. We should remember that in the fourth and fifth centuries CE aristocratic pagans regarded Christianity as nearly beneath notice and noteworthy *only* in being the irrational cult of the proletariat.

There is one further question that our hypothetical perceptive observer might pose: *Why television rather than the movies?* We reply to this question fully in our concluding chapter. Suffice it here to say that, whatever its intrinsic limitations, television has at least one advantage over cinema. A typical entertainment film runs two hours. A serial television program might, so long as it sustains itself through multiple seasons, run into hundreds of hours. Quantity never guarantees quality, but it does, as in epic poetry or the monumental novel, open up the possibility of tracing human cause and effect over a vast distance—down through the generations. Science fiction, dealing as it does with cosmic vistas and millennial eras, must therefore find in the seriality of television drama a natural medium for development of its visionary largeness.

The six television shows that we have selected for our investigation of the way in which science fiction assimilates the themes of faith stand in this tradition of serious "middle culture," as it might be called, a dimension where the forms of popular culture and the content of high culture communicate with one another to the enrichment of both. Few of our readers will be thoroughly familiar with all six shows (we list them below), but most will have a good, even an enthusiastic, grasp of at least one of them, and probably an awareness of the others. Precisely in offering both the familiar and the unfamiliar, our selection, we hope, will entice readers to explore beyond the horizons of their existing interest. We hope, indeed, that we will ultimately entice readers to explore beyond the merits of television science fiction, as such, into the merits of the *literary* science fiction that inspires it.

We begin with the classic British television series *Doctor Who*. Saint Paul warns the early Christian congregations that they must be vigilant against the "powers." Paul is speaking not only of direct solicitations by malicious beings, but other, ostensibly intellectual allurements, such as those of Gnostic system builders. *Doctor Who* features a protagonist whose mission is to help ethical people who have succumbed to the glamour of spiritually baroque promises disguised as utopian or redemptive schemes. Many of the Doctor's nemeses bear a strong resemblance to the competitors of Christianity in Paul's day. The Doctor's own moral principle is humble and commonsensical, springing ultimately from his love for humanity. Parallels between the Doctor's fantastic antagonists (the emotionless Daleks, the Simon Magus-like "Dark Master") and twentieth-century ideologues permit viewers of the series to see that Paul's critique of false creeds applies just as well to the doctrinal struggles of the modern period.

Our next chapter takes us from the continuing battle between good and evil to a life of pursuing the good, showing how television's most famous science-fiction series, *Star Trek,* consistently portrays broadly Christian ethics. The dynamics between Spock and McCoy show how neither pure reason nor pure emotion are adequate to direct our actions, but every time they clash, they must compromise and cooperate to pursue the good. The Prime Directive that attempts (imperfectly) to guide the humans in their dealings with other species is a codification of respect and humility, though one that also must bend to the spirit and not the letter of the law. Finally and most impressively, in episode after episode, mercy, empathy, and selflessness win out over their opposites, no matter how well armed or technologically advanced the latter may be.

The relation or conflict between the individual and the community is an ethical problem occasionally touched on in *Star Trek,* but it is the fundamental and recurring theme of the odd and inventive series *The Prisoner.* The series focuses on the dehumanizing idolatry of making the state the object of devotion and worship; but if it stopped there, it would be merely a cold war period piece. Instead, it profoundly considers the individual's responsibilities, especially the call to nonviolent resistance, and even shows that Number Six's fanatical selfhood results finally in alienation, unless he can build a real community that worships neither the state nor the individual.

Moving from ethics to consider the larger world and God's relation to it, we look at how the supernatural scenarios of *The Twilight Zone* are often stories of sin and grace. First, the series' depiction of evil is predominantly and unmistakably Christian: most of the evil characters and forces depicted in the episodes are merely impotent, parasitic, repetitive, and oblivious to the past. And when the show turns to consider truly happy or saved lives, they are ones of innocence, community, love, and right memory. These stories are not ultimately about ethics, however, but about the characters being (or not being) receptive to grace, a supernatural force that can cure their restlessness and actualize the good that they had hidden from themselves.

The series *The X Files* takes us to a world deeply imbued with the imagery and urgency of Christian apocalyptic, wherein the examination and conversion of the soul—the confrontation with moral truth—may not be postponed. Faith consists of the openness of the soul to the transcendent vision vouchsafed by God, a divine message that shows the pettiness and transience of all social and political concerns. Yet one who opens oneself to this vision can be isolated from or even persecuted by others. *The X Files* follows the lives of two spiritually sensitive "investigators" of paranormal and supernatural phenomena. As they experience conventionally inexplicable events, they come to see social and political institutions as humanity's collective resistance to a transcendental dispensation, and they learn to redefine themselves in opposition to customary (and, as they see it, erroneous) assumptions about life and existence. As in Revelation, the vision experienced by Muldur and Scully forces them to make a decisive leap into novel spiritual conviction.

Finally, we consider the universality of the Word, both as incarnation and as scripture. Jesus addresses a universal humanity: the human spirit is the same wherever it appears, notwithstanding that it manifests itself culturally in seemingly disparate ways. Indeed, the story of the tower of Babel contends that humanity once *was* unified, even in its communicating in *one* language, but sinful humanity brought on itself the catastrophic confounding of languages. The series *Babylon 5* takes up this vision of an ecumenical humanity divided into warring factions and teetering on the verge of annihilation. The purpose of the Babylon station is to provide a neutral ground on which antagonists in the cosmic wars can rediscover a common, moral language and vision. The common morality and humanity of all the different species of the inhabited galaxy is the insistent message of those who have committed themselves to the Babylon Project. Commanders Sinclair and Sheridan are exemplary moral figures who inspire others through their dedication to peace and their willingness to risk all for the sake of the community.

From the classics of ancient Greece to the classics of modern literature, television, and films, science fiction has shown itself not to be a genre of storytelling that deals only with engineering marvels with cardboard characters to attend them, but a revival of the moral and theological imagination against a cosmic background. Let us now explore that imagination and vision as it is expounded in these classic television series.

I

Grappling with the "Powers"

Doctor Who in the Earthly and Celestial Dominions

Again, the devil took him up to a very high mountain and showed him all the kingdoms of the world and their splendor; and he said to him, "All these will I give you if you will fall down and worship me." Jesus said to him, "Away with you, Satan! For it is written, 'Worship the Lord your God, and serve only him.'" Then the devil left him. And suddenly angels came and waited on him.

Matthew 4:8—11[1]

Even Satan disguises himself as an angel of light. So it is not strange if his ministers also disguise themselves as ministers of righteousness.

1 Corinthians 11:14–15

> The system of powers Satan has engendered is . . . spiritual, religious in a very special sense, [and] efficacious and illusory at the same time . . . Expressions like "powers *of this world*," "kings *of the earth*," "principalities," etc. assert the earthly character of such powers. . . . [But] expressions like "princes of the kingdom *of the air*," "celestial powers," etc. emphasize [their] extraterrestrial, "spiritual" nature.
>
> René Girard, *I See Satan Fall like Lightning*[2]

Anthropology, Theology, and the Powers

Satan, according to the biblical exegesis of the literary and religious scholar René Girard, exemplifies the immemorial means by which, in the long ages before prophecy and the gospel, *all* communities, polities, kingdoms, and empires organized themselves at their foundation and by which, again in a regular and ritualistic manner, they sustained that aboriginal establishment. A consequence of Christianity's displacement of overt paganism in the Western world is that modern people live lives that are largely "de-ritualized," as Girard sometimes puts it in his spoken remarks; Protestants tend to be even less attached to a ritual calendar than Catholics and followers of Eastern Orthodoxy. In order, then, to understand what might at first strike us as an unusual preoccupation in episode after episode of the long-lived BBC science-fiction serial *Doctor Who,* we need to consider in some detail the relation among pagan notions of divinity, the meaning of ritual, and the power of priesthoods in pre-Christian societies. Girard's analysis of this knot of anthropological phenomena is particularly enlightening. Let us first turn to Girard's discussion of *myth.*

When we examine myth, Girard asserts, we discover that the pagan gods are inevitably *made* and that the process of their manufacture is an invariable one: the resolution of a violent crisis (the mythic *chaos,* plague, civic insurrection, or Titanomachy) through the arbitrary designation and subsequent immolation of an innocent party on whom those threatened by the violence of their fellows place the blame for their terror and misery. On this same victim—after his death has quelled the conflict of *all against all* by transforming it into the agreement of *all against one*—the murderers subsequently bestow the paradoxical status of a magical intercessor. To this now (falsely) supernatural entity, whose *being* seems to encompass the extremes of existence, those who see themselves as rescued from violence by its death feel compelled to ascribe the power either to inflict crisis on, or to bring serenity to, the vulnerable human scene. A clear example of this occurs in Sophocles' well-known Oedipus tragedy, about the ill-fated king of Thebes. In the first play, Oedipus fulfills the oracle that says he is doomed to slay his father and marry his mother, and he becomes an intolerable scandal who must be expelled from the community. In the second play, in a mysterious flash of light, the old, blind, wandering Oedipus rises to heaven to take his place with the gods.

Kingship has a relation to these things. In Girard's analysis, kingship develops from primitive sacrifice when priestly specialists take over governance of the rites and begin to appropriate to themselves the authority of the supernatural being, in whose honor the people undertake the ever-necessary immolations of the increasingly crowded sacred calendar. Girard builds on insights achieved by Sir James G. Frazer (1854–1941) and Émile Durkheim (1858–1917) a century ago. Frazer saw the king as the victim whose immolation had been deferred, and Durkheim saw myth as a legitimizing projection of the social reality. In a sequel to the Oedipus story, a succession of kings follows Oedipus in Thebes, as waves of crisis and civil war sweep over the city with ritualistic regularity. Presuming this instability of primitive and ancient rulers to be a fact, at some point in social and political development, the community or someone within it must have found a way to stabilize kingship. Perhaps a substitute victim could be found, whose death would satisfy the need of the society for catharsis, leaving the king untouched.

We indeed see this development—in which the Big Man, as the potential victim, manages to avoid his sacrifice by arranging to have others immolated in his stead—working its way to settlement in the numinous-bureaucratic organization of the ancient Egyptian kingdom. Kingship is a stable institution in the Nile Valley, but at a price for the kingdom's people. It was against the ornate cruelty and oppressive falsehood of the Egyptian monarchical *cum* theological dispensation that the Hebrews, under Moses's leadership, at last rebelled, removing themselves from Pharaoh's dominion to begin their forty years of desert wandering. Pharaoh does not merely *stand in* for the god Amun-Re; he *is* Amun-Re, an actual deity regnant on this earth. Montezuma, the last of the Aztec rulers, likewise enjoys divine status: servants carry him on a litter so that contact with the earth will not pollute his exaltedness. Egypt had largely dispensed with human sacrifice at the time of the exodus, but the myths, such as those of Osiris and Set, reveal its presence in earlier centuries. In any case, Pharaoh's officers might dispense capital punishment in the monarch's name on any person at a whim; such a person is a sacrificial victim in effect if not in name. Moses's sense of the kingdom's deep-seated injustice and his decision to switch his loyalty from Pharaoh to the downtrodden stem all at once from his sight of a soldier brutalizing one of the Hebrew brick makers for no reason except to demonstrate power.

For Montezuma's part, when he presided over the regular massacre atop the step-pyramid in Tenochtitlán, spectator-worshipers could hardly distinguish him from the bloodthirsty divinity—Huitzilopochtli, Tlaloc, Quetzalcóatl, or whatever name he bears according to the occasion. When the chief Aztec fails to stem the Spanish conquest under Hernán Cortés, his own people stone him to death in his palace.

If a king, as Girard writes, were a victim whose execution had been indefinitely postponed, and who therefore requires substitutes on the altar, a victim might well be a king who has failed. Both Oedipus and Montezuma provide examples; the fate of Moses, who never reaches the promised land, remains vague, but more than one commentator—most elaborately the French poet Alfred de Vigny—has speculated that he became a victim of his own people. His stammer, says Girard, is a typical sign of a victim. The power of the king, as representative of the supernatural being, rests in his ability to manipulate and exploit an organized violence, of which all remain in fear, and to convince the tribe, through the charisma of the dreadful rites, that interfering in his arrangement would entail a greater danger than submitting to it.

Propitiating the gods ensures their goodwill and so holds chaos at bay. The gods do not really exist, but belief in them, bolstered by participation in the rites, engenders real social effects; the idolaters therefore understand sacrifice as entirely righteous and necessary. In rebuking the Pharisees, Jesus laments: "Jerusalem, Jerusalem, the city that kills the prophets and stones those who are sent to it" (Matt. 23:37). As the befuddled Caiaphas later says to the riled crowd, "You do not understand that it is better for you to have one man die for the people than to have the whole nation destroyed" (John 11:50). Acts recounts how, after the orthodox party martyrs Stephen,

Paul (who was still called Saul) "approved of their killing him" (Acts 8:1).

The delusion that killing a victim produces magical effects—insuring the body politic, averting plague, or quelling insurrection—has had a strong grip on the human imagination. Thus, the ritual organization of the community, the participation of all in the sacred rites, might well be said to have structured consciousness until Hebrew prophecy and the Gospels offered a new, liberating way of looking at the human scene: the nonsupernatural way, which, as we noted in our introduction, coincidentally made science possible.

Girard invites us to consider the noble Brutus and his fellow conspirators against Julius Caesar in the Ides of March of the fateful year 44 BCE. All of them ranked as men of refined learning, who would never have polluted themselves by spilling blood before an idol. Barbarians might do such things, but not Epicurean philosophers or Stoic moralists. Yet they can think of no other way to secure the tottering Roman Republic, for which they fear, than by felling a victim. They do so by collective blows in a quasi-sacred, conspicuously public locale, namely, the foyer of the Roman Senate. The gesture is a fiasco: for by a terrific irony the murdered Caesar swiftly becomes the transfigured foundation on which the Roman Empire (itself brutal and sacrificial) will rise, as it supersedes the ill-fated republic. In a vote, the Senate later "*deifies*" the assassinated Caesar, while all subsequent emperors take his name, as though to reincarnate him. The Severan emperors of the late second and early third centuries go so far as to identify themselves with Sol Invictus, a Latin variant of the Persian sun god Mithras.

The totalitarian regimes of our own era, from the Parisian Directorate of the 1790s to the Khmer Rouge of the 1970s, have always required mass executions and gaudy show trials of high-profile "enemies of the state" to consolidate their hold. Bloody theatricals solidify the fractious people by redirecting their ire and so ensure the unquestioned sway of correct ideology and obedience. Is there a food shortage? Let us blame the "saboteurs" or the "bourgeois reactionaries." Theories that existence is itself evil and requires total transformation—or, barring that, destruction—abound in the modern world. If only some blocking agent were liquidated, as such theories would have it, liberty and equality and fraternity would prevail and utopia would arise.

More than one scholar has called attention to the resemblance of the twentieth-century totalitarian doctrines to those ancient Gnostic speculations that pitted themselves against Judaism and Christianity in late antiquity. Political tracts gain status as a type of false scripture, while devotees mummify dead party heroes and keep them on public display. Pilgrims may to this day see a pickled Lenin in Red Square or purchase copies of his speeches in red leather covers with gold-embossed titles. Scattered fanatics even inveterately proclaim an admiration for Mao or Hitler, quite possibly *because of* rather than *despite* the bloody carnage once committed in their names.

The Gospels, as Girard writes, remark such things critically: "Though not identical with Satan, the powers [Paul's term] are all his tributaries because they are all servants of the false gods that are the offspring of Satan, that is, the offspring of the founding murder."[3] In this spirit, Jesus invokes the martyr tradition stemming from "the blood of righteous Abel" (Matt. 23:35), in whose martyrdom all kingdoms that are *not* the kingdom of God have taken their foundation. In this stalwart line stands the Christ himself, the "Omega" of all prophets, who, being already God, cannot be deified by his execution under the governing power. The crucifixion, supervised by the plenipotentiary of the Pax Romana in Jerusalem, merely and vainly repeats the essential pagan gesture for forging renewed solidarity out of militant, divisive factionalism. The attempt to make Jesus a victim *for the sake of the Roman Empire* and for the sake of its grip on Judea nevertheless fails. The apostles, overcoming their initial lapse, refuse to endorse the otherwise unanimous justification of the monstrous deed and begin again to preach the old prophetic admonitions against sacrifice and against god-kings. The gospel testimony begins the process whereby the empire of the Caesars will stand in the clear light as simply one more among an endless succession of *powers,* grander than previous ones and possessing a fearsome ministry of propaganda, but no less bloody in its characteristic methods.

The Gospels deliver men and women from such powers by helping them to see that imperial grandeur and tyrannical luster alike take nourishment from a false transcendence. Despots, like Montezuma atop his pyramid or Caesar at the gladiatorial games, use the fascination of the victim to generate the pseudodivine charisma in which they then clothe themselves so as to appear, in their own persons, as a sort of god. Despots need victims and endlessly designate them: think of Herod's slaughter of the innocents during the infancy of Christ. Jesus uniquely demands *no victim* but offers himself in the place of the victim to show the vanity of all blood-stained idols, of every righteous persecutor, pretended superman, self-alleged demon-master, would-be man-god, perfected one, ascendant cult, bellicose state, or conquering empire.

Powers—in Greek, *dynamoi*—hover in swarms over the antique Mediterranean world. Writes Girard:

> On the one hand, to say of the powers that they are worldly would be to dwell on their concrete power within this world, which is an essential dimension but to the

> detriment of their other dimension, the religious one. Although the latter is illusory, it has effects too real to be conjured away. On the other hand, to say of the powers that they are "celestial" is to insist on their religious dimension, namely, on the prestige that thrones and sovereigns enjoy among humankind and that is always perceived as a little supernatural. We see this even now in the toadyism that bows and scrapes at the feet of our governments, no matter how unimpressive the latter are.[4]

Wonder workers and utopian prophets appear, like Apollonius of Tyana (born circa 4 BCE), celebrated in a popular biography written a century and a half after his death as a pagan Christ. Mani, a Zoroastrian reformer of the third century, preached the absolute evil of creation and foretold its liberating dissolution in a fiery judgment. Mani founded a religion, whose adherents included a Persian king, Shapur I, and thousands of converts in North Africa, Italy, and Europe. Manichaeism still commanded a sizable following in the early fifth century and probably reappeared as the Albigensian heresy in thirteenth-century Provence. Like Simon Magus and the later Gnostic holy men, Mani saw himself as a messiah, or savior. The Hellenistic kings of Syria and Egypt had likewise styled themselves *soter,* or "savior," as though to indicate their assumption of superhuman status. So too do the Magian and Manichaean doctrines promote, in antiworldly terms, the worldly power of a self-nominating elite cadre. As for the Gnostics themselves, they claimed a special knowledge (*gnosis*), unavailable to others, that marked them out as spiritual *perfectissimi*—gods in exile, as it were—owing no allegiance to any existing legal, religious, or political order. Gnostics tended to regard other people as less than fully human, mere automata in service of the evil lord of matter.

Doctor Who as Discoverer of False Gods

The universe cheerfully inhabited, enthusiastically celebrated, and playfully explored by the renegade Gallifreyan Time Lord called Doctor Who (never referred to, however, as anything except "the Doctor") resembles the troubled ecumenic world of late antiquity, in which many powers—political, technical, quasi-supernatural—contended with one another for dominion. In *Doctor Who*'s imaginary but curiously familiar cosmos, conquerors, envious of power beyond their own, aspire to be gods; schemers succumb to the luster of ancient rites and revive them; bizarre doctrines corrupt whole planetary communities; and nihilistic zealots threaten existence. Not physiologically human, except in his outward form, the Doctor nevertheless preserves a special fondness for humanity, Earth being his favorite planet.

The Time Lords of Gallifrey are the most technically and ethically refined race in the universe, or so they claim; by their ability to travel not only in space but also in time, they have positioned themselves to be caretakers of the cosmos and of its people, a duty which, to the best of their ability, they discharge. They try to be guided, in conscience, by the will of "The White Guardian," a benevolent quasi-deity representing, as David J. Howe and Stephen James Walker put it, "an unknown power . . . above the Time Lords themselves."[5] There is likewise a "Black Guardian," who can, however, disguise himself as his opposite number, making identification difficult. Like any priestly bureaucracy, the Time Lords show a tendency to take their own rules and exegeses with an unbending, Pharisee-like seriousness; while not Gnostics, they display at times a characteristically Manichaean hauteur. Putting the spirit before the letter, the Doctor has criticized the reigning literal-mindedness and conceit of his colleagues. In a fit of supercilious offense, they unanimously expel him from the sacred precincts, whereupon he goes into exile on Earth. "I am a pariah," he says in the story called "The Two Doctors" (1985), "an exile of my society." If the Doctor sympathized with scapegoats, as he resolutely does, this might be connected with his personal experience as a gadfly dissenter among the Gallifreyans. Two related multipart stories, "The Deadly Assassin" (1976) and "The Invasion of Time" (1978), support this hypothesis. The dissenting Time Lord has a dearly bought insight about how communities reconsolidate themselves in a crisis—or merely under criticism. *Doctor Who*'s producers founded the first season of the show on this premise when it premiered on the BBC forty years ago, and they sustained it thereafter. The Doctor would later be reconciled with his contemnor peers, more or less. Yet he would never cease—to borrow Paul's phrase—to act the role of a "light . . . hidden in darkness" (1 Cor. 4:5), sometimes clownishly and sometimes with grim determination.

Doctor Who, with its distinguishing quirky style, enjoys the distinction of having run longer than just about any other serial program on television. It aired every season from 1963 to 1989. It returned as a made-for-television movie on the American Fox network in 1996 and production has recently begun on a renewed regular program for the BBC. The original television program also spun off two *Doctor Who* movies in the mid-1960s, courtesy of an American producer working in Great Britain. In all, ten actors have taken turns portraying the nonconformist genius, whose Gallifreyan physiology permits him occasionally "to regenerate," as the convention has it. These actors are William Hartnell and Patrick Troughton (both deceased), John Pertwee, Tom Baker, Peter Davison, Colin Baker, and Sylvester McCoy, all on television; Peter Cushing (also deceased), in the two "Dalek" movies (1965 and 1966), Paul McGann in Fox's

American production, and Christopher Eccleston in the 2005 BBC revival. By a peculiar coincidence, Tom Baker and Sylvester McCoy, the fourth and seventh Doctors, trained for the Catholic religious life in youth, before rejoining the world and making careers in theater.

From the beginning, *Doctor Who*'s writers demonstrated what would prove an abiding interest in religious-archeological issues interpreted from a broadly Judeo-Christian perspective. Such stories as "The Daemons" (1971), "The Pyramids of Mars" (1975), "Image of the Fendahl" (1977), "The Talons of Weng-Chiang" (1977), and "The Stones of Blood" (1978), which fits into the season-long *Key to Time,* belong to the trend. A prototypical example—and one of the best *Doctor Who* episodes for its writing, acting, and production—is "The Aztecs" (1964).

In the current era of politically correct reticence about non-European cultures and civilizations, one must speak frankly about the Aztecs. Whatever the merits of their architectural and other aesthetic achievements, however attractively baroque their myths and fables, and despite their status as "victims" of Iberian colonial policy, they ran their empire as a sacrificial theocracy, making war on their neighbors to keep the altars refreshed and the gods satisfied, for five hundred years. The priests *ate* the hearts of the victims. In these things, the Aztecs continued the style of their Mesoamerican precursors, the Olmec and the Maya. Cortez conquered the Aztecs as easily as he did, in his campaign of 1520, because the peoples living adjacent to the Valley of Mexico eagerly joined him in making a war of liberation against their long-time oppressors. Bernal Diaz, who traveled with the expedition, mentions in his *Conquest of New Spain* Cortez's discovery of a pyramid consisting of 100,000 human skulls, collected from the sacrifices and put on display to awe the subject peoples with the startling image of Aztec fearsomeness. The nineteenth-century American historian William H. Prescott (1796–1859), a Protestant with scant affection for the Spanish-Catholic regime in New Spain, nevertheless recorded, in the epilogue of his pioneering two-volume study (1848) of the conquistadors, that if forced to choose between the colonial inquisition and the Aztec regime that it replaced, he would opt for the former, so abhorrent was the latter.

The *Doctor Who* scriptwriter for the Aztecs story, John Lucarotti, materializes the Time Lord's conveyance, the TARDIS, inside the burial chamber of a legendary priest named Yetaxa. The artifice of Yetaxa, a fictional character, contradicts no known facts about the last pre-Colombian civilization but permits a piquant tragedy to work itself out. Lucarotti's script establishes the date as the late fifteenth century, a generation prior to Cortez's arrival.

John Crockett's thoughtful direction confronts viewers immediately with the Aztec paradox: his morticians have preserved Yetaxa inside a jade-and-obsidian carapace of exquisite beauty, but alongside his remains on the slab lie scattered the daggers, amulets, and related implements of sacrificial procedure; the bejeweled mummy is also the last thing we see as the travelers depart at the end of the story. The clues suggest, even though the story never directly establishes, that Yetaxa was a dissenter among the priests, who spitefully killed and then deftly deified him—made him, that is, a nucleus of their own *power*, lest they lose it. One of the Doctor's traveling companions, Barbara Wright (actress Jacqueline Hill), has formerly taught history in a girls' college; she possesses both the knowledge to understand the circumstances and the connoisseurship to appreciate the finesse of what she sees. Startled by the wonderful ornaments, she absentmindedly places the bracelet of "The Coiling Serpent," a sacred badge, on her left arm. This leads to the Aztec clerisy's mistaking her for a messenger from the gods, and the others for her servants. Barbara becomes the pivot between two contending *personae* of the Sacred College, Tlotoxl (actor John Ringham), "High Priest of Sacrifice," and Autloc (actor Keith Pyott), "High Priest of Knowledge." These two in their opposition anticipate the later *Doctor Who* development of the morally contrasting "Guardians" in *The Key to Time* (1977/78).

The Doctor and his companions have arrived at a moment of crisis. A drought has afflicted the land for some months, threatening dire consequences. Yet the climatic pressure on the society is hardly distinguishable from a chafing social unrest. The elites plot against one another (Tlotoxl plots against Autloc); ambitious aristocrats eye the opportunity to seize control. Barbara provokes the fractiousness when she exploits her mistaken identity as a divine messenger to try to end sacrifice; rejecting the Doctor's opposite counsel, she reasons that the pleasing refinement of Aztec life, which director Crockett represents as utopian (his Tenochtitlán features a "Garden of Peace"), can be purged of the repellent barbarity. The squint-eyed Tlotoxl, little believing in the gods, nevertheless understands that one might most effectively maintain an autocratic regime, as he aims, through ostentatious sacrifice. His charisma derives from the victim's plight, quite in the pattern described by Girard, on the basis of the gospel analysis of prebiblical institutions. Tlotoxl says menacingly of Barbara that a false messenger "has come among us to destroy us." One is reminded of the hostility of the Neoplatonists, such as Porphyry and Iamblichus, to Christianity; they too saw the novel theology of the Sermon on the Mount as threatening destruction.

Autloc, a genuinely pious and "sensitive" man, finds himself convinced by Barbara's prophecy (historically informed, after all) that a time will soon come "when there shall be ten thousand sacrifices in a single day," the mass of them insufficient to keep the state from cataclysmic dissolution. The High Priest of Knowledge can see the trend in Tlotoxl's increasingly bloodthirsty behavior and in his cabal with the military leader Ixta, the "Chosen Warrior." Autloc agrees with Barbara that "the gods' ways" differ from Tlotoxl's; Autloc hopes to inaugurate a new, nonsacrificial ethos for his people. Lucarotti inserts a subtle hint about the identity of the new ethos in a scene where Susan Foreman, the Doctor's granddaughter, submits to instruction in the ways of Tenochtitlán. The Aztecs divide their calendar into millennial "Suns," or Ages, as Autloc tells Susan (actress Carole Ann Ford). First came "The Sun of the Four Tigers," then "The Sun of Air," then "The Sun of Fire and Rain," and then "The Sun of Water"; next—its epoch is the eclipse predicted for a few days hence—will come "The Sun of Man."

Lucarotti has ingeniously punned: "The Sun of Man," as he writes it, sounds to the ear like "The *Son* of Man," one of the rhetorical tropes of Christ in the Gospels. Thus, Jesus avers in Matthew: "For as the days of Noah were, so will be the coming of the Son of Man" (Matt. 24:37). Lucarotti's Aztec drought, like the Old Testament's universal deluge, is the metaphor of a social crisis—the final, holocaustic breakdown of the sacrificial order—and, like Noah's flood, it uses large-scale geophysical imagery to suggest communal upheaval, death, and suffering. We speak, after all, of "waves of violence" and "the drying up of charity." Sacrificially organized societies indeed always incline to crisis, because the fear of becoming a victim prompts people to leap ahead of the designation by defensively designating someone else. When in Genesis-related folklore Noah's neighbors revile him for his peculiar hobby of building the ark, they are preliminarily singling him out in an ominous way. The old habit of ostracism, frequently a prelude to sacrifice, is why the Ten Commandments forbid the bearing of false witness against one's neighbors. When the New Testament's "Son of Man" declares that one should positively *love one's neighbor,* he breaks the cycle of ritual lynching by demonstrating its hollowness and, in so doing, necessarily weakens the hoary underlying mechanism of the ritual society.

In striving to suppress the exaggerated bloodiness of the Aztec order, Barbara increasingly understands that she has implicated herself in it. Tlotoxl knows Barbara for no divine messenger; he hesitates to move against her only because she has promised to "destroy" him should he reveal her merely mortal status. To prevent Tlotoxl's attempted sacrifice of Ian Chesterton, her fiancé, who also travels with the Doctor, she puts a knife to the priest's throat, saying, "If my servant dies, so shall Tlotoxl." The impasse breaks without bloodshed, but Barbara sees the impossibility of her plan. Ian (actor William Russell) chastises Barbara for "insisting that Tlotoxl's the odd man out" when "he's not." Tlotoxl, in other words, fills the role of canny functionary and rabble-rousing demagogue in a society where the rabble majority responds with hearty eagerness to being cannily roused. The Doctor tells Barbara that she cannot change history. With great vehemence he confesses to her: "Believe me! I know. I've tried." The suspicion arises that the Doctor has visited Tenochtitlán before, that his meddling then was what led to the killing of Yetaxa by a frightened orthodoxy. If Tlotoxl were no exception, Autloc really would be one, but he cannot effect change *from within* the ritual order that he has so long served. He can only go into exile. "I have lost my faith in our traditions," he says. Leaving Tenochtitlán, he will "seek truth in the wilderness, away from other men." The Doctor, too, in a hot moment with Tlotoxl, has said that his way, in contrast to the priest's, "is . . . truth." The Doctor's words suggest that *knowledge* counteracts *power,* as *truth* counteracts *sacrifice.* This invocation of the moral truth points to the real meaning of the new age of "The Son of Man."

Yet More False Gods

The notion of a "new age," somewhat differently intended, lies at the heart of another exemplary *Doctor Who* story, "The Daemons," from the years of the third Doctor, John Pertwee. Here, the Pauline admonition that "even Satan disguises himself as an angel of light" acquires a peculiar aptness, as when the Doctor's recurrent nemesis, the Master, disguises himself as an Anglican vicar. A passage from Galatians also applies: "Formerly, when you did not know God, you were enslaved to beings that by nature are not gods," whereupon it becomes meet to ask, "how can you turn back again to weak and beggarly elemental spirits?" (Gal. 4:8–9).

Writer Guy Leopold's script assumes a contemporary setting and concerns the excavation of a Bronze Age tumulus called "Devil's Hump," near a remote English village, entirely fictitious, named "Devil's End." The early 1970s witnessed a craze not only for magical lore and witchcraft—Colin Wilson's study *The Occult* had maintained a place on the best-seller lists in Great Britain and America since its appearance in 1969—but for all manner of theosophical and mystical curiosa, from UFOs to Atlantis. Alongside Wilson's *Occult,* Erich von Däniken's *Chariots of the Gods* (1968), with its "ancient astronaut" hypothesis, enjoyed conspicuous popularity. "But it really *is* the dawning of the Age of Aquarius just about now,"[6] says the Doctor's assistant, Jo Grant (actress Katy Manning). "The Daemons" nourishes its plot on this odd mixture while taking the view that the "new" might well conceal the *old* in the sense of something atavistic—a *turning back,* to adapt Galatians, to primeval forms not unrelated to those that blemish the outward serenity of Aztec life in the earlier *Doctor Who* excursion. Even the quaint custom of the Morris Dance, a seemingly harmless vestige of Anglo-Saxon paganism, takes on a sinister, but not implausible, color in Leopold's clever five-part tale.

Leopold's story has one additional affiliation with, of all unlikely things, a novel by Fyodor Dostoyevsky (1821–81). In the Russian writer's *Daemons* (1880),[7] from which Leopold appears to have borrowed his title, nihilistic schemers try to foment political revolution in a provincial town by exacerbating social divisions and, at last, by arson and assassination. Dostoyevsky, a Russian Orthodox Christian, sees revolutionary politics prophetically as a lapse into prebiblical religiosity. The features of the twentieth-century totalitarian regimes bear out Dostoyevsky's intuition. We need only consider the way in which, under the ideological dictatorships, a complicated cult of the personality (as it was called in the case of Stalin) tends to form around the leader, complete with quasi-priestly ritual. We earlier remarked how insurrectionary manifestos become substitute scripture in an ideological context. It is not difficult to see why modern tyrants require an ersatz gospel. Persecuting the religious homicidally and dynamiting houses of worship, as Hitler and Stalin did, suggest that the tyrant finds the revealed faith intolerable; this, in turn, suggests that despots think of themselves in godlike terms. No *two* gods, of course, can ever inhabit the same cultural or political space at the same time, as tyrants see it.[8] Such contemplations have gone into the making of the Time Lord's archenemy.

The Master is at once a cosmic Tlotoxl and a violence-intoxicated rebel against the moral order, like Dostoyevsky's nihilist-insurrectionist, Stavrogin. A renegade Time Lord like the Doctor, the Master has distinguished his exile by evil rather than by charitable deeds. Barry Lett's novelization (1971) of Leopold's teleplay describes him as cherishing "one overwhelming objective [that] always remained the same: Power!"[9] Like the theurgists and spirit-conjurors of late antiquity, and like Tlotoxl, the Master wants "the power of the tyrant . . . the power of the despot . . . the power of the demigod."[10] Having murdered the real vicar so as to slip into his role, the Master exploits the fascination generated by the dig at Devil's Hump while stirring up among his parishioners cleverly planned resentments and frustrations. The prehistoric tumulus, like the Aztec step-pyramid, marks an ancient sacrificial site. Leopold's science-fictional twist, in the mode of von Däniken, is that the place first became sacred to the ancients who raised the mound there because it marked the spot on which extraterrestrial beings, whom they mistook for gods, once landed and where the deluded people, thrown in a panic, made human offerings to the interlopers. Entirely "amoral," as the Doctor explains, the "Daemons" once assisted *Homo sapiens* to "kick out Neanderthal Man,"[11] an original radical expulsion—race murder, really—reminiscent of Cain's killing of Abel.[12] Pagan deities like the Egyptian Khnum, the Greek Pan, the Cretan Minotaur, and the medieval European "Horned Beast" enshrine the Daemons as myth. One such creature, with superhuman powers, remains in suspended animation in the barrow; the psychic emanations of this dormant entity, "Azal," have inspired local rites and superstitions for centuries, or even for millennia, giving the region its peculiar impish reputation.

The Master attempts to revive Azal with a Black Mass, evoking him with shouts of *"Io! Evoé!"*[13] These syllables form the ritual cry of the celebrants of Dionysus in the sacrificial orgies devoted to that god during the early period of Greek culture and later outlawed in the Greek city-states as intolerably primitive and bloody. Girard reminds us in *Violence and the Sacred* (1972) that Dionysus, the sacrificial deity par excellence, owns "no proper being outside the realm of violence."[14] The violence of mythic divinities merely projects, however, the violence of the human community. Leopold's invented alien presence—whether in the historical or the contemporary setting—does nothing more than activate tendencies that, from the perspective of biblical anthropology, we recognize as fully, although tragically, human.

The Master summons the townspeople to tempt and cajole them: "In troubled times like these," as he says, "it behooves us to stick together."[15] He sees "decadence . . . on every side," and he urges against a symptomatic trinity of "democracy, equality, and freedom" his own anodyne values of "decision, power, and strength."[16] The word choice is significant, even if Leopold never intended anyone to examine his locution etymologically. "Decision" and "to decide" come from the Latin *decidere,* literally "to cut the throat." The Master talks like the existentialist he claims to be, when he tells Miss Hawthorne (actress Damaris Hayman), the locally much disparaged "white witch," that "the soul" represents "a very dated idea."[17] In self-inflating Gnostic fashion—"existentially," in his term—the Master prefers *will* to *soul:* "As my will, so mote it be," goes the refrain of his demonic incantation. After first setting the representatives of the community against one another by publicly recounting petty crimes and pointless grudges kept secret by their perpetrators, so that all "fear . . . what the next few moments might reveal,"[18] the Master then assures them all that "everything is possible if you follow me,"[19] a noticeably Stavrogin-like pronouncement.

Squire Winstanley (actor Rollo Gamble) dissenting, the Master commands Bok, a gargoyle, to kill him, leaving the others to feel guiltily that they have themselves participated in the homicide, which, by their assent to it, they effectively have. Stavrogin, in Dostoyevsky's *Daemons,* uses the same murderous technique to bolster solidarity among the revolutionary conspiracy that he heads. It is, to coin a phrase, a *decisive* gesture. At every stage in the foundation of the Master's new order, sacrificial through and through, he must destroy something of the existing biblically rooted, nonsacrificial order. The ironic spokeswoman for the latter, the white witch Miss Hawthorne, shows herself a resolutely moral and courageous character, whom the Master conspicuously hates as a major obstacle in his path. The climax occurs when the Master belatedly discovers that the forces of violence he has unleashed threaten even him.

Jo destroys Azal when, at risk to her own life, she interposes herself between the creature and the Doctor. The Doctor explains: "Azal couldn't handle a fact as illogical and irrational as your being prepared to give up your life for me."[20] While Leopold has kept the Judeo-Christian theme in the background, the invocation of self-sacrifice as the "ridiculous and foolhardy"[21] deed that undermines the homicidal "logic" of blood offerings tells all.

In "The Stones of Blood" (1977), from the middle years of Tom Baker's tenure as the Doctor, a great megalithic circle on the pattern of the familiar Salisbury Plain monuments replaces the tumulus of "The Daemons" and the step-pyramid of "The Aztecs." Ancient sacred architecture crops up frequently in *Doctor Who,* which is simply to say that the *Doctor Who* writers grasp the fascination that the genius loci of pagan religious sites exercises on popular imagination. The roughly hewn stellar temples of Neolithic humanity betoken a lingering power even after two thousand years of the biblical dispensation; folklore, perhaps cannily, affiliates such relics of the past with trolls, devils, imps, and a lingering malign influence. In "The Stones," it is the fictitious "Nine Travellers," looking appropriately Stonehenge-like, said to be located on the actual Boscombe Moor.

Director Darrol Blake edits together location footage with shots of designer John Stout's lovingly wrought, darkly atmospheric studio set. Instead of the Master, David Fisher's script gives us Leonard DeVries (actor Nicholas McArdle), a self-nominated Druid hierarch trying to revive the Celtic demigod called "the Cailleach," a "Stones" counterpart of Azal, through sacrificial offerings at the Travellers. These prove effective, not for any supernatural reason, but because two of the Travellers are dormant "Ogri," nonsentient but dangerously hungry creatures imprisoned anciently in situ, who feed on blood (hence, "The Stones of Blood.") The Cailleach, too, a technologically proficient criminal, has been incarcerated in a time warp—linked "transdimensionally" to the megaliths—after a beastly destructive career, from which punitive limitation she wants liberty in order to resume her depredations on the cosmos. She is manipulating gullible parties to this end, exploiting the allure of primitive rites and of esoteric doctrine. Paul once assented to the proposition that "there may be so-called gods in heaven or earth, as in fact there are many gods and lords" (1 Cor. 8:5). Thus, while the Cailleach, like Azal, is a real being, a real power, but *not* the real God, those concupiscent souls driven by their *libido dominandi* to win sovereignty over others will nevertheless seek her alliance in their schemes, as DeVries does, to become despots.

DeVries characterizes himself as "not in the conventional sense" a Druid but, rather, "a keen student of Druidic lore."[22] Archeologist Amelia Rumford (actress Beatrix Lehmann), who befriends the Doctor, finds DeVries "a most unpleasant man," made no less so by the fact that, in his fascination with "all that mumbo jumbo and antiquated nonsense,"[23] he appears more than slightly ridiculous. A little man, he wants to be a Big Man. When viewers see him in ritual regalia amidst the flames of a nocturnal ceremony *in camera* and with knife upraised, they recognize him as in line with Tlotoxl and the Master, with Soutek in "The Pyramids of Mars," and with Kassia in "The Keeper of Traken."

The flames of sacrifice feature in a surprising number of *Doctor Who* stories. They flicker like a ghoulish reminder in the background of many an eldritch scene. Peter, after denying Christ, seeks anonymity in a crowd that has formed around a flaming brazier; he wants to *stick together,* as one might say, with those who uphold the normative gestures of society that Jesus is trying to undo. Girard comments that, in the scene of Peter in the temple courtyard, the Gospels (all four) illustrate "the usual," the pre-Christian "religion"; this old way "is inevitably mixed with sacrifices . . . the purity of the familial cult."[24] The fire reminds us of "the ancient gesture of the Aztec sacrificers and [of the medieval] witch-hunters as they forced their victims into the flames."[25]

In explaining to the Doctor that the Cailleach is goddess "of War . . . of Death . . . of Magic,"[26] in whom he fervently believes and whom he ardently serves, DeVries identifies himself, despite his unprepossessing mien, as an amoral power seeker. Like many another political schemer, he has fled, out of resentment against his betters, to the consolatory embers of a lowly devotion. The pattern repeats itself elsewhere in the *Doctor Who* canon. "I should have been a god," shouts the invidious Omega (actor Stephen Thorne) in "The Three Doctors" (1973), voicing the bedrock delusion of the disaffected. "I shall be a god!" proclaims Maximillian Stael (actor Scott Fredericks) in "The Image of the Fendahl." The self-pitying

Stael, "unable to feel part of the rest of humanity . . . would rule it."[27] That the actor playing DeVries in "The Stones" has made himself look like a pudgy Heinrich Himmler only underscores the impression. When the power that DeVries has summoned turns on and destroys him, it strikes one as inevitable. Those who live by sacrifice shall perish *as sacrifices*. The sequence of Caesars, particularly the later Byzantine ones, offers a study in the phenomenon, with the disgruntled next-in-line plotting to hasten the demise of his soon-to-be predecessor, while his own successors plot against him.

The philosopher Hannah Arendt (1906–75) wrote of *the banality of evil*. Arendt's phrase refers to stunted cases—like Caligula or Commodus, like Hitler or Himmler, like the French or Russian revolutionaries—who, espousing grandiose doctrines, sometimes of their own godhead, manipulated violence to control whole societies, as though in service to bloodthirsty demons. In the twentieth century especially the bonfires of immolation have leapt high at the behest of the paltriest of men.

"There Is No Such Thing as Magic"

"There is no such thing as magic," the Doctor confidently tells Jo in the opening scene of "The Daemons," "magic" being another word for a "mumbo jumbo," an objectively meaningless pagan image. In "Meglos" (1978), one of the "Savants," or scientists, of Tigella complains of the planet's *other* ruling faction, the priestly "Deions," that he sees no reason to defer to a group that practices "primitive sacrifice." The denouement of the story establishes that the Deions have indeed held back the sensible rearrangement of Tigellan society and that the Savants, predicating their recommendations on the facts, have argued better policy for their people. One might make the mistake in reviewing a mass of *Doctor Who* stories casually that the program's writers espouse the typical modern position of "scientism," assuming, as "enlightened" people have done since the eighteenth century, that *science* is simply another word for all-encompassing truth, and *religion* simply another word for crass superstition. Nothing could be further from the case, as the Doctor's words in "The Daemons" to Jo—or in "The Robots of Death" (1977) to Leelah (actress Louise Jameson)—well suggest. Not *religion* but *magic* is the contrary term to *science;* science is about direct observation of the world, and magic is about illusion and deceit. The Doctor generally describes himself as a scientist (a status that his moniker implies), and he likes to unmask sacred illusions by discovering their empirical basis.

Yet for all its interstellar cruising and planetary exploration, the fundamental science in *Doctor Who* remains *human science;* and the fundamental human science is that which, like biblical revelation, recognizes the immemorial structures of the community prior to the Decalogue and the Gospels as those of the scapegoat and of sacrifice. It is the Decalogue that reveals the relation of covetousness and idol worship with murder; it is the gospel that lifts the veil from the hocus-pocus of sacrificial rites and makes way for the new social principle of love. Prebiblical sacrality often presents a learned face, as in the complex of gods and myths in the pyramid religions of Mexico or Egypt; the gods and myths justify the eternally repeated ritual gestures. Each of the many gods has his proper ramifying nomenclature and his peculiar elaborate rites.

The God who speaks to Moses out of the burning bush, by contrast, *has no name*—he calls himself only by the minimally declarative sentence "I am"; nor has he any rites, his sole concern being with morality and justice. The philosophical coteries and mystery religions of the

Hellenistic period, like the Mexican or Egyptian cults, crowd their formulations with esoteric pronouncements and ceremonious punctilios. Priests dedicate their lives to learning the doctrine and pose as experts in the sacred. Paganism never parodies science, because it comes before science and, as Girard argues, actually prevents the formation of science. Paganism nevertheless tends to look like a parody of science; and much of postbiblical pseudoscience (theurgy, theosophy, alchemy, Atlantology, ufology) looks suspiciously like a lapse into prebiblical magical thinking. The Gnostics of Alexandria and Rome took the trend to its conclusion when they argued that a mystical knowledge (*gnosis*) could itself transform the one who laboriously acquired it.

The Doctor, like a good evangelist, opposes such nonsense, but he never excludes the genuine—as opposed to the false—transcendence. He might easily say with the apostle that "knowledge (*gnosis*) puffs up, but love builds up" (1 Cor. 8:1). His visits to Gallifrey, his home world, invariably disturb Time Lord complacency in the way that the Sermon on the Mount disturbed the normative religiosity of first-century Galilee. In "The Deadly Assassin," Time Lord society has degenerated into a dogmatic orthodoxy, not above the use of torture to preserve itself against any threatened change; the torturers practice their art on none other than the one who has challenged their orthodoxy, the Doctor. The process has gone further in "The Invasion of Time." The name of the particular type of degeneration is *idolatry:* a community invests mere forms and formalities with a sacred status and begins to serve these as though they, rather than something transcendental, constituted either the object of worship or a morally based law ordained by a just God. Time Lord society on Gallifrey in these corrupt moments resembles nothing so much as Aztec society in Tenochtitlán. The Doctor, having encountered idolatry many times in his Odysseus-like travels, recognizes the cultural affliction immediately and administers a therapeutic shock.

Here again we perceive a gospel principle in the background, the notion that the new social order based on love entails the abandonment of long-standing, much reified ritual law and of the petrified attitudes that sustain it, these being incompatible with love. This social transformation will appear to those who fail, in the beginning, to understand it as unmitigated destruction; just so Barbara's attempt to reform sacrifice appears to Tlotoxl. Jesus must carefully say: "Do not think that I have come to abolish the law or the prophets [for] I have come not to abolish [the law] but to fulfill [it]" (Matt. 5:17), lest his hearers recoil in terror from his preaching. They do so anyway. The unraveling of established *power* must terrify those who imagine themselves as dependent on power.

The *Doctor Who* team produced, over forty years, some of the most inventive and thoughtful programming ever to grace that most dubious of entertainment media, television. Drastically constrained BBC budgets seem not to hamper but to stimulate those involved with the project. The moral consistency of the *Doctor Who* saga, even as many different hands carry it out over the decades, contributes much to the show's success, as does the intelligence of the writing and the obvious enjoyment that the actors bring to their *Doctor Who* roles. Sometimes a player's return in a new role itself enriches the overall "texture" of the series. Margot van der Burgh, who plays the refined Aztec lady Cameca returns in "The Keeper of Traken" as one of the philosophical rulers of the planet Traken, whose society the Master has determined secretly to subvert. Jacqueline Hill, who plays Barbara Wright in "The Aztecs," returns in *Meglos* as Lexa (a name meaning "the Law"), leader of the sacrificing Deions. When the actors and actresses appear again, viewers have the sense of becoming reacquainted with old friends. Even the villains strut across the stage with panache. Recurring nemeses like the Daleks or the Cybermen have their own wicked charm. The metallic, rasping motto of the Daleks—*"Seek, locate, exterminate!"*—is a perfect formulation of the victimary principle on which, as we have seen, *power,* in the gospel sense, rests.

Many of the anthropological and theological themes or motifs that appear in *Doctor Who* will reappear in the other science-fiction TV series that we discuss in subsequent chapters. The crew of the starship *Enterprise* in *Star Trek* encounters a number of sacrificially recidivist societies; they also periodically confront seeming contraventions of physical law that tempt the label of *magic* but which turn out to be applications of science and technology beyond the level known to those who are at first bewildered by them. Once the causal mechanism is discovered, however, the aura of magic vanishes, to be replaced by understanding. Like their *Star Trek* counterparts, the explorers in *Babylon 5* must preserve their postritual social order against incursions by those who either have not yet advanced beyond sacrifice or have lapsed back into it. We invite readers to think about the recurrence of these plot gambits because, in our opinion, they strongly associate the science-fiction genre with a gospel context. There are a few anticipations of science fiction in antiquity, as we have indicated in our introduction, but the genre only really develops in the context of European Christendom, in such works of moral satire as Cyrano de Bergerac's *Voyage dans la Lune* (1657) and Jonathan Swift's *Gulliver's Travels* (1726). Indeed, the twin spirits of Cyrano and Dean Swift are often at their satirical work in the episodes of *Doctor Who*.

In the 1980s most *Doctor Who* episodes became available on videocassette, and many of these are still obtainable in the market. In more recent years, the BBC has begun issuing classic episodes in the new DVD format, typically with a wealth of additional material, including spoken commentary by participants in the episode, which is often a source of rich information. The classic William Hartnell story, "The Aztecs," and the wildly imaginative Tom Baker sequence of *The Key to Time* (which encompasses "The Stones of Blood"), are good starting points, after which initiates will grasp the basic principles of the series and can explore on their own. Families looking to avoid the stupidity and crassness of current commercial television will find much to delight them in the ultimately quite serious escapades of the redoubtable Time Lord.

II

Christian Virtues and Human Nature

Star Trek

> Space—the final frontier. These are the voyages of the starship *Enterprise*. Its five-year mission: to explore strange new worlds, to seek out new life and new civilizations, to boldly go where no man has gone before.
>
> Opening narration, *Star Trek*

> Be perfect, therefore, as your heavenly Father is perfect.
>
> Matthew 5:48

Star Trek is not only the most popular science-fiction series ever on television, but one of the most popular television series of any kind. Its place in television history, however, was by no means immediately apparent. The original series ran only three seasons on NBC, from

1966 to 1969, but since then there have been four sequel (or prequel) series—*Star Trek: The Next Generation, Star Trek: Deep Space Nine, Star Trek: Voyager,* and *Star Trek: Enterprise*—and a whopping ten feature films.[1] Add to that an animated series, books, comic books, games, toys, fan clubs, fanzines, Web sites, scholarly articles and books, and frequent and enormous conventions of "Trekkies" or "Trekkers," and it is clear that *Star Trek* is truly a phenomenon, having become a part of American culture that is as recognizable and influential as Elvis or John Wayne.[2]

Why is the series so popular? On the one hand, it is possible to become so enthralled by its popularity that one is almost reduced to silent, awestruck reverence before the show: "For the multitude of fans, *Star Trek* is a vision for our future, a vision for humanity, a vision indeed for the entire cosmos."[3] But what, specifically, is this "vision"? And what—besides a fan's devotion—would lead us to embrace it? *Star Trek*'s consistent vision seems to be its intense morality. Of the shows we are examining, only *The Twilight Zone* was equally adamant and consistent in its moral vision and in its didacticism.[4] *Star Trek*'s creator, Gene Roddenberry (1921–91), though often quite vocal in his hostility toward organized religion of any kind, acknowledged that each *Star Trek* episode was basically "a morality play."[5] This moral tone, this sense that the show is not just there to entertain us, but to proclaim what is good and just in life, is a definite part of its attraction even after all these years.

Is *Star Trek*'s morality specifically Christian? Given Roddenberry's own beliefs, and the series' consistent lack of explicit references to any known, human religion, many critics have said no. They would maintain that *Star Trek* remains steadfastly and exclusively secular and humanistic, even dismissing religion in general as a kind of backward, intolerant superstition practiced by the less developed planets visited by our heroes, who sometimes need to "enlighten" the natives to abandon their "primitive" beliefs.[6] As we will see, however, several of the virtues repeatedly praised on the show, while by no means unique to Christians, are most often associated with Christianity as some of its defining moral values: these are humility, compassion, and self-sacrifice. And the other virtues practiced by the crew of the *Enterprise*—courage, self-reliance, and moderation—are certainly compatible with Christian ethics, as well as necessary to living a good and happy life.[7] This is not to claim that *Star Trek* is specifically Christian, only that there are several points in its moral vision that are inclusive of and compatible with a Christian perspective. Even more than that, the morals of *Star Trek* generally are helpful, even fundamental to living a Christian life. Neither Roddenberry nor the other *Star Trek* writers were thinking "What would Jesus do?" when they crafted their characters and scripts, but they nonetheless have given us many examples of characters who very much practice Christlike love, humility, and sacrifice.

In all the analysis below, we will be looking only at the original *Star Trek* series. Partly this is done out of sheer practicality: with four more series and ten motion pictures, the phenomenon would be too enormous to treat in its entirety. But it may also be justified on the basis that the original series provides the template for the others: character types, villains, themes, and plots from the original series are constantly recycled in the subsequent series and movies. And the overall concept or ambiance of any *Star Trek* vehicle is contained in the narration that begins each episode of the original series. Each episode may be "new" in some small sense, but at the same time, whether the episode is set in the twenty-second, twenty-third, or twenty-fourth century, and wherever the *Star Trek* characters may be boldly going at the time, the moral questions posed in the original series are the same ones that have occupied the subsequent series and movies, because they are the same questions of life, love, and value with which humans (and, apparently, even nonterrestrial humanoids) have always struggled.

Though the characters are almost certainly familiar to our readers, let us review them briefly. The *Enterprise* is captained by James Tiberius Kirk (played by William Shatner), a headstrong but courageous and oft-decorated officer of Starfleet Command, an organization that carries out the military and scientific endeavors of the peace-loving and egalitarian United Federation of Planets. His second-in-command is Spock (played by Leonard Nimoy), whose mother is human and whose father is from the planet Vulcan. Because of his Vulcan lineage, Spock has greater strength, endurance, and sensory perception than normal humans. But the mental capabilities of Vulcans are what most set them apart: they can perform long and elaborate mathematical calculations mentally, they have an encyclopedic memory, they can both send and receive information telepathically,[8] they can render humanoid opponents unconscious by pinching the base of their necks, and they are nearly incapable of feeling emotions. Although not part of the chain of command, the ship's doctor, Leonard "Bones" McCoy (played by DeForest Kelley) is a close friend of the captain and is frequently consulted when there is a crisis (though he also can be counted on to offer his opinion even if unbidden). He is the most compassionate of the main characters, but prone to emotional outbursts that can render his decisions suspect. Finally, the myriad mechanical components of the ship are overseen by Montgomery Scott, a.k.a. "Scotty" (played by James Doohan), a hard-drinking but dedicated and capable officer, who is repeatedly shown forcing the *Enterprise* to perform beyond its specifications, almost as if by sheer will. Let us see now how we can learn about the virtues from these and the other characters of *Star Trek.*

Unmasking False Gods and Paradises: Freedom and Responsibility

The crew of the *Enterprise* frequently encounters powerful alien beings who have pretensions to godhood. Either through telekinetic ability (e.g., "Where No Man Has Gone Before," "Plato's Stepchildren"), or more advanced technology (e.g., "The Gamesters of Triskelion"), or superior intellect and subterfuge (e.g., "Space Seed"), they are able to capture and control the *Enterprise* and its crew, demanding obedience and even love and devotion from them. Each such encounter ends with Kirk and his friends vanquishing the godlike beings, winning their freedom, and continuing on their mission. This oft-repeated plot of rejecting worship in favor of independence has led some to propose that *Star Trek* is against religion per se, regarding it as an infantilizing burden or trap.[9] But an examination of the "gods" so rejected shows *Star Trek* to be more like the biblical tradition of tearing down false idols than it is an atheistic denial of any divinity.[10]

Let us consider perhaps the paradigmatic episode of this kind, "Who Mourns for Adonais?" The *Enterprise* is grabbed by an enormous hand in space. The crew members then see on their viewing screen a man wearing a crown of laurel leaves. He demands that a landing party come down to his planet, though significantly, he excludes Spock from this invitation. When Kirk and his party arrive, they find that the man is the Greek god Apollo, or, rather, that the Greek god Apollo was really this alien, who had used his technology to trick the ancient Greeks into worshiping him and his fellows as gods and goddesses. He is initially overjoyed to meet these new Earth people, expecting them to be a new generation of eager worshipers. When they refuse, however, Apollo turns to rage and violence, and finally must be destroyed with a blast of phasers from the ship. Compared to the false gods of other episodes, Apollo is not such a bad fellow: he is not overtly cruel or lecherous, he would just like Earth men to defer to him and Earth women to fawn on him, almost simply for old time's sake. His lack of more predatory qualities causes Kirk at the end to wonder out loud, "Would it have hurt us, I wonder, just to have gathered a few laurel leaves?" No, it wouldn't have, but in a way, the episode shows that you get what you pay for with gods as with everything else: a god who needs only a little bowing and scraping is also a god who can offer nothing more impressive or lasting than what human ingenuity has already achieved. Only the real God, who needs nothing from us, can rightfully deserve our complete love and devotion; and only such a God can deliver to us what our technology never can—eternal life, love, and happiness.

As described, it is clear that the godlike beings of *Star Trek* bear little resemblance to any God of love and compassion, whether it is the biblical God, or Allah, or Vishnu. They are incapable of real love and can only threaten and use their followers. They are "little more than cosmic bullies."[11] Choosing Apollo as their representative was highly apt, for this is exactly how the Greek gods behaved—bullying, seducing, raping, and tricking people. Such gods also have little to offer, beyond a promise not to kill those from whom they demand worship. In fact, these false gods seem to need humans much more than humans need them. Although their powers are frightening, they are quickly revealed as clingy, whiny, overgrown children: in one episode, "The Squire of Gothos," this is presented literally, and the powerful alien being who was tormenting Kirk and his friends is eventually stopped by his parents, who apologize for his naughty behavior.[12] The episodes that present adult humans who have obtained godlike powers (e.g., "Where No Man Has Gone Before," "Space Seed") show them as no better: even adult restraint breaks down if coupled with greater power. As Spock observes in "Space Seed," "superior ability breeds superior ambition." It would be the religious duty of any person to reject and despise such false idols, just as the Hebrew Bible repeatedly commands the Israelites not to worship Baal and Asherah, Canaanite deities similar in demeanor and weakness to those of the Greek pantheon. Even worse than empty, stunted idols, there is a demonic side to such beings, as Khan, a superman who attempts to take over the *Enterprise* in the episode "Space Seed," slyly insinuates. Kirk rightly understands that Khan models himself on Satan as presented in Milton's *Paradise Lost,* who claims that it is "better to rule in hell than to serve in heaven."[13] It is the height of piety, not atheism, to reject and fight against such a figure.

A more difficult and ambiguous scenario is raised when the crewmembers of the *Enterprise* destroy a seeming paradise, rather than a supposed but false god. As with the theme of the rejection of false gods, this is a recurring plot on *Star Trek.* Sometimes it can be dealt with fairly easily, as in "The Way to Eden," where the paradise is unfortunately filled with lethal, poisonous plants and must be abandoned, or "Shore Leave," where the planet of infinite delights and dangers turns out to be a highly advanced kind of amusement park, which one can enjoy nonfatally only if one is very careful. Sometimes the writers basically short-circuit the discussion by having the inhabitants or rulers of the paradise threaten the *Enterprise* (e.g., "The Apple"): there is much less compulsion to discuss the nature and value of vacuous, blissful ease if the people enjoying it are also trying to kill you.[14] None of these scenarios raises any serious moral or philosophical dilemmas.

But in "This Side of Paradise," we have one of the most poignant moments in the *Star Trek* universe, precisely because the paradise offered to the crew is so attractive and not coercive or threatening. The *Enterprise* approaches a planet where they believe that all the human colonists have died from exposure to Berthold rays (a fictitious kind of radiation fatal only to animals, not plants). Upon investigating, they find that the colonists are alive and even in perfect physical health, because they've been sprayed with spores by a plant that gives them immunity to the rays as well as enhanced physical health overall. However, it also makes them listless and content with whatever is at hand. A similar kind of happiness in "The Return of the Archons" is described by Spock as "mindlessness, vacant contentment . . . soulless," but here the situation is made more interesting by the fact that Spock himself is infected, and he seems undeniably happy. The spores quickly infect everyone on board the *Enterprise,* including Kirk, though he then discovers that violent emotion rids him of the spores' effects. He insults and physically assaults Spock—a risky tactic to attempt against a Vulcan with the strength of several human men—and thereby angers and "cures" him of the spores as well. Together they contrive to bombard the planet with waves that will send everyone into a rage and end the rule of the spores, "curing" everyone. Spock ends the episode with the evaluation—delivered matter-of-factly and stoically by him, but heard as poignant and devastating by the audience—"For the first time in my life I was happy." Rejecting a simple, physical kind of happiness is not without cost or difficulty, and "real" happiness is not necessarily simple or easy. The colonists, infected crew members, and even Mr. Spock tried to live like the lilies of the field (Luke 12:27), lolling about all day staring at clouds or flowers. But what God demands of human beings is that they "strive for his kingdom" (Luke 12:31), or even that they "enter it by force" (Luke 16:16), or, at the very least, that they just plain work for a living as coregents of God's creation (Gen. 2:15). Spock himself evaluates his situation in these terms, calling his return to normalcy a "self-made purgatory"—not a hell, mind you, as though his life were a punishment, but rather that it is a long and arduous process of self-improvement, growth, and responsibility: "The humans reject protective custody and easy illusions, preferring perilous freedom and the hard-won lessons of genuine discovery."[15] It is a particularly combative, Faustian vision of following God, but it is a Christian one nonetheless: we were not meant to be content with purely temporal, earthly joys—especially if those come to us with no effort—but rather we must strive for these and for higher, eternal joys, such as freedom, service, and love, as difficult and demanding as these are.[16]

Human freedom is threatened not only by our dreams of a lazy paradise, but also by our own creations, when we trust them too much to make our lives easy, comfortable, and happy. This is obvious in the episodes where a robot or computer goes berserk and starts killing people (e.g., "The Ultimate Computer," "The Changeling"). It is perhaps more pertinent and frightening, however, when the machine is just plain stupid but people slavishly continue to believe in its infallibility, as in the episode "Court Martial." When Kirk is wrongfully accused of negligence based on evidence from a faulty computer, the court officers are fully prepared to believe the machine's testimony and convict Kirk. There is also a disturbing tendency on the part of the judges to brush aside Kirk's rights—the rights of the individual—if they conflict or hinder "the good of the service," that is, the good of their group, or, more accurately, the good of their jobs and their bureaucracy.[17] But Kirk's defense attorney—a quaint but brilliant rhetorician who still relies on law books rather than computers—launches into an impassioned tirade asserting human rights and freedom. Although the futuristic court does not have witnesses swear on a Bible, when the lawyer rattles off a list of normative, sacred documents that defend "humanity fading in the shadow of the machine," the Bible is significantly and appropriately at the top of his list. According to the Bible, humans have freedom, rights, and responsibilities because they are made in the image of God (Gen. 1:27): they are meant to have dominion over creation (Gen. 1:28), and are not meant to be the lazy thralls of spore-spewing plants or misguided machines.

Kirk repeatedly rejects idolatry and devil worship, not religion per se, because idols and devils threaten the crucial human value of freedom. The human need for freedom is symbolized on the bridge of the *Enterprise* by the communications officer, Lieutenant Uhura (played by Nichelle Nichols), whose name means "freedom" in Swahili,[18] and with whom Kirk shared the first interracial kiss on United States television, showing that the show's metaphysical pretensions also included a dose of practical social comment and criticism.[19] Only a God who respects human freedom would be appropriate for Kirk or us. Such a God is found in the Bible, where God is the author and guarantor of human freedom, creating human beings who are free to have a relationship with him, but who are equally and emphatically free to reject communion with God and go their own way. And just as Kirk rejects "gods" who seek to take away human freedom, he flees from or destroys "paradises" that are built on enslavement or lethargy, no matter how pleasant they may seem. Such lives of oblivion or servitude are incompatible with human nature, which yearns for freedom, and which even yearns for the responsibility that comes with freedom, as Kirk proclaims in "Return of the Archons": "Freedom is never a gift, it has to be earned!" A passive, limp "paradise" would even be impious, rejecting the freedom that God has built into human nature and abdicating the responsibility that God demands of his real followers in their growing, living relationship with him.[20]

Kirk, Spock, McCoy, and the Prime Directive: Humility and Moderation

Kirk is most often helped in his quest for moral excellence by his two close friends on the *Enterprise,* Spock and McCoy. The three are, in fact, so deliberately integrated on the show that they almost function as one whole being, "a highly articulated symbol of wholeness."[21] Like a successful, integrated "family, if not, at times, one personality,"[22] they make up for each other's deficits, complement each other's opposing qualities, and accentuate each other's good points. Their complementarity is a commonplace in both fans' comments and academic analyses of the series,[23] and it is obviously of perennial appeal, as variations on the triad also occur in the later series. Besides one of the most wonderful images of profound and dedicated friendship, and of the whole being greater than the sum of its parts, the image of the three functioning together as one is another part of the show's examination of human nature, using each of the three to personify one aspect of a person's mind or soul, and thereby to focus and sharpen the analysis.

This analysis of the human soul in three parts is essentially a modified version of that proposed by the ancient Greek philosopher Plato (427–347 BCE), who distinguished between reason, appetite or desire, and a hard-to-define quality of "spiritedness" or "passion" (*thymos*).[24] Of all the Greek philosophers, Plato has frequently been deemed the most compatible with Christian beliefs, and several of the church fathers, most notably Saint Augustine (354–430 CE), showed how Platonism pointed toward many of the same truths as Christianity.

In *Star Trek*'s appropriation of Plato's scheme, Spock represents reason. He is almost always seen at Kirk's side, providing a logical analysis of the myriad of factors in a given situation, often even including the probability of success of each proposed course of action. But as detailed and detached an adviser as he is, consulting Spock is not just the same as consulting the ship's computer. Unlike a computer, Spock can express preferences that go beyond mere mechanical calculation, and he can make moral judgments. The efficacy and morality of Spock's decisions are repeatedly portrayed. For example, when Spock is absent from the bridge in "Spock's Brain," a critical decision must be made as to which of three planets to investigate in a limited amount of time—in order, coincidentally, to save Spock's life. Kirk consults three other officers on the bridge—Uhura, Chekov (actor Walter Koenig), and Sulu (actor George Takei)—but it is obvious from their suggestions that he might as well go "eeny-meeny-miney-mo": unlike Spock, they almost comically lack any ability to sift, weigh, or deliberate over the data, and their choices are completely arbitrary and conflicting. Almost exactly the same scene is played out in "A Private Little War," this time with Uhura, Chekov, and Scotty, who are equally incapable of helping Kirk in his deliberations. And Spock's analysis is not just efficacious; it is moral. In "A Taste of Armageddon," Kirk and Spock are confronted with a civilization that practices a bizarre kind of virtual warfare, in which a computer model calculates who would have died in a real attack, and then the people on the list dutifully commit suicide. When Spock says that he understands their system, the local official is pleased, but Spock corrects him: "I do *not* approve. I understand." Spock shows how a soul governed entirely by reason is both effective and serene, but without being indecisive or nonjudgmental. Using reason, Spock can discern what course of action is right—"right" both in the sense of "effective" and in the sense of "morally correct"—and follow it vigorously.

But the character of Spock just as frequently and vividly presents the limitations of reason. Spock reminds his fellows several times that Vulcans were not always peaceful and logical, but became so only through extreme discipline and training, following on a history and an inner nature every bit as savage as that of humans.[25] This self-control is made more difficult for Spock by his less logical, more emotional human side, but even his Vulcan half can sometimes be unruly and uncooperative. This is shown in "All Our Yesterdays," when Spock and McCoy are transported back in time. Spock feels his reason faltering and slipping away, as he has been transported to a time when Vulcans were unbridled, murderous brutes, and he is himself making the transition to this state. This all-too-easy stripping away of Spock's veneer of reason and control nearly costs McCoy his life when he crosses Spock. In "Amok Time" we again see the fragility of Vulcan reason even more graphically exploded, and without the convenient and artificial excuse of time travel. Spock's mental and physical health deteriorate until he is on the brink of death, and he explains that this is because his time of *Pon farr*—the Vulcan mating ritual—has arrived. When Kirk, Spock, and McCoy arrive on the planet Vulcan, they find that the ritual is anything but logical: following on an insane, dissociated state of "blood fever," it moves on to combat to the death using the most primitive of weapons. In exchange for being completely governed by their reason more than 99 percent of the time, Vulcan males have to submit to an unstoppable descent into bestial madness for the other part of their lives. In "Mirror, Mirror," Kirk and McCoy find a parallel universe where there are evil counterparts to all the *Star Trek* characters. On the one hand, the episode is highly optimistic, showing how the evil Spock seems to be persuaded by Kirk to quit his low-down ways; but on the other hand, there is a dose of realism when the evil Spock calculates that the barbarous empire of which he is a part will continue for another 240 years. Perhaps reason can overcome evil, but only on a rather long and painful schedule of centuries, not in the short-term horizon of a person's lifetime. Spock shows how it is good to control one's baser instincts with reason, but that control probably cannot be maintained at all times, nor can it naively be relied upon to quell base desires in a reasonable amount of time. Reason may be the higher part of a person, but it is not the strongest or the most durable.

Even when not overcome by his desires, Spock's reason is not always sufficient to the task at hand. When Spock takes command of a shuttlecraft in "The Galileo Seven," his decisions are, as always, completely logical, but the situation spirals more and more out of control. On the planet surface, Spock and his crew are attacked by huge yetilike creatures. Spock's logical response of firing warning shots rather than killing the natives outright only enrages them further, till they are standing on top of the shuttle, pounding it with boulders. Spock incites his own crew to the brink of mutiny by refusing at first to bury a dead crew member, as he deems it illogical to risk further carnage to attend to a corpse that is beyond their help. Not only does Spock lack emotions, but their presence in others throws his calculations into a fatal disarray.[26] Further, Spock lacks all sense of wonder,[27] or of the sacred: when he pulls a spear from his dead comrade's back, he can impressively pontificate on the spearhead's physical properties and workmanship, while oblivious to the mystery or sanctity of the human corpse at his feet. Spock admits to being equally unmoved by the wonder of natural beauty in "This Side of Paradise," when he sadly notes that he never before noticed the beauty of clouds.[28] In "The Savage Curtain," we find that Vulcan reason also turns out to be quite inadequate when dealing with unmitigated evil. In this episode Kirk and Spock are joined by replicas of Abraham Lincoln and Surak, the legendary founder of Vulcan civilization and devotion to reason, to do combat with a quartet of cosmic villains, the least offensive of whom is Genghis Khan. Surak unwisely attempts to reason with the unregenerates, appealing to their logic and self-interest, but completely overlooking the illogical, inconvenient, but utterly undeniable fact that they just plain like to be bad.[29] They then simply murder him and get on with the business of trying to kill Kirk, Spock, and Lincoln as well. Like the elves in Tolkien's universe—who are similar to Vulcans in both demeanor and physical appearance—reason and the Vulcans who represent it seem better suited as auxiliaries and advisers than as leaders. In all these instances, reason is shown not just to be weak, but to be inadequate; it is not equivalent to wisdom.

Taking both the triumphs and the failures of Spock's reason into account, it seems that the exchange between McCoy and Spock in "The Galileo Seven" well summarizes the show's evaluation of rationality: when McCoy objects that not all problems can be solved by logic, Spock responds, "I know of no better way to begin." As often happens in the series, McCoy and Spock are both right. In approaching a problem, or just living our lives, reason is the right place to begin, but it is not the whole process or the only way to proceed. All in all, Spock clearly shows how reason is an absolutely necessary, but insufficient and very fragile element of human virtue and happiness.[30]

McCoy consistently represents the desires, not just the physical, but certainly including those. In his capacity as a physician, McCoy necessarily has more to do with basic physical needs than do the other characters. Even within his medical duties, the doctor seems mostly known for his bedside manner, not for his technical prowess. One senses that Spock's frequent jibes that the doctor utilizes potions and witch-doctor-like quackery are not totally unfair: if he could cure people just by doting on them, by being kind and loving and reassuring to them, McCoy probably would prefer it to his lasers, machines, and drugs. Technological marvels remove the humanity and intimacy of the doctor-patient relationship and make it more mechanical and impersonal, like servicing an automobile. McCoy himself belittles futuristic medicine, preferring such ancient and maternal treatments as exercise, rest, and good diet ("The Omega Glory") and admiring feminine manipulations of herbs and magic ("A Private Little War"). He is famously and frequently discomfited by the transporter and other physical inconveniences of life onboard a starship. McCoy is also more realistic as to how people's bodies affect their minds, and vice versa, eschewing both Kirk's lackadaisical manner and Spock's rigid self-denial. In "Charlie X," McCoy is the only one to notice the fairly obvious fact that a teenage boy who's never seen a woman before might be experiencing some problems adjusting to life onboard a starship full of young ladies in short skirts, and he urges Kirk to give the boy a talk about the birds and the bees. Because of such physicality and loving care, it has been observed that McCoy seems more in touch with his feminine side than are the other male characters.[31] On the bridge of a military vessel, surrounded by men performing stereotypically masculine functions—Kirk commanding, Spock analyzing data, Sulu firing weapons, Scotty fixing machines—McCoy is a welcomed, sensitive, maternal counterbalance. In a universe of machines that act like people and alien beings who have no bodies, McCoy is a solid foundation in physical reality, acknowledging its limits, easing its accompanying pain, and enjoying its pleasures and beauty.

Such enjoyment of physicality leads us to the other, less physical human qualities that McCoy embodies: emotion and intuition. McCoy is perhaps the most consistently and overtly happy crew member on board the *Enterprise,* labeled by one critic "the eternal bon vivant."[32] He keeps a special stash of Saurian brandy in sick bay ("The Enemy Within"), and when presented with the possibility of having his heart's desire, he orders a mint julep ("This Side of Paradise"). His southern drawl appears only infrequently in the series (and is really rather annoying), but it too conveys a certain comfort or ease, and another kind of counterbalance, especially to Spock's almost Zen detachment and to the Protestant work ethic so vigorously and relentlessly championed by Kirk and Scotty.[33] McCoy proudly and frequently displays outbursts of many emotions, whether anger, frustration, righteous indignation, fierce loyalty, or romantic love, having his fair share of love interests in the series (e.g., "The Man Trap," "For the World Is Hollow and I Have Touched the Sky"), despite being older than Kirk and Spock. None of this is to portray McCoy or his qualities as soft or weak—any more than calling him maternal implies weakness: as we will see in the next section, he saves the *Enterprise* and his friends as many times as any other character, and his bravery is equally unquestionable, as when he coolly stares down the scalpel-wielding, megalomaniacal superman Khan ("Space Seed"). When

Kirk is believed dead in "The Tholian Web," Spock and McCoy play a prerecorded message from Kirk that summarizes McCoy's quiet strength: Kirk counsels Spock to seek out McCoy's advice, thereby to "temper [his] judgment with intuitive insight." McCoy's emotions and intuitions are as necessary to the mission of the *Enterprise,* or to the healthy functioning of a human soul, as are Spock's reason and logic.

But exactly as with Spock, McCoy's qualities of emotion and intuition are also shown to be incomplete and sometimes detrimental to his own well-being and that of his shipmates. His emotional outbursts are not always endearing: they can cloud his judgment and endanger others. His maternal side proves dangerous in "And the Children Shall Lead," when he is put in charge of five demonic children and unwisely and perilously puts their care ahead of the interests of the crew. His jibes at Spock are usually corrective, but they can turn outright nasty and counterproductive, as in "The Tholian Web," where McCoy indulges in an absolute paroxysm of illogic, first accusing Spock of lusting after command of the ship, then reminding Spock that he will have command if he simply leaves Kirk behind, then finally accusing Spock of trying to get command by *not* leaving Kirk behind. Exactly as in the case of Spock and his reason, McCoy and his emotions seem best suited to advise and influence, not to command the ship or a person completely.

The synthesis and integration of these conflicting faculties of reason and emotion falls upon Kirk, who represents spiritedness.[34] He is the embodiment of the original meaning of *virtue,* which is "manly excellence" (the root is still visible in words such as *virile*). Kirk commands, strives, and advances—always with the help of reason and emotion, but not because of them: he is the one who provides the drive and the goal. We can see this is the essence of Kirk by the fact that when presented with his worst fear, it is the fear that he might become incapable of command ("And the Children Shall Lead"). Kirk's essence is even the subject of its own episode, "The Enemy Within," in which a transporter malfunction produces two Kirks, one "evil" and one "good." But as they are further examined, these initial labels prove misleading.[35] The nasty Kirk is, rather, an exaggerated, uncontrolled version of McCoy's appetitive, animal, emotional side of human nature: his first action onboard is to get drunk; then he attempts a rape, and ends by shrieking, "It's my ship! It's mine!" Significantly, it is McCoy who sticks up for the nasty Kirk: "It's not really ugly, it's human." The nice Kirk is much like Surak in "The Savage Curtain," but even weaker: Surak could at least decide (foolishly) to parlay with the evil characters, while the nice Kirk lacks all decisiveness and can only stare dumbly at the facts of a situation, without any ability to decide which course to pursue. Both halves, significantly, lack spiritedness, for the nasty Kirk is also a craven coward who can only attack from ambush. He too lacks decisiveness and can only rampage around pursuing his momentary lusts; he is as incapable as the nice Kirk of forming a plan or solving a problem, unlike the "real," complete Kirk. Somehow in the splitting of Kirk, the most crucial element of his humanity has been lost, leaving only two maimed and unviable thirds, not halves. It is only when the two Kirks willingly submit to going through the transporter again simultaneously that they are reunited, forming again a spirited Kirk who can make decisions.

The essence, then, of Kirk's humanity and virtue is his admirable self-control, his ability to moderate the extremes of reason and desire: to desire, but within the bounds of what is reasonable, and to reason and desire in a purposeful, deliberate way. This is a description of virtue as basically moderation and maturity, with the corollary that sin is essentially childish, immature behavior.

This is shown vividly in another episode that dissects a human soul, "Charlie X." The *Enterprise* takes onboard a teenage orphan, Charlie, who has been raised on a planet by Thasians, an alien race whose exact character and capabilities are unknown. Among people for the first time right as he hits puberty, Charlie is confused, moody, and aggressive. With McCoy pressuring him to do so, Kirk attempts to train the boy in how to control and restrain himself and get along with others. Kirk tries to do this by physical training in judo, a good outlet for aggression, and one that by its nature requires literal, physical give-and-take with an opponent, rather than just striking and dodging, as in karate or boxing. He also gives a succinct summary of moderation: "There are a million things in this universe you can have, and a million things you can't have!" Describing the universe as 50 percent indulgence and 50 percent denial is hardly the most rigorous, demanding level of self-control, but it is not a bad starting place for the kind of training in moderation that would lead to a normal and even virtuous life. Unfortunately, Charlie is both too old and too immature to respond, and the situation turns lethal when it is revealed that he has developed telekinetic powers under the training of the mysterious Thasians and can kill or maim people with his mind. As we shall see, it is exactly the same scenario as the crucial *Twilight Zone* episode "It's a Good Life," and the point is exactly the same: children are definitely not innocent. They are as sinful and desirous as adults.[36] Virtue is not innate; it must be learned by long and often arduous training, but a child with supernatural powers could refuse such training and wreak havoc. The *Enterprise* is saved from this child/monster only by the fortunate appearance of the incorporeal Thasians, who apologize for letting their dangerous charge escape, and they take him back to their planet. It is one of the sadder moments in the series, as

Kirk has been unable to train an unfortunate youngster to follow the path of virtue that he himself does.

Besides Kirk's two friends, the Prime Directive is another powerful reminder of virtue to Kirk, and it is one of the most frequently recurring plot devices in the *Star Trek* universe. The Prime Directive is the categorical command to all starships and their crews that they are not, under any circumstances, to interfere with the development of an alien culture. Such interference would constitute an infection or contamination, and the deleterious effects on both the contaminated and the contaminator might be so far-reaching and unpredictable that this situation must be avoided at all costs. *Star Trek*'s writers clearly had in mind the awful consequences of earthbound imperialism and colonialism in the eighteenth and nineteenth centuries. Even when outright warfare and genocide were avoided (which was rarely), mere physical contact could be fatal—smallpox epidemics among Native Americans, beriberi among Dutch settlers in Java, malaria among white missionaries in Africa. Even if not fatal, there could be strongly negative effects from supposedly benevolent "cultural imperialism"—economic exploitation, the introduction of dubious political regimes such as communism, the use of colonized peoples as proxies in the colonizers' wars, and the extinction of all indigenous forms of belief or worship. If these were the awful disasters that happened within the human species when one tribe naively tried to "help" or "civilize" or "improve" another, then much greater care would have to be exercised when interacting with the myriad of life-forms in the universe. The strict noninterference of the Prime Directive could also prevent the kind of inadvertent idolatry that is almost forced on Paul in Acts 14:8–18 by well-meaning natives, another awful scenario of mutual destruction used in the *Twilight Zone* episode "The Little People," but successfully avoided by the crew of the *Enterprise* through their obedience and self-restraint.

But, as any viewer knows, the Prime Directive is violated so many times in the course of the series and its sequels that it is in danger of becoming a running gag, where the Prime Directive is either invoked or ignored based only on the exigencies of the plot. There is surely much to this criticism, as the show, like any other, had first to attend to dramaturgical matters rather than philosophical ones: the stories have to "work" before one can worry about the consistency of their "meaning." On the other hand, *Star Trek* so clearly wants to present a moral message as well as an aesthetic experience, that one is right to investigate or question its message if this appears to be presented inconsistently or uncritically.[37] Even within a plot-driven universe, there is a relative consistency of the Prime Directive's importance and meaning on the show. No matter how insanely self-destructive the aliens are behaving, Kirk tries his best to remain aloof and uninvolved, though he will always retaliate in self-defense if the locals attack the *Enterprise* (e.g., "A Taste of Armageddon") or otherwise threaten the safety of innocents (e.g., "The Cloudminders," "For the World Is Hollow and I Have Touched the Sky"). When the *Enterprise* arrives too late to stop a planet from destroying itself in the episode "Let That Be Your Last Battlefield"—an episode pointedly aimed at racial tensions in the United States—it hardly seems a triumph of the Prime Directive, but merely a tragedy that any humane person would've done anything to stop if given the chance. Most of Kirk's violations of the Prime Directive are only in response to previous violations by other humans (e.g., "The Omega Glory," "Patterns of Force," "A Piece of the Action"), or by the even more meddlesome and much less conscientious Klingons (e.g., "A Private Little War"), that have resulted in horrible perversions of alien cultures that send them down the road of endless warfare or even genocide. Such remedies are not really violations of the spirit of the Prime Directive, which seeks ultimately the health and well-being of both the alien culture and the whole universe. Instead, they are equivalent to the use of "unnatural" drugs or treatments to cure the smallpox that one's fellows have inflicted on a foreign race. Such interference by Kirk or a doctor is embarked on with humility, caution, and regret that the situation has come to this. Such treatments are also done out of love and concern for the alien race, not out of a desire to control, manipulate, or use them.

The ultimate reason for the Prime Directive, therefore, is an accurate and humble assessment of human limitations. Kirk states this clearly to another starship captain who has violated the Directive: "I don't think we have the right or the wisdom to interfere" ("The Omega Glory"). Kirk generalizes his criticism to "we," showing clearly that it is not just a shortcoming of this particular captain—as though a person who were wise enough might have the right to "fix" an alien culture, or perhaps that Starfleet could approve of it by a vote—but that no human being could ever have such a right to play God in this way, because no human being could ever attain to such godlike wisdom.[38] This humble acknowledgment of human fallibility and insufficiency in the face of a universe with nearly limitless challenges and dangers is praised repeatedly throughout the series, and it is what often saves the characters from turning into the kind of monsters and bullies against which they fight: "It is, in large part, the humans' lack of godly pretensions that saves them. Humans have self-doubt; they know they are not perfect."[39] Humans are weak and fallible, but so long as they are aware of this, it makes them stronger than the arrogant and misguided entities—human, alien, or mechanical—who wrongly believe in their own infallibility and moral superiority. The Prime Directive is an important and constant reminder to all the characters of such human weakness.

In an especially important episode, the series even has the good moral and aesthetic sense to show Kirk himself falling prey to such hubris, in the episode "Errand of Mercy."[40] Kirk offers to protect the seemingly primitive inhabitants of the planet Organia from the evil Klingons. The Organians politely but emphatically refuse and allow themselves to be invaded and even abused and murdered by the Klingons. Kirk and Spock on the planet surface square off against a squad of Klingon troops, while Starfleet and Klingon battle cruisers close in on each other in the space overhead. At this point, the Organians finally reveal themselves not to be primitive and cowardly, but rather to be advanced, incorporeal beings whom Spock estimates are as far beyond us as we are beyond amoebas. The Organians neutralize all Klingon and Federation weapons, and Kirk and the Klingon commander impotently sputter against them, "You're talking nonsense!" "What gives you the right?!" With a truce forced on him, and his own bloodlust and shocking similarity to the loathsome Klingons embarrassingly revealed,[41] Kirk is sheepish and stunned, finally admitting to Spock, "I'm embarrassed. I was furious with the Organians for stopping a war I didn't want." It is part of Kirk's heroism and appeal that he has the wisdom to be "embarrassed" by his shortcomings and hypocrisy, and that he can therefore learn to avoid them in the future and better live out his ideals of mutual respect and freedom. As he humbly and beautifully states it in another episode, "We're all vulnerable in one way or another" ("Is There in Truth No Beauty?").[42]

Guided by the humility of the Prime Directive and by their own counterbalancing qualities, Kirk, Spock, and McCoy together serve as one of the greatest paradigms and inspiring exemplars of the humanistic virtues of humility and moderation. They are respectful of others and even capable of learning from them and thereby correcting their own shortcomings. Working together, they successfully avoid the extremes and moderate their reason and emotion into a synthesis that is both virtuous and highly effective. But deeper and more divine than moderation and humility, Kirk and both of his friends constantly live their lives in the service of others, even at great expense and sacrifice to themselves. These are the higher, "Christian" virtues of compassion and self-sacrifice, to which we now turn.

Christian Virtues: The Golden Rule—Compassion and Self-Sacrifice

Part of *Star Trek*'s appeal is in its characters' wonderful restraint, so sadly lacking in much of the rest of television or the movies. Kirk and his crew never pursue revenge and never use excessive force. An incapacitated opponent, no matter how much damage he has done, is always spared by Kirk (e.g., "Space Seed," "The Omega Glory"): "Do to others as you would have them do to you. . . . Be merciful, just as your Father is merciful" (Luke 6:31, 36; cf. Matt. 5:48; 7:12). As we saw above concerning humility, sometimes Kirk himself falters in this respect, and has to be taught such mercy by superior alien beings, as in "Arena," which begins with an enraged Kirk pursuing an alien ship which has destroyed a human settlement. Spock counsels restraint, observing that the aliens may not be as bent on aggression as Kirk assumes, but Kirk is incorrigible and overcome again by his bloodlust. As the two ships pass by a star system, both Kirk and the alien captain are whisked off their ships by aliens called the Metrons, who put them on an asteroid and instruct them to do single combat to the death. The captain of the alien ship is a Gorn, a seven-foot-tall lizard who can take anything Kirk can dish out—including having a boulder dropped on him—and who can toss Kirk around like a rag doll. Kirk retreats and finds the ingredients for gunpowder, which he uses to build a mortar. He blasts the Gorn, incapacitating but not killing him. Kirk then refuses to finish off his opponent, acknowledging that he himself had been too hasty in his judgment and too eager to kill. The Metrons are so impressed by this show of mercy—a quality which they had assumed humans too primitive to possess—that they spare both ships and send them on their way. Once again, Kirk has shown himself noble enough to learn from others and from his own mistakes.

But even higher than the quality of mercy is the Christian ideal of compassion, of not just sparing another being from suffering, but of actually alleviating another's suffering by willingly sharing in it, as Jesus shared in our humanity and suffering. As noted above, such a quality is especially prevalent in McCoy, who shares his patients' sufferings and is a better healer because of it. McCoy lives out daily the ideal of the good Samaritan, who compassionately helps a wounded stranger.[43] But Vulcan physiology also affords Spock a unique opportunity to experience compassion, despite his own lack of emotion. In "The Devil in the Dark," Kirk and Spock investigate the horrible deaths of miners on the planet Janus VI. They find that a creature made of living rock, the horta, is responsible, incinerating the hapless miners with the acid that it uses to burrow through rock. But after Kirk wounds the creature with his phaser, Spock performs the Vulcan mind-meld with it, feeling everything that it feels. Spock cries out in agony, making audible the pain that the horta is feeling. Both Spock and Kirk are deeply moved by the experience, now knowing that the horta acted to defend itself and its eggs, and realizing how wrong it would be to kill it. Having felt the creature's pain and understood its motives, they recognize and seek to protect its rights: they no longer treat it as a monster or "devil," but as a person, which it is, even if it is not human. Kirk calms the angry miners and negotiates for them and the hortas to live in peace and cooperation. Compassion expands the circle of those we can call neighbor or friend, just as it does in the story of the good Samaritan (Luke 10:29–37), who, once he was overwhelmed by compassion, could not help but come to the aid of a member of another tribe, despite their preexisting animosity: "Jews do not share things in common with Samaritans" (John 4:9).

An almost inevitable concomitant of compassion is self-sacrifice, the giving up of one's own well-being and even life for another, in imitation of Jesus's perfect sacrifice: "If any want to become my followers, let them deny themselves and take up their cross and follow me. . . . For the Son of Man came not to be served but to serve, and to give his life a ransom for many" (Mark 8:34; 10:45). Kirk echoes this exactly in "Metamorphosis": "Love sometimes expresses itself in sacrifice." Each of the main characters—Spock (e.g., "Operation—Annihilate!"), McCoy (e.g., "Spock's Brain"), and Kirk (e.g., "The Tholian Web," "Amok Time")—repeatedly shows himself possessed of such a great and self-sacrificing love as to lay down his life for the others: "No one has greater love than this, to lay down one's life for one's friends" (John 15:13). Showing how important this virtue is to the series, it is not reserved just for our heroes but is frequently seen in guest characters—for example, Dr. Dehner in "Where No Man Has Gone Before," Lazarus in "The Alternative Factor," and Commodore Decker in "The Doomsday Machine." This highest, most divine love is very rare, but it is widely and unpredictably bestowed on creatures all over the universe, as a grace, we could say.

The most intense and dramatic example of self-sacrifice is in the episode "The Empath." It is clearly the most overtly Christian episode in a series that otherwise prefers its religious dimension to be discrete and indirect, as we have seen.[44] The episode begins with a quotation from the Old Testament (Ps. 95:4) and ends with a quotation from the New Testament (Matt. 13:45). In this episode, it is not a matter of one of the three main characters sacrificing himself for the others, but each in turn offers to die to save the other two, and the torture scenes of Kirk and McCoy are deliberately staged as crucifixions.[45] In this episode again, our heroes are shown not to be the only ones capable of self-sacrifice, for the episode revolves around the beautiful interplay between the three main characters and another, alien character who is coming to learn about their love and compassion.

While investigating a planet orbiting a dying sun, Spock, McCoy, and Kirk are captured by big-headed aliens named Vians, who calmly subject them to torture while a beautiful, frail, mute woman looks on. McCoy names the woman Gem, and she shows that she is able to absorb their pain and wounds into her body, which can then heal in a matter of seconds.[46] Between bouts of torture, she kindly performs this service for the officers of the *Enterprise,* but the Vians increase their torture of McCoy to the point where Gem may die if she empathically absorbs his fatal wounds. We then finally learn the reason for this seemingly pointless sadism: the system's sun is about to explode, and the Vians have the technology to save only one planet's population from destruction. The Vians have rightly judged that the most valuable qualities of a person or a civilization are compassion and self-sacrifice, so if Gem can learn and practice self-sacrificial love, then her race will be saved: "For those who want to save their life will lose it, and those who lose their life for my sake and the sake of the gospel, will save it" (Mark 8:35; cf. Matt. 16:25; Luke 9:24). Their actions show that the Vians themselves are less accomplished at practicing these virtues, a hypocrisy for which Kirk passionately berates them. By witnessing how Spock, McCoy, and Kirk act toward each other, Gem herself learns how to love in this way, and she is finally willing even to take on McCoy's fatal injuries, though, good doctor that he is, he pushes her away before she can complete the process. The Vians relent and give the best summary ever of what the series does overall: "You were her teachers. . . . Everything that is truest and best in all species of beings has been revealed by you." Just as "Charlie X" is sad because Kirk cannot teach the boy to practice moderation, the end of "The Empath" is one of the most triumphant in the series, because the *Enterprise* officers have fully educated another being in their most valuable lesson of how to practice the highest form of love.

Conclusion

More than almost any other television series, *Star Trek* self-consciously and deliberately poses philosophical and moral questions. "*Star Trek* is the only television show to have directly posed the question: 'What is the Good?' . . . *Star Trek* may be the only television show that has attempted to convey the peak joy of philosophic contemplation and philosophic friendship."[47] For all its camp and Shatner's frequently dreadful acting, it presents one of the most sustained explorations of moral philosophy on television to date. It repeatedly examines the nature of good and evil, human nature, progress, reason and emotion, and, most of all, virtue. *Star Trek* became and remains so popular because it does not just entertain but inquires into questions of ultimate meaning and purpose with thoughtfulness, ambiguity, and insight. Because of the idiosyncrasies of its creator, the show would not do so in an explicitly Christian or even a religious way, but this should not obscure its overall message, which is both humanistic and Christian, in the broadest and best senses of both.[48]

Another, perhaps simpler way to describe the show's moral appeal is to note that *Star Trek* has, for almost forty years, satisfied our longing for heroes, for people who live virtuous lives that inspire us to emulate them. The crew members of the *Enterprise* are—unlike most characters on television—admirable, and their morality is both a challenge and an encouragement to us: "Here was a program which said that heroism is not a providential gift to a certain elect, but a quality attained through difficult and painful choices. This does not diminish heroism's glow, but enhances it; for it places the possibility for true heroism within the grasp of anyone, not merely the strong or gifted."[49] We love and keep watching *Star Trek* because—like a good sermon, or like the morality plays or epic poetry of previous ages—it teaches us how to be better and inspires us to be so.

III
Human Freedom

The Prisoner

Prisoner: Where am I?
Voice: In the Village.
Prisoner: What do you want?
Voice: Information.
Prisoner: Whose side are you on?
Voice: That would be telling. We want information. Information. Information!
Prisoner: You won't get it!
Voice: By hook or by crook, we will.
Prisoner: Who are you?
Voice: The new Number Two.
Prisoner: Who is Number One?
Voice: You are Number Six.
Prisoner: I am not a number! I am a free man!!
Voice: <triumphant laughter>

Opening dialogue, *The Prisoner*

And you will know the truth, and the truth will set you free.

John 8:32

The Prisoner is considered by many to be the most inventive, unusual television show ever produced, so unusual that it is surprising that it ever aired, even for such a short run as it had. Its seventeen one-hour episodes premiered in 1967. In the United States it was first shown on CBS, though subsequently American audiences could see it on PBS stations, and it is now available on VHS and DVD. Although there are so few episodes, they have inspired fan clubs, an annual meeting at the site where the series was filmed in Wales, fanzines, Web sites, a comic-book adaptation, a song by the heavy-metal group Iron Maiden,[1] several commentaries,[2] novelizations, and frequent talk of a feature film adaptation.[3] The show's influence is felt in one of the other series analyzed in this volume, as the creator of *Babylon 5,* J. Michael Straczynski, is an avid *Prisoner* fan and frequently puts references to it in his series.

The main outlines of the show's premise are given at the beginning of each episode, where we see dark storm clouds while hearing claps of thunder. We then see a long, deserted stretch of highway. A car races by, driven by the main character of the series, the Prisoner, also known as Number Six, played by Patrick McGoohan, who was the series' executive producer, as well as the writer and director for three episodes. The car weaves through narrow London streets and into an underground parking garage. We then see Number Six striding down a long corridor, his loud footsteps the only sound, his expression angry and determined. He reaches double doors, flings them open, and storms into an office. He confronts the man sitting there, shouting at him, pacing back and forth in front of the desk. Number Six pounds his fist on the desk, upsetting and breaking the teacup and saucer there. We hear none of the shouting and crashing, however, but only thunderclaps. Finally he pulls out an envelope and slams it on the desk and strides out.

We see a typewriter putting Xs across an ID card with Number Six's picture on it. Then the ID card is carried by a mechanical arm down a long track between two rows of file cabinets that almost seem to stretch back to infinity. One of these file cabinets opens by itself as the mechanical arm approaches and the card slides down a chute into the drawer, which closes on its own. We see that the drawer is labeled "Resigned." The envelope must have contained his resignation—from what, we do not know.

We then see Number Six arrive at a townhouse, but with a large black car pulling up ominously behind him as he gets out of his car. He goes into his apartment and hurriedly packs a suitcase. As he shuts the suitcase, we see a man approaching his apartment door; then a cloud of gas floods into the apartment through the keyhole, the room begins to spin, and our hero collapses, unconscious. When he awakes and opens the blinds, he sees a lovely, peaceful, perfectly manicured resort town called simply "The Village," where he is now a prisoner.

This opening sequence is repeated at the beginning of almost every episode. It establishes the premise for the series. Our hero is a prisoner in a perfectly comfortable Village that usually offers no mistreatment, but from which he cannot escape. His incarceration has followed upon his resignation from some supersecret organization that does not tolerate such insubordination or self-assertion: it makes no difference whether he was an agent of MI5, OSI, Area 51, or Her Majesty's Secret Service. As Number Six quickly finds out, the Village is populated by other spies and officials, from all over the world and both sides of the Iron Curtain. Like Number Six, their previous identities are irrelevant within the Village, and they are all referred to by only their numbers. They are held in the Village by some unknown entity that is either a cooperative venture of all world governments to contain and neutralize people who are dangerous to the status quo or is an organization that somehow transcends all governmental ties and allegiances, an Illuminati-like group similar to that in *The X Files* (though *The Prisoner*'s wardens are without ties, so far as we can tell, to extraterrestrials). Further complicating and frustrating the prisoners' situation is the fact that it is impossible to tell which of them are "moles" or traitors planted or bribed by the Village administration to spy on other prisoners. Also, the threat of force or torture, while subdued and not overt, is always subtly present. The overall tone of the series is one of suspicion, paranoia, unease, and disorientation.

The opening sequence in London is usually followed by the opening dialogue given at the beginning of this chapter, playing as a voice-over to scenes of Number Six trying to escape. In every episode, a new Number Two comes to the Village to run it; his or her special mission, of course, is to break Number Six and get the "information" as to why he resigned. Even Number Two is somehow a prisoner as well as a warden within this system, however. As one elderly Villager summarizes it in the first episode, "Arrival," "We're all pawns." Or as Number Two himself observes in "A Change of Mind," "Nobody is above investigation." Only Number One would be the "king" in this game, but his or her identity—or even whether such a person exists—remains a mystery even at the end of the series.

If the scenes of the Prisoner's resignation and imprisonment in the Village provide the background to the action, this dialogue provides the underlying themes and questions of the series, which constantly returns to the problem of the individual relating to society and the sometimes unfair, dehumanizing demands that society puts on the individual. Human freedom is a frequent theme in *Star Trek,* but there the threats to freedom are always extrinsic—for example, aliens unfairly and arbitrarily kidnap the *Enterprise* or its crew and enslave or torture them; Starfleet and the Federation are always shown to be basically benevolent—if sometimes inept and demanding—entities that would never threaten or degrade people in such a way. But *The Prisoner* presents us with the more disturbing and potentially more revealing scenario of a man whose freedom is constantly threatened by our own institutions and inventions. Not only are we our own worst enemies as a species, but in the end he finds out that he is his own worst enemy in a very personal, psychological sense. Number Six's struggles against these human and personal challenges are what makes the series so compelling and relevant, and it is to these challenges that we now turn.

The False Idols of the State and Technology

As the setup of the series shows, the Prisoner faces a state or institution that possesses virtually infinite power, technology, and resources and that has no scruples whatsoever about using these for its own mysterious ends. The administration of the Village possesses weapons and technology far in advance of anything known in the outside world. They can whisk hundreds or even thousands of people from all over the globe away to some undisclosed location and keep them there indefinitely. They apparently have been doing so for at least decades, if not longer, and they plan on continuing forever, as the Village is equipped with a hospital, a nursing home, and a cemetery; one episode ("The Girl Who Was Death") reveals that there are even children born and raised there, as bizarre as that may seem. No one has ever tried to stop the Village administration, or even interfered with its machinations. It is, in fact, implied that all or most world governments cooperate with the maintenance of the Village, for their own selfish ends, and with no concern for their citizens' well-being or for anything as abstract, sentimental, and quaint as "human rights." It is shown several times in the series that the Prisoner's own former employers and colleagues collaborate in his imprisonment and persecution ("Arrival," "The Chimes of Big Ben," "Many Happy Returns"). But, as we shall see, the message and hope of the series is that one man can defeat all this—that a moral, virtuous individual can use his reason and will to withstand any assault made on him by a dehumanizing, immoral state. No matter how much coercion or technology is brought to bear on him, Number Six can outlast their schemes, keep his integrity intact and his mind free, and eventually win his freedom.

First, before turning to individual episodes, let us consider a recurring character that tangibly and terrifyingly embodies the threats posed to human freedom by the state and technology—the Village's "watchdog," a creature known as "Rover." It is seen during the opening dialogue of each episode and at the closing credits, and it usually appears during every episode proper, as the final and unconquerable obstacle to any of Number Six's escapes. As it was originally conceived, Rover was to be some kind of vehicle or contraption, but the proposed device failed its most crucial test: it couldn't maneuver across water, a necessity if it were to chase and capture Number Six in his many escape attempts.[4] But the final version of Rover—ably played by a variety of weather balloons—turned out to be much more effective and memorable, appearing on the show as a giant, bouncing sphere that could outrun any human or vehicle, glide through or over water, and could capture or kill people by swallowing them. It also seemed to have a hypnotic effect on people, even when it was not attacking, as everyone besides Number Six is paralyzed when Rover appears, and even our hero is sometimes temporarily incapacitated by its presence.

This version of Rover is a brilliant, provocative image. Unlike the original conception of a robotic police vehicle, a large orb turned out to be much more mysterious and menacing. Although Rover appears to be manufactured, a horrible, technological marvel engineered by whoever runs the Village, it is never clear what exactly it is. Whenever it appears on the show, Rover first emits a loud roar, somewhat resembling the sound made by the movie monster Godzilla, but it then glides by with an electronic whining or whistling sound. It seems that it could be either mechanical or biological, a robot or a strange, alien creature; certainly its endearing name is more appropriate to an animal than a robot. During its attacks, Rover seems the most biological and least mechanical, as it absorbs its victims like an amoeba or like the white blood cells in the movie *Fantastic Voyage* (1966). It also seems able to split, amoebalike, into smaller Rovers ("Free for All"). The Village authorities' control or understanding of their watchdog seems less than total. Although they often release it underwater so that it can rise to the surface and attack Number Six when he is in the water or on the beach, Rover is frequently shown patrolling the Village on its own, without human direction. In the episode "Schizoid Man," it kills an agent of the authorities before they can stop it. In the penultimate episode, "Once upon a Time," Rover even sits in Number Two's control chair, as though it were in charge. And in one bizarre and mysterious scene in "Free for All," several Villagers are shown seated around Rover, mesmerized by it, apparently worshiping or communing with it.[5]

All of this serves to make Rover a potent symbol of human creativity and intellect run amok, for humans have created something that they now can neither control nor understand. Like the suprastate entity that controls the Village, and like a plethora of technological devices and methods shown in the series, Rover must have begun as something to protect and serve human beings, but it has evolved into something that perpetuates itself, while trapping and killing people. Certainly the enormous advances in computers and biology since the show was first filmed make it seem even more likely that there could one day be a creature like Rover—a robot or an animal made by humans to serve us, that instead helps to destroy us. And while we may have "won" the cold war during which *The Prisoner* was made, and we may calm ourselves with the reassuring mantra that "freedom is on the march," it is still abundantly clear that states and rulers are as eager and capable as ever of enslaving us, lying to us, manipulating us, and disregarding our rights. When we see Rover melting or dissolving in the last episode of the series,[6] it is the most tangible image of the Prisoner's victory over everything that has sought to degrade and dehumanize him: he has destroyed his most inhuman enemy, an enemy made all the more dangerous and threatening for having been invented by humans.

The Village authorities' idolization of technology and the Prisoner's dismantling of it figure in several episodes. Although the series grants a certain efficaciousness to behavioral sciences (e.g., "It's Your Funeral," "Checkmate"), it is usually mocking and critical of modern ideas of psychology, insofar as they diminish the person to a machine whose thoughts and actions can be predicted, manipulated, or "fixed." In "A, B, and C," the authorities have tried to calculate what Number Six would have done if he had not resigned and been brought to the Village. They predict that he would have sold his secret information to one of three people. The authorities have condensed the images and vital statistics of these people onto little reels marked "A," "B," and "C." On each of three successive nights, Number Six is drugged and one of these reels is plugged into a machine that will force that person to appear in Number Six's dreams that evening, though the "plot" of the dream will still be under the control of his own subconscious. The authorities have at their disposal technology that even today is beyond anyone's expectation, for they can then watch the Prisoner's dreams projected onto a screen, thereby using his subconscious to learn the secrets that his conscious, waking mind protects. Their dream apparitions, however, are quickly detected as false by Number Six, who knows how the people are really "supposed" to act in his dreams. In the third dream, when he unmasks the shadowy figure "C" (of whose exact appearance and identity the authorities are unsure), the Prisoner gives him the face of the Number Two who has engineered this nightly torture. Number Two's attempts fail, because the human subconscious is just as sacred and in control as the conscious, and both are beyond the powers of idols as weak and trivial as their drugs and gadgets.

The authorities are somewhat more successful in "The Schizoid Man," where they try to drive Number Six mad by bringing to the Village an impostor, Curtis, who looks and acts exactly like him. By treating the real Number Six as though *he* were the impostor, they hope to make him doubt his own identity and eventually break his will to resist. Through drugs and electric shock, they condition Number Six's behavior in certain ways to make him seem less like himself: they make him act left-handed when he's really right-handed, and they rather humorously give him an insatiable desire for pancakes. Their plan begins to degrade Number Six's mind, but not so much because of their technology or the psychology behind it, but because of good, old-fashioned human emotion:

they turn a female friend of Number Six against him, and the betrayal thoroughly unsettles him. Number Six also subverts their plan in a very low-tech, physical way: he ambushes the impostor and beats him till he divulges the plan. In the end, Number Two also resorts to a human, nontechnological solution: believing that Number Six has taken the place of the impostor and is now going to escape, Number Two asks him to give his regards to his wife, Susan. When Number Six mistakenly says he'll do so, Number Two has him stopped, saying, "Susan died a year ago, Number Six." In the actions of both Number Six and the authorities, it is clear that even technology as advanced as that found in the Village is very fallible and limited indeed. Besides pointing up the weakness of science, in this episode Number Six makes a statement that could be the epitaph for science in the series as a whole: "The trouble with science is that it can be perverted." The accuracy of this evaluation can be seen in our world every day, in a myriad of abuses or misuses of science, both large and small.

Mind control is again criticized as both evil and ineffective in "The General." In this episode, we find out that the Village has functions other than just holding and interrogating dangerous ex-spies: the Villagers can also be used as guinea pigs for experiments. As in Nazi concentration camps or Soviet gulags, the Villagers are an especially tempting group for such experiments, as there are no intrusions or restraints put on the mad scientists' work, and the subjects cannot object to or withdraw from the study. In this case, however, the experiment seems quite benign, at least at this preliminary stage. By means of a "sublimator" and television broadcasts, the Villagers are subjected to subliminal messages that are indelibly imprinted onto their minds. The process is called "speed learn," and it impressively conveys encyclopedic knowledge in seconds to everyone who watches it:

even Number Six, upon being asked the next day when was the Treaty of Adrianople, cannot help but blurt out "1829." But the flaw of this "education" is later shown, when Number Six is asked *what* was the treaty of Adrianople, and he realizes that he has no idea. While being touted as a wonderful replacement to rote memorization, this process is even worse. Now the students wrongly believe in their own omniscience, while they cannot even regurgitate the full set of facts, but only disconnected snippets of them. The only "advantage" to speed learning is mockingly shown as the Villagers have a huge, Mardi Gras-like party the night before final exams, rather than studying: speed learn would turn all of education into one long spring break, a tempting but empty descent into hedonism, similar to what we will see criticized in another episode ("Free for All").

The creator of the process, the Professor, himself realizes his terrible mistake and attempts to warn others, exclaiming that "speed learn is an abomination! It is slavery!" Number Six of course immediately sees the awful potential for such dehumanizing "knowledge" being force-fed to people, observing that "Napoleon could've used it." (As in our comments below on the use of dark humor, the series seems to prefer comparisons to the more comical tyrant Napoleon, rather than to the more monstrous and terrifying ones of the twentieth century.) Both the Professor and Number Six are aided in their attempts to stop speed learn by a humane and sympathetic Village administrator, Number Twelve, but they are unsuccessful at stopping its broadcast. In the end, they find that speed learn has been taken over by "The General," an enormous computer created by the Professor. Number Two brags that the General can answer any question put to it. Number Six accepts the challenge and destroys the computer by asking it a question that he claims is "insoluble—for man or machine." Number

Six's query was simply, "Why?" The scene is, of course, as hokey and deserving of eye-rolling as any of the times when Captain Kirk destroys monstrous machines with some clever trick. But the lesson is still noteworthy: only people can meaningfully ask—as the Prisoner does in every episode—questions such as "Why?" Such a question does not madden and destroy us, even if we cannot answer it, the way it destroyed a machine like the General. Such a question is exactly what makes us human, for we are beings who passionately long for and relentlessly pursue meaning, rather than just data, wherever such a pursuit takes us and whatever it costs.

Number Six's battle against the pervasive evil of a state run amok is vividly shown in "A Change of Mind." In this episode we see a common tactic of totalitarian regimes: to curry favor and lessen their own punishment or win rewards, the citizens themselves cooperate in their own oppression by reporting or even persecuting those whom the state singles out as scapegoats for the community. Number Six underestimates the orgiastic, mob-driven savagery to which his fellow Villagers will descend: he calls them "sheep," when in this episode they are really much more like rats or hyenas, turning on each other and tearing one another apart to please their captors. Like any mob, they have lost all reason and restraint, and they shout down Number Six with no concern that their labels are contradictory: "Reactionary! Rebel! Disharmonious!" Number Two, who is stirring up all this hatred against Number Six, feigns concern for him, reminding him that "the slowest mule is nearest to the whip," a sentiment that will be spelled out again in "Checkmate": "In a society, one must learn to conform." After they label him as "unmutual," the fury of the mob is fully unleashed against Number Six, and they beat and drag him through the streets; the savagery of their attack is shocking to both Number Six and us, and it is made more shocking and monstrous by the fact that the leaders of the mob are matronly old ladies wielding umbrellas as clubs. The idea that your neighbor's teenage son could somehow be stirred up enough to commit violence is alarming, but not nearly so frightening as the idea that, under the right circumstances, the kindly old lady down the street could also be whipped up into a frenzy of murderous rage against you.

Once the mob has spent itself, Number Two can apply more direct, focused, organized brutality to Number Six. Here we see the ultimate, most monstrous example of the state overstepping its bounds: against those who have been declared "unmutual," the authorities declare themselves duty bound—for the sake of both the accused and the community—to perform a lobotomy on the wayward citizen. The authorities euphemistically call this procedure "social conversion," hijacking the language of religion and faith onto their own sinful ends. It is the ultimate and complete disregard of individual rights: if one's mind is against the state, the state will simply take that mind away. Fortunately for Number Six, his mind is so valuable to the authorities that the "social conversion" is a fake: the authorities hope that by tranquilizing him enough with drugs and talking to him as though he were a lobotomized imbecile, they will weaken his will and he will speak freely to them. Unfortunately for them, Number Six figures their ruse out, first using their drugs against his "doctor" to render her harmless; Number Six then adeptly uses the mob to his advantage. He docilely and meekly asks Number Two if he can make his "confession" before all the citizens, but when allowed to do so, Number Six instead turns on Number Two and shouts him down as "unmutual," knowing that it is in the nature of a mob to turn against their master just as quickly and savagely as against anyone else. The mob chases Number Two through the streets, either to his own lobotomy or his escape via helicopter; either way, he has been toppled as leader of the Village, his own weapons of terror and oppression used against him to end his evil rule.

A similar situation of Number Six turning the tables on his tormentors is shown even more graphically in "Hammer into Anvil." The episode begins with a woman, Number Seventy-three, being cruelly interrogated by Number Two. When she screams, Number Six tries to run to her aid, but she throws herself from a window and dies. Number Six is clearly outraged by the cruel and unnecessary death, and to Number Two's threat of "You'll pay for this," he responds, "No. You will." Number Six then begins to perform strange actions all over the Village, knowing that Number Two monitors his every move. In full view of the shopkeeper who he knows will report his behavior, Number Six listens to the beginning of a musical piece on several different records, checking his watch while doing so. He writes a message on a pad of paper, knowing that Number Two will be able to read it from the impression made on the sheets underneath: "To X. O. 4 Ref your query via Bizet record. No. 2's instability confirmed. Detailed report follows. D. 6." Number Two is panic-stricken, knowing that his own actions can be monitored and censured, and now believing that Number Six is an agent sent by his superiors to do so. Since there is no plot against him, Number Two's paranoia and fear are the seeds of his own destruction.

Knowing this weakness of tyrants and bullies, Number Six continues his random, mysterious actions, and increasingly uses them to implicate others in his supposed plot—a conspiratorial-sounding phone call to the hospital supervisor, which Number Six knows will be monitored; erroneous birthday greetings read on the radio, which he knows will make it seem that the radio broadcaster is part of the conspiracy; whispering to Number Two's most loyal servant, when he knows that others are watching and will report the incident to Number Two. Number Two believes all of it, firing and attacking people all around him, committing actions that are increasingly unstable and irrational. In the end, Number Six walks into his office, and rightly diagnoses his problem, the fatal problem of all tyrants: "All this power at your disposal, and yet you're alone. . . . You destroyed yourself." Still believing that Number Six is an agent of those in command, Number Two picks up the phone to his superiors and asks to be replaced, admitting that he has lost the ability to command. Having used intimidation, lies, and paranoia against the Villagers, and having fatally done so with Number Seventy-three, Number Two has now had these weapons used to destroy him. The state's dehumanizing weapons of terror have again been ironically and righteously turned back against it by Number Six, exposing its idolatrous magnification of itself and its callous sacrifice of its own citizens. Number Seventy-three has been avenged, but more importantly, Number Two has been punished, and the state he represents has been chastened and its powers curtailed, however briefly.

The message in these episodes is clear: the individual human being—made by God in the image of God, Christians and Jews would add—is greater than any human-made state or technology. Governments and technologies are useful and necessary when they serve women and men, but these entities are idolatrous and evil when their perpetuation and growth are regarded as the goals of human life: as in Jesus's saying about the Sabbath (Mark 2:27), human-made institutions were made for human beings, not human beings for the institutions. This is the exactly reversed, perverted situation of the Village and its mad scientists and governors, or of any dehumanizing state or technology: they do not serve their citizens, their citizens serve them, men and women endlessly sacrificed to insatiable and useless idols whose only purpose is to continue their own worthless existence. The individual has a spiritual and eternal value, while human institutions or accomplishments can be only physical and temporary. The demands they can legitimately make on people are therefore limited to physical, temporal things; as Jesus observed to those who sought to accuse him either of unduly selling out to secular authority or of treason against the secular authority: "Give therefore to the emperor the things that are the emperor's, and to God the things that are God's" (Matt. 22:21; cf. Mark 12:17; Luke 20:25). With such limited demands and legitimacy, the power of the state or of other human-made entities, while often terrifying, is also ultimately limited and temporary: in every episode, Number Six lives out Jesus's exhortation "Do not fear those who kill the body but cannot kill the soul" (Matt. 10:28; cf. Luke 12:4). Throughout the series, his soul is fully and fiercely alive, and in the end he has helped us to see the value and purpose of ours.

War and Violence

The Prisoner was produced during the cold war, when the threat of complete destruction by nuclear war hung over all of us; the show's original run was also during the Vietnam War, a war widely considered to be unjust, and which brought actual, present killing and dying into our homes nightly on television. Given this milieu, it is inevitable that the show would return several times to the issues of war and violence. In particular, it asks the probing questions of how to live a virtuous life when the threat of violence hangs over one constantly, how to respond to the state's demands that one perpetrate violence on its behalf, and whether one should retaliate against state-sponsored violence in kind. Never is Number Six shown to be reluctant to use violence: an expert marksman, fencer, and pugilist, he shows in every episode that there are very few problems that he cannot solve with a good shellacking. But neither is the Prisoner eager to use violence against his tormentors, and he is as restrained and nonlethal as the situation allows.[7] (We will later discuss the one exception to this, the final episode, which seems to stand in a class by itself because of its surreal, hallucinatory quality.) In this, Number Six more closely resembles the Chinese martial artist Caine from the television series *Kung Fu* (1972), than he does his fellow British spy James Bond. And since Number Six is frequently outnumbered and beaten unconscious in the course of an episode, the series clearly shows that violence is more often the recourse of the ignorant, inhumane, and more powerful than it is the tool of justice and righteous indignation that we too often imagine it to be. The show unmasks and disarms such oppressive, unjust violence with two strategies—humor, on the one hand, and active, nonlethal resistance, on the other.

A recurring image of the ridiculousness of violence is the fictitious martial art "kosho," which is practiced by some people in the Village gymnasium. Number Six is especially adept at it, as he is at every athletic or mental endeavor. The playing field for kosho consists of two trampolines in a room, with an open tank of water between them, and a small, slanted ledge all along the walls of the room, several feet above the surface of the trampolines. The two combatants, wearing helmets and padding, bounce between the trampolines and the ledge. They hit and grab each other until one is knocked into the water. All of this is punctuated by ceremonious bowing, while there is Asian-sounding music playing in the background. There must be rules as to how many steps may be taken on the ledge before jumping down to the trampoline, what varieties of contact or holds are allowed, and so on, but these are never stated and would be moot anyway. As with the identity of the organization from which the Prisoner resigned, we have all the information we need to judge kosho: it is a ridiculous parody of combat. If the point were to show Number Six excelling at some martial art, there could have been karate or judo at the Village gym. Instead, we have a spectacle that probably resembles countless bouts with impromptu props and rules dreamed up by adolescent males everyday. It combines the catharsis, aggression, flamboyance, and slapstick of professional wrestling and a carnival dunking booth and is intended to remind us of how silly and childish violence often is, despite its danger.

Violence is shown to be even more childish in one of the most violent and conventionally entertaining episodes, "The Girl Who Was Death." The episode follows Number Six—inexplicably outside the Village and back in the real world—as he chases a mysterious woman. The episode's scenes are punctuated by shots of hands turning the pages of a children's picture book, the pictures corresponding to what is going on in the chase. Throughout the chase, the woman tries to kill Number Six in various ways—poison, explosives, an out-of-control sauna. Using radio, she compliments him on his skills at avoiding death, saying that she has longed for a "worthy opponent." She leads Number Six to a deserted town for the climax of her trials of his survival skills, saying that they "were made for each other . . . you are a natural survivor; I am a natural killer." He is put through a series of deadly traps involving machine guns, electrified spikes, and finally an airtight room full of exploding candles that produce cyanide gas. When he defeats all these, Number Six takes a bulldozer and drives it toward his opponent, using the blade as a shield against her machine-gun fire (seemingly a parody of John Wayne's similar maneuver in *The Fighting Seabees* [1944]), but she disables the vehicle with a bazooka. She continues to fire at him until she believes that she has killed her "lover."

Number Six now follows the woman to a lighthouse, which he learns is a missile aimed at London. The missile is the creation of the woman's father, a mad scientist with a group of henchmen, all humorously dressed as Napoleon. Number Six defeats most of the guards by using a Bugs Bunny-like trick to rig their guns so that they shoot backward and kill themselves. He is nonetheless captured, and with the woman still quipping ("Think of me when you hit town!"), he is tied to a chair in the nose cone of the missile, which is about to be launched. Number Six breaks his bonds, sabotages the missile, and escapes on a boat. As he is leaving, the mad scientist and his daughter try to stop him by throwing grenades at him, but as with the guards' guns, Number Six has improbably rigged these to explode in their hands. They and their missile are destroyed. Number Six is then shown closing a picture book, and Number Two (who looks like the mad scientist) is disappointed that their plan to have Number Six tell a story to children did not cause him to lower his guard at all. It did, however, underscore the lesson of how silly and childish violence can be. If kosho does not rise above the level of professional wrestling, "The Girl Who Was Death" treats violence like a Road Runner cartoon—an empty, immature amusement, "eye candy" in current slang. Like a teenager driving a car recklessly and too fast, violence often hurts people badly, but it is ultimately something most of us outgrow when we find better things to do with our lives, even though we still have to remain on our guard against reckless, dangerous teenage drivers, especially the one lurking inside each of us.

Humor is not the only response used on *The Prisoner* to disarm violence and curb our appetite for it. Two episodes portray Number Six as adamantly opposed to lethal force, and they are two episodes in which Number Six most unambiguously and fully triumphs over the authorities and over his own self-centeredness. "It's Your Funeral" presents us with the not-unlikely scenario that within the Village some Villagers have come to be known as "jammers": they talk about schemes and escape plans constantly, out in the open, so much so that the authorities have come to ignore them as harmless cranks. But now the authorities are using this situation for sinister ends. They have aided some of the jammers in concocting a real plot to assassinate an elderly Number Two, who has angered his superiors for some unknown reason. The move is not at all unlike many plots in Stalinist Russia or other totalitarian states: rather than quietly having a disagreeable or inconvenient subordinate just disappear, why not help the opposition to kill him, then honor him as a hero and martyr for the father- or motherland, and end by hauling up the opposition for punishment at a show trial? It gives better publicity and more complete control all around, over both the opposition and one's own terrified followers.

Before Number Six knows the authorities' involvement in the assassination, he sets out to stop the plot, though he surely sympathizes with the jammers' urge to rebel. Once he knows that the whole plot is organized by the authorities for their own ends, however, and that they will use it as an excuse to punish and terrorize the Villagers further, his opposition becomes much more determined. In his conversations with the targeted Number Two, there is some hint that Number Six has some sympathy for another man doomed and persecuted by the authorities; this is especially so near the end, when the death threat has past, but Number Six continues to help the old Number Two to escape from the Village. But Number Six's main concern is his fellow Villagers, to keep them from being punished for their ineffective and misguided rebellion. This episode shows Number Six as much less antisocial, uncaring, or disruptive than in other episodes. His fellow Villagers—as intrusive and annoying as they may be most of the time—are, for the most part, innocent prisoners, like him, and Number Six feels a real sense of community and responsibility for them. His commitment to nonviolence, in other words, springs from his best and most humane impulses—his sympathy, caring, and identification with other people, even those he would be inclined to regard as enemies or nuisances. Violence therefore is shown to be most often selfish and self-serving, while refraining from violence is shown to be part of feeling for others and building a community with them.

The series' most striking meditation on violence and nonviolence is the episode "Living in Harmony," in which we are mysteriously presented with Number Six dressed as a cowboy in the Old West. He is beaten and dragged into the ironically named town of Harmony, where he witnesses a vicious lynching perpetrated by bestial townspeople. Exactly as in the Village, Number Six is then interrogated by the chief authority of the town, the Judge, as to his motives and especially as to why he will not join the Judge's henchmen. Number Six attempts to leave town, but the townspeople are so violent toward him that the Judge uses this as an excuse to lock him up for "protective custody." A stereotypical "prostitute-with-a-heart-of-gold," Kathy, helps him escape, but he is recaptured and the Judge says that Kathy will be jailed if Number Six does not become the town's sheriff; the Judge intimates that the Kid—the Judge's sadistic, mute, chief enforcer—will rape her if she remains in jail. Number Six finally agrees to cooperate, but he refuses to carry a gun. The Judge's henchmen repeatedly try to subdue him, but he fends off all their attacks without a firearm. When the Kid callously kills a man without provocation in the saloon, however, the townspeople demand that their sheriff use a gun to stop the violence (rather conveniently forgetting their own savagery at the beginning of the episode). One of them even offers to help, but the Judge has this man killed too. Number Six plans to escape all this madness and brutality with Kathy, but the Kid kills her in an insane, jealous rage before they can do so. Number Six finally gets his gun, killing the Kid first, then the rest of the Judge's henchmen, before the Judge shoots him in the back. When the fatal shot rings out, Number Six collapses, and wakes up on the saloon floor, now in his usual Village garb. He finds the western town populated only by cardboard cutouts of people and horses. He walks down the dirt road to find the Village still there, and within the authorities' headquarters, three people resembling the Judge (Number Two), the Kid (Number Eight), and Kathy (Number Twenty-two), who had played parts in the violent hallucination of Harmony that they had inflicted on Number Six with drugs and electronics. Unfortunately for them, they continue to play their parts, as Number Eight and Number Twenty-two return to the fake western town later that evening, where he kills her, then falls to his death from the saloon balcony.

"Living in Harmony" combines two distinct issues about the use of violence. First, there is the question of how much one should resist the state's unjust demand on its citizens that they use violence on its behalf. On this question, the show is clear that the truly heroic person will never give in to the state's demands that he or she kill on its terms, for its reasons, against his or her own conscience. Since the series aired during the Vietnam War, this message seemed to hit too close to home, and the episode was not aired during the original broadcast run in the United States.[8] There is also the issue, as in "It's Your Funeral," of whether it is right to use violence against an oppressive police state. (On both these issues, the episode is closely paralleled in the Sam Raimi film *The Quick and the Dead* [1995], with the Prisoner in the same role as Cort, the mysterious preacher who is beaten and dragged into the sadistic town of Redemption, where he is unwilling to participate in their mindless violence until pushed too far.) On the issue of violent resistance, the episode shows our hero repeatedly trying his best to avoid or escape confrontation, but finally using force to end the violence against others. Even Gandhi (1869–1948), perhaps the most famous advocate of nonviolence besides Jesus, significantly allowed for the use of violence in such cases:

> I have been repeating over and over again that he who cannot protect himself or his nearest and dearest or their honor by non-violently facing death may and ought to do so by violently dealing with the oppressor. He who can do neither of the two is a burden. He has no business to be the head of a family. He must either hide himself, or must rest content to live for ever in helplessness and be prepared to crawl like a worm at the bidding of a bully.[9]

If anything, Gandhi would blame Number Six for not resorting to violence sooner, as several people have died while he remained inactive, and his rampage of violence, coming only after Kathy has died, seems tainted thereby with revenge rather than strictly achieving justice. But it nonetheless serves to neutralize the forces of evil and end their future predation on the townspeople, and Number Six embarks on it with grim resignation, not gladness or triumph. He is a most unwilling but effective warrior, like a police officer shooting a criminal or an animal-control agent shooting a mad dog. Number Six has once again behaved with virtue, dignity, and respect for life, even when everyone else around him has not.

Rather than embrace the extremes offered in the popular culture of the 1960s or the present day, *The Prisoner* presents us with one of the most humane, realistic, and Christian responses to violence, one that combines humor and more serious resistance. Humor has often been used by those who oppose violence to show how childish and ridiculous it is. Rather than confront violence head-on—which usually results in more violence—such humor seeks to defuse or sidestep the situation, to provide the oppressed with a cathartic outlet, one that they may even eventually be able to share with their oppressors. Such humor is usually dark indeed, as in the accounts of Holocaust survivors or in a classic antiwar film like *Dr. Strangelove* (1964). Besides such current manifestations, we see such a deprecating attitude toward violence and bigotry in some Old Testament books, such as Jonah and Esther. It is also found in Jesus's life, as when Jesus refuses to confront Roman legions with violence, which some of his followers advocate, but casts a "legion" of demons into a herd of pigs (Mark 5:1–20; Luke 8:26–39; cf. Matt. 8:28–34). Some of Jesus's teachings include this kind of humor, as when he counsels his hearers to strip naked before those unfairly demanding the repayment of a debt (Matt. 5:40; Luke 6:29), thereby making the oppressor into a laughingstock, rather than opposing him with violence.[10] Such a parody shows the impotence and emptiness of violence and makes it into an object of ridicule, not fear or admiration. It makes the Prisoner into a hero for combating it without sinking to its level.

When the show turns from humor to principled resistance, it must be said that Number Six is no pacifist. But neither is pacifism, as admirable as it is, the only Christian response to violence and injustice over the centuries. As noted above, one of the greatest advocates of nonviolence, Gandhi, allowed for violence in those cases when others were threatened. John the Baptist and even Jesus himself are occasionally portrayed as using violent rhetoric or actions, especially against those who abuse their authority to corrupt religion (Matt. 3:7–10; 21:12–13; Mark 11:15–19; Luke 3:7–9; 19:45–48; John 2:13–17), while the Prisoner is more frequently forced to use violence against those who have corrupted the state and technology to degrade and destroy his life and the lives of others. It is also instructive to see how the Prisoner does not fall into the other extreme of an eager, inhumane indulgence in violence, despite its attraction in our culture. At exactly the time that James Bond and John Wayne were cultural icons who embraced state-sponsored violence and gladly killed on the state's behalf, Number Six resigned from his career of committing violence and espionage for his state and brought upon himself unjust persecution by his own country. But even then, he resisted retaliating against the oppressive state with deadly force. If, as we saw in the previous section, patriotism could well be said to be the last refuge of scoundrels—an idolatrous excuse for their sins and excesses—then violence could well be said to be their first recourse, the first avenue they turn to in order to solve a problem. The truly wise person knows, like Number Six, that in such a world of scoundrels, violence may become necessary, but it should never be celebrated or even enjoyed; and the truly humble and humane person puts the lives of others—even those who are at present violent scoundrels—ahead of his or her own. Just as surgery, chemicals, radiation, or other "unnatural" procedures may sometimes be necessary to restore health, violence should be tolerated only so long as the threat it opposes outweighs its own intrinsic danger and evil. Number Six teaches us such wisdom and humility in a way that is more compelling than almost anywhere else on television or film.

Alienation and Real Community

Number Six is, however, hardly perfect. While his unique personality—defiant, stubborn, suspicious, cynical—especially suits him to surviving the degradations of a prison, it is easy enough to see how in a more normal situation he could lapse into an unhealthy and unhappy lifestyle of distrust and loneliness. As with a soldier or a police officer, certain skills and attributes necessary to dealing with the darker side of human nature have been cultivated in the Prisoner to the point where they could become monstrous and dangerous, rather than useful and virtuous. Number Six triumphs over the dehumanizing Village by making himself as nonconformist and individualistic as possible, but there is always the danger that individuality can grow into arrogance, alienation, and misanthropy. The series handles this deftly by showing how the very traits that enable the Prisoner to survive with his humanity intact and his spirit unbroken are also what cause him to fail in several of his attempts to escape. These are the most psychological and personal of the episodes: especially in the case of the last two episodes of the series, they become so hallucinatory and nightmarish that it is fair to say that they are more about what is going on in Number Six's mind, his internal struggle with himself, than they are a resolution to the ostensible plot going on in the outside world, or in the Village, which is left ambiguous on several important points.

Perhaps Number Six's most noticeable and recurring Achilles' heel is his consistently poor judgment in choosing whom to trust or distrust. This is repeatedly shown in several episodes, starting with the first, "Arrival." There, after being attacked by Rover, Number Six is in the hospital next to a friend from the outside world, another secret agent named Cobb. Number Six then hears that his friend has killed himself. At the funeral, Number Six meets a woman who later claims that she and Cobb were planning an escape, and she wants Number Six now to take part. She offers him an electronic device that will neutralize Rover so he can get past it and into a helicopter to escape. Number Six is suspicious of her, but makes the attempt, which fails when the helicopter, remotely controlled by Number Two, simply circles back to the Village. But Number Six was not betrayed by the woman: instead, at the end we see that Cobb has cooperated with Number Two by staging his own death to trick both the woman and his old friend. Number Six has let personal feelings cloud his judgment and has trusted the wrong person.

This pattern is repeated in other episodes. In "Schizoid Man," Number Six comes close to losing his mind because he unwisely trusts a woman, Alison, also called Number Twenty-four. The beginning of the episode shows that he and the woman are able to perform some extrasensory perception (ESP) or mind-reading tricks: he can look at a card, and she can tell what it is without seeing it. So when the impostor who looks exactly like Number Six shows up and bests him at other challenges—fencing and shooting, though not at quoting Shakespeare, since that is purely mental, and Number Six's mind cannot be conditioned as his body can be—the real Number Six thinks to use the psychic bond that he has with Alison to prove his identity. She is in on the plot to break him, however, and has therefore arranged to guess all the cards wrong with Number Six, and all of them right with the impostor. Although Alison eventually repents of her mistake in a very touching scene of real remorse (cf. Judas's repentance in Matt. 27:3–10, and the repentance of Number Twenty-two in "Living in Harmony"), the betrayal is perhaps the worst and most damaging in the series, and Number Six is saved only by an accident—seeing the bruise on his fingernail that is not where it is supposed to be brings the memories of his brainwashing flooding back. Although never explicitly romantic with any other Villager, Number Six always seems quaintly gallant by our standards, and here he has probably let such a romantic, unrealistic idealization of women mislead him. Again, a quality that makes him more humane in comparison to the Village authorities—who treat men and women equally as mere instruments or "pawns"—also makes Number Six more vulnerable and alone when in conflict with them.

Number Six's faulty evaluation of people also cuts the other way, however, in the direction of cynicism rather than naiveté. So far we have seen how he has trusted too quickly or naively, and the authorities have used this against him. But he can also be so stubborn and domineering that he foils his own escape plans, as in "Checkmate." After one of the Village chess games that use humans as pieces, Number Six approaches the Villager known as the Rook, an electronics expert, and introduces him to a group of conspirators planning escape under Number Six's leadership. Number Six shows the Rook how he has picked these men. He approaches several Villagers and is belligerent and demanding with them: if a Villager pushes back, then he must be a "warder" working for the authorities; if a Villager is cowed and submissive, then he is really a prisoner and can be trusted. The group prepares for their escape, which involves the Rook building a radio transmitter to lure in a nearby ship by calling for help as though they were a downed aircraft, and then paddling out to sea on a raft to be picked up by the ship. The preparations fail, however, when the Rook withdraws from the plan, because he mistakenly believes that Number Six is working for the authorities. Why does he think this? Because Number Six displays the exact same intimidating and ruthless attitude that the authorities do. Number Six's assertive, self-sufficient personality makes him adept at handling the authorities and thwarting their many attempts to destroy him, but it also makes him clumsy at handling other prisoners or at making the friends that he will need to escape this prison, a prison made harder and more lonely by his personality.

Besides his faulty evaluation and treatment of others, Number Six's motives seem less than entirely pure. Throughout the series there is the nagging suspicion that his fierce individualism and refusal to conform stand right at the edge of being willing or even desirous to take the next step of dominating others. If he thinks himself too superior to obey, perhaps he thinks himself superior enough to give orders to others? Although Number Six frequently and steadfastly refuses the authorities' inducements to help them rule the Village if he cooperates, it seems that this refusal is mostly because they offer these privileges on their terms, not his; they come with too many strings attached, but they may not necessarily be unattractive to the Prisoner. Certainly Saint Augustine (354–430 CE) would notice very little qualitative difference between self-assertion and independence, on the one hand, and the sinful urge to dominate, oppress, objectify, and use others—the *libido dominandi*—on the other. At the very least, the latter is the sinful expression of the former, and the transition between them can be subtle and hard to resist indeed.

We are given a glimpse of Number Six's susceptibility to this temptation early in the series, long before the final two episodes that are focused on this weakness of his.[11] In the episode "Free for All," Number Six is first tempted to run for the office of Number Two, and then brainwashed with drugs and some electronic device to do so. (Contemporary audiences will have to content themselves with the lack of sophisticated special effects for the latter device: it consists of a blinking light.) But one cannot discount everything Number Six does in the episode with the excuse that he is being controlled by the Village authorities and their mad scientists: brainwashing is tried on the Prisoner several times in the series, but at no time is it ever as effective and complete as in this episode. Something in his mind and personality must have been especially receptive to this particular suggestion. Indeed, the episode is full of double entendres that contain under their irony a partially true diagnosis of Number Six's egoism and selfishness, as when Number Two chides him, "You mustn't think only of yourself," when encouraging him to run for office. Number Six does seem obsessed with himself and his needs, and seldom has any concern for the other Villagers, whom he refers to as subhuman "cabbages" (in this episode and in "The General") and "sheep" ("A Change of Mind"). And when Number Six throws himself into the campaign, his choice of slogans seems to reveal a dark side of his mind and his expectations. The highest-minded goal he claims for his future leadership would shame even the most debased huckster: "Less work and more play!" The title of the episode also points to this anarchic, hedonistic, self-indulgent aspect of Number Six: his monomaniacal insistence on his own freedom—noble in the face of tyranny and mindless conformity—does run the risk of reducing human life to a "free for all." The episode also shows this by referring to card games several times, when the rest of the series constantly refers to the game of chess: card games are "free" in the sense of being random and frivolous, not like the mental contest of chess that is "free" within a very strict set of rules and calculations. In the end, Number Six completely parodies his own noble-seeming goals and reduces them to an oxymoron, as he shouts into the loudspeaker system, "Obey me and be free!"

The way out of this egoism is painfully demonstrated to Number Six at the very end of the episode. The cheerful and subservient woman who had been following him around as his campaign assistant now turns on him and beats him with increasing ferocity, her pretty face now cold, hateful, and contemptuous at how foolish he was. Stunned by the attack, Number Six flees from her and runs into several guards, who continue the beating, until the Prisoner sinks into unconsciousness under the blows. Although there are many fight scenes in the series, this one stands out as especially brutal and prolonged.[12] As they are beating him, he is very deliberately held with his arms straight out, and the focus is on his face as he winces in pain and slowly passes out. This staging makes the scene clearly and explicitly into a crucifixion. Number Six is beginning to realize that his quest for freedom cannot succeed through rhetoric and manipulation, through playing the game of the Village authorities as he had tried to do with the election. Real freedom will be had only through suffering and self-sacrifice, through taking up his cross and submitting to the authorities' abuse: "If any want to become my followers, let them deny themselves and take up their cross and follow me" (Mark 8:34; cf. Matt. 16:24; Luke 9:23). What he must further learn, beyond the lessons of this episode, is how to build a community, rather than just to fight and suffer on his own. He has learned not to manipulate and control others; now he must learn to trust and love them.

In the final two episodes of the series, this earlier exploration of Number Six's weakness and his partial overcoming of it expands into a full odyssey to learn the lessons of humility and his need for other people, so that he can withstand and reject the final temptation to dominate and abuse them. The penultimate episode, "Once Upon a Time," has a Number Two return from a previous episode ("The Chimes of Big Ben," with Number Two played by the veteran actor Leo McKern) to try again to break Number Six. Number Two's plan is to go to "degree absolute," a complete immersion of himself and Number Six into a regression and recreation of Number Six's life. Number Two, Number Six, and the mysterious, midget Butler (played by Angelo Muscat, he appears briefly in every episode, but never with so much prominence and importance) will be locked into an underground bunker for one week, unable to leave or have interference from the outside. With the electronic brainwashing, Number Six is regressed back to a receptive, childlike state; he is not, however, rendered nonaggressive or completely compliant. Number Two plays out various authority relationships with Number Six—father and son, teacher and student, coach and athlete, judge and accused, captain and bombardier on board a plane, interrogator and prisoner of war. His goal is that of deep psychoanalysis—to build trust and identification between himself and Number Six. Number Two is only partly successful. The week runs out without Number Six answering the crucial question of why he resigned, and Number Two dies, either worn out from the ordeal or poisoned by the Village authorities. But Number Six is clearly hurt and angered by the death of his interrogator/therapist, with whom he did form a deep, human bond. He wanted to win, but certainly not to kill this man who is also a victim of the system. Number Two's death is only another victory for the authorities, not for Number Six. But at the end of the episode, he is escorted away with the promise that he will now meet Number One.

The deep, psychological investigation of Number Six and Number Two in this episode reveals several things about the exact implications of Number Six's refusal to submit. First, there seems a deep problem with the definition of community that Number Two tries to force on him. Number Two starts with the quite bland and unhelpful truism that "society is a place where people exist together," but moves almost immediately to the unacceptable and unnecessary conclusion that, therefore, "you must conform!" But the most heated exchanges have to do with exactly what Number Six values and where his values conflict with those of society. Surprisingly and revealingly, the conflict is not because of Number Six's obsession with his own personal freedom and nonconformity, but because of his devotion and loyalty to other people whom society somehow oppresses or persecutes. Regressed to the role of a boy, Number Six is asked to turn in a fellow student for a minor infraction, but steadfastly refuses to do so, even when threatened with being blamed and punished himself. As an adult arrested for speeding, he defends the moral rightness of his actions against their illegality: according to him, matters of life and death are "above the law," as they should be. Later, as a bombardier, Number Six repeatedly refuses to release the bombs, then suffers as a POW for doing so. In his childlike state, he and Number Two are shouting "Pop!" at each other, and together they free associate and interpret it as an acronym for "Protect Other People," a principle that guided Number Six's actions in many episodes and is now revealed as his deepest subconscious urge. Since this motto should also be the guiding principle of any healthy society, Number Six's conflicts with the authorities are revealed as damning evidence against them, not him, no matter how much Number Two tries to convince him that he is at fault. Despite his flirtations with dominance and egoism, Number Six reveals that his problem has never been with community, but with authority. In a real, healthy society that did not abuse authority, Number Six would be a highly productive citizen and the most loyal friend.

But in the last episode, "Fall Out," he must undergo and reject one final temptation to his dark, egoistic, domineering side. After Number Two's death, Number Six is led to an underground cavern filled with robed figures wearing black-and-white masks. The cavern also has numerous armed guards and is dominated by an enormous, smoking cylinder that looks like a giant rocket or missile, with a huge, red number "1" on it.[13] Number Six is seated on a throne with the Butler next to him to watch the proceedings. Number Six is introduced to the group as having "survived the ultimate test." According to them, he has "gloriously vindicated the right of the individual to be individual" and has earned "the right to be a person." Here is the ultimate indictment of the Village authorities and their sick society: they regard individuality and personhood as privileges one earns for good behavior rather than what they are, the intrinsic rights of every human being. They have more than usurped God's prerogatives, they have claimed an ability that not even God has, for not even God can deny or take away our personhood: God respects our personhood and desires us to live in real community with him. We also see in this scene that the authorities' technological powers are even beyond what they have displayed thus far, and which again encroach on God's prerogatives: they resuscitate the dead Number Two, an act that he rightly does not regard as a favor, but only as an attempt to use him further, as he scoffs at them, "You couldn't even let me rest in peace."

The authorities now indict Number Two and another Villager, Number Forty-eight (actor Alexis Kanner, who had appeared in "Living in Harmony," but not as the same Villager), as examples of improper, destructive rebellion, and they reincarcerate them. Number Six is again praised for his rebellion, which the group hails as the "right" kind, though their leader has trouble articulating what exactly that means. Number Six is offered the choice of either to leave them or to rule them. Although we would think that the choice would be obvious, Number Six does not state his decision. He ascends the podium to address the group, but every time he begins his speech with the word "I," the whole crowd bang their fists and chant "I! I! I!"[14] Number Six is then lowered into a tunnel beneath the room, from which he can ascend into the cylinder marked "1." At the base of the cylinder, he sees Number Two and Number Forty-eight imprisoned in clear tubes. Number Six climbs a spiral staircase into a room full of globes, with a masked figure there with "1" on the front of his robe. Number Six tears off the mask, as the figure shrieks "I! I! I!" Under the mask, the figure is a gorilla, still shrieking. Under the gorilla mask, the figure is Number Six himself, cackling insanely. Number Six chases the figure around the room and up a ladder, then closes a hatch behind the figure, trapping him at the top of the missile. The scene, as surreal as it is, shows Number Six first denying his animal side and all the reductionistic explanations of human nature that he has spent sixteen episodes combating: humans have an animal side, but they are not *merely* animal. Number Six then defeats himself, denying and imprisoning his solipsism, egoism, and lust for power.[15]

For him to accept being Number One would be to descend into a self-absorbed, lonely existence of shrieking "I!" as he ruled others through animal force or insane dominance. To borrow the line that all coaches use in pep talks to their teams, there's an "I" in "Prisoner," but not one in "freedom": real freedom is by nature communal, as it liberates and fulfills others together with oneself.

Having defeated his dark, individualistic side, Number Six builds his little community by freeing Number Two and Number Forty-eight and accepting the help of the Butler. Number Six begins the missile's launch sequence. He and his friends overpower some hooded figures and some guards, taking the former's clothes and the latter's guns. They burst into the meeting room and begin a frenzied shootout with the remaining guards as the Beatles' "All You Need Is Love" plays in the background. The leader of the assembly sounds the alarm, and we see the Village frantically being evacuated as the missile lifts off. We see Rover dissolving, but otherwise the fate of the Village is unclear: given the episode's title and Number Six's earlier threat to "wipe this place off the face of the earth" ("Chimes of Big Ben," repeated in "Once upon a Time"), it seems likely that the missile is a nuclear one targeted at the Village, but it may be that Number Six's victory has simply now rendered the Village useless, since the secret, escape-proof prison is now no longer either secret or escape-proof. Meanwhile, Number Six and his friends escape in a tractor trailer. They arrive in London and happily go their separate ways, all to triumphant music.

Unbeatable at combat and problem solving, Number Six begins the series with people skills that are not nearly so well developed, to say the least. He is like a modern-day Oedipus: mentally able to solve the most difficult riddles and challenges and physically able to fight off multiple assailants, he is nonetheless hopelessly inept and misguided in his personal relationships and blind to his own shortcomings. He is unwilling to be a follower, but equally unsuited to being a leader. Although usually peaceable and not oppressive, he is so arrogant and condescending in his dealings with other people that they are repulsed and mistrustful of him, to the detriment of both him and them. He can even be tempted with the lust for power that his tormentors embrace so much more willingly and sinfully. But in his shortcomings, the Prisoner teaches us what may be the show's most valuable lesson: that even—or, perhaps, especially—a person with almost superhuman mental and physical abilities is doomed to fail if she or he cannot humbly accept vulnerability and weakness in order to forge real bonds of love and trust with other people. By the end of the series, Number Six has learned to do that, and we see the final victory of all his virtues over both his outer and inner demons, when he rightly orders his virtues in the hierarchy Paul described: "And if I have prophetic powers, and understand all mysteries and all knowledge, and if I have all faith, so as to remove mountains, but do not have love, I am nothing" (1 Cor. 13:2). Number Six was right all along that the essence of human existence and meaning is freedom: "For freedom Christ has set us free. Stand firm, therefore, and do not submit again to a yoke of slavery" (Gal. 5:1). Seventeen episodes of painful lessons have taught Number Six the right goal and purpose of freedom: "For you were called to freedom, brothers and sisters; only do not use your freedom as an opportunity for self-indulgence, but through love become slaves to one another" (Gal. 5:13). In one of the most triumphant and uplifting moments in all of television, the Prisoner is finally free—and more fully human and alive than even he had imagined possible.

Conclusion

Much like *Star Trek, The Prisoner* provides us with one of the few truly heroic characters in television, or in modern culture in general. Number Six's heroism is perhaps more accessible than that of Kirk, Spock, and McCoy, however, for he confronts many of the demons of modern life and society that face us all—alienation, superficiality, violence, injustice, the loss of individuality. His is a solitary, private quest for dignity in a dehumanizing world, rather than the more remote and fantastical quest of the *Enterprise* officers to save the galaxy from constant, extraterrestrial, superhuman predation. Number Six's rebellion against the status quo and his final forging of his own little community of rebels and misfits are powerful inspirations to all of us who find ourselves imperceptibly but inexorably slipping into the boring anonymity and numbing ennui of our own "Villages" of cookie-cutter housing developments and strip malls.[16] His world and ours both beguile and torment us with empty promises of secular happiness and fulfillment, while he shows us the way to reclaim a real humanity, sacredness, and spirituality. McGoohan himself is said to have intended such a prophetic meaning for his masterpiece, insisting on the refrain, "Hear the word of the Lord!" (Ezek. 37:4) for the final episode.[17]

It is also instructive to compare Number Six to another contemporary "hero" who bears a superficial resemblance to him—another superspy of the 1960s, James Bond. McGoohan has expressed contempt for the Bond character and twice turned down the role himself,[18] and it seems that he makes a valid point. There is something slightly embarrassing and distasteful that Bond made it as high as third place on the American Film Institute's list of fifty greatest movie "heroes,"[19] for it shows an essential confusion about our idea of "hero," about what we value and admire. If "hero" means someone who does exceptional, extraordinary things—for example, kill armed, three-hundred-pound assailants with his bare hands or have incredible sex with unbelievably beautiful women while underwater or in outer space—then Bond could reasonably be called the greatest "hero" of all time. But under the more narrow and important meaning of "hero" as someone who does virtuous and self-sacrificing deeds to help others, then Bond is nowhere near heroic: he is simply a highly talented and lucky assassin and gigolo. As escapism into a thrilling world of spies and terrorists whose morals are even lower than Mr. Bond's, this is probably harmless enough, but it really shouldn't be confused with identifying with a hero, with a person we would like to emulate and from whom we think we can learn valuable lessons about how to live our lives. McGoohan himself could be adamant on this point: "I abhor violence and cheap sex . . . we need moral heroes. Every real hero since Jesus Christ has been moral."[20] Here again, Number Six's story is truly heroic and relevant, showing us a man who struggles to unmask and tear down some of the false idols of the modern world and who also struggles to overcome his own ego and self-centeredness. This is not an escapist story, as is Bond's or as so much of science fiction is accused of being: this is a story that helps us to escape from the spiritual bonds put on us by the modern world and by our own sinful selves.

IV

Sin and Grace

The Twilight Zone

You're traveling through another dimension, a dimension not only of sight and sound, but of mind, a journey into a wondrous land whose boundaries are that of imagination. Next stop—the Twilight Zone!

One of several opening narrations for
The Twilight Zone

Say to those who prophesy out of their own imagination: "Hear the word of the Lord."

Ezekiel 13:2

Ever since the creation of the world his eternal power and divine nature, invisible though they are, have been understood and seen through the things he has made. . . . For there is no distinction, since all have sinned and fall short of the glory of God; they are now justified by his grace as a gift.

Romans 1:20; 3:22–23

If *The Prisoner* could be hailed as the most original television series ever broadcast, *The Twilight Zone* can hold a title nearly as august and, in the end, more influential—the most original *and widely popular* television series. The series originally ran for five seasons (1959–64), still runs regularly on the Sci-Fi Channel—including frequent daylong and two-day marathons—and in the 1980s spawned a feature film produced by Steven Spielberg, two revived television series, and a very helpful and popular commentary.[1] The series was one of the few successful anthology shows, with no common character, writer, or plot running through the episodes. Every week viewers would see new characters entering the "twilight zone," a broad concept that over the show's run could mean any experience that was scary, unfamiliar, or that did not obey the laws and expectations of our normal world. The phrase has become part of American vernacular English, meaning any indistinct and indefinite place or, more often, a frame of mind that is similarly unmoored and chaotic, as in the song "Twilight Zone" (1982) by the rock group Golden Earring.

Part of the show's appeal was certainly in the enormous and wide range of talent that worked on it, personified and concentrated in its creator, Rod Serling (1924–75), as well as spread out over an abundance of brilliant actors, writers, directors, and composers. The show's popularity has also benefited from offering such a wide variety of premises and experiences to its viewers. Many of us remember the series most vividly for its scenes of ominous, abiding terror, whether from murderous dolls ("The Dummy," "Living Doll," "Caesar and Me"), invading aliens ("People Are Alike All Over," "The Monsters Are

Due on Maple Street," "Elegy," "The Invaders," "To Serve Man," "Black Leather Jackets," "The Fear"), dangerous robots and machines ("The Lonely," "A Thing about Machines," "The Lateness of the Hour," "In His Image," "Uncle Simon," "Steel," "The Brain Center at Whipple's"), malevolent spirits ("Perchance to Dream," "The Jungle"), the grim reaper ("One for the Angels," "The Hitch-Hiker," "Nothing in the Dark"), or the less fantastical but often more real horrors of flying in airplanes ("The Odyssey of Flight 33," "Nightmare at 20,000 Feet"), conventional war ("The Purple Testament," "King Nine Will Not Return," "A Quality of Mercy"), nuclear holocaust ("Time Enough at Last," "Third from the Sun," "Two," "The Shelter," "One More Pallbearer," "The Old Man in the Cave"), or ecological disaster ("The Midnight Sun"). It is ample testimony to how effectively *The Twilight Zone* tapped into primal fears that it exploited such premises with minimal budgets and almost nonexistent special effects—scaring millions of people into nightmares or sleepless nights—decades before the ersatz killer doll Chucky went on his rampage in *Child's Play* (1988) and its sequels and almost a half century before tens of millions of dollars were spent on the special effects of a frozen Earth in *The Day after Tomorrow* (2004) or on the menacing automatons of *I, Robot* (2004)—none of which were very frightening. Perhaps less satisfying were the series' attempts at humor ("Mr. Bevis," "A World of His Own," "Mr. Dingle the Strong," "Will the Real Martian Please Stand Up," "Once upon a Time"), but they too have given the show a certain endearing quality, by helping it to avoid the mistake of taking itself too seriously and falling into pretentiousness.

As we think of the series' relevance to our Christian faith, however, one theme stands out as uniquely and emphatically Christian as it is depicted in *The Twilight Zone*—the struggle between good and evil or, more precisely, the triumph of good over evil. Though people often have very unpleasant things happen to them in the series, the show is adamant that evil will always finally fail, and evil people will always pay for their crimes, unless good people are complicit in the evil through neglect or cowardice. Indeed, whenever there are identifiably good and evil characters in an episode, the show is unambiguous and unrelenting in its morality. Dolls, aliens, robots, the grim reaper, and irrational fears make such frequent appearances in the series precisely because they are beyond or beneath morality—and therefore can be relied upon to do the dirty work of scaring us with their amorality. But the real human characters are clearly part of a moral world that is not only good and just in some ultimate sense, but is so even on a daily or weekly basis.

The Twilight Zone's Christian perspective goes a bit deeper than just asserting good's triumph over evil, however. This would, after all, be fairly unremarkable, perhaps even overly optimistic. The show repeatedly and lyrically embodies the uniquely Christian idea of original sin, both as to its presence in all people, and as to its deadly effects in our world. We will see this in the show's depiction of evil, which is almost always parasitic and repetitive, but also beguiling and all-pervasive. At the other end of the spectrum of human experience, the series seems acutely and beautifully aware of the Christian idea of grace, of supernatural assistance that makes people realize their own goodness and that of others, and helps them overcome sin. We will see this in the series' depiction of people saved from some evil in their lives by their innocence, humility, and openness toward others and to new experiences—qualities that they are miraculously reminded of through some supernatural event and that then prompt them to acts of compassion, love, and sacrifice. As Marc Scott Zicree well puts it in the preface to his *Twilight Zone Companion,* "Repeatedly, it [*The Twilight Zone*] states a simple message: The only escape from alienation lies in reaching out to others, trusting in their common humanity."[2] In the words of Serling's opening narration, *The Twilight Zone* may be conceived of as "a wondrous land whose boundaries are that of imagination," but it is unmistakably a part of our world, a part from which we can learn better the difference between good and evil, and in which we witness uplifting examples of people growing closer to God and other people.

Evil and Hell: The Reality and Legacy of Original Sin

How the various world religions depict good and evil is, to a large extent, the defining difference between them. The Eastern religions of Hinduism, Buddhism, and Taoism tend to look at the distinction between good and evil as ultimately invalid, as dire and destructive as it may seem to us during this life. For them, things that appear to us as good and evil are really better described by complementary, intermingled, and relative forces, rather than implacably opposed and easily distinguished ones. This can be seen graphically and in an aesthetically pleasing way in the Chinese symbol of yin and yang—a circle divided into equal white and black halves, but the white and black halves overlap, showing unity and mutual support, not conflict. Rather than depict the world as a battleground between good and evil, the Eastern faiths would see it more as a cycle and balance between various forces that appear opposite and opposed from our finite, limited perspective, but which really function together for the good of the whole universe. For them, describing the world as a complex interplay between such forces as wet/dry, light/dark, hot/cold, and male/female—any of which may be "bad" for us at a given time, but none of which are "evil" per se—is a better, more accurate description of what is going on in the world than a conflict between good and evil. In science fiction, such an interlocking duality is close to the worldview of the *Star Wars* universe, in which "the Force" is not to be confused with "the Good" or God, for it has both light and dark sides. Symbiosis and ambiguity characterize the Eastern perspective, while the Western perspective—whether it is religious or merely philosophical—emphasizes dualism, objectivity, and conflict.

The two other major, Western, monotheistic religions—Judaism and Islam—are therefore much closer to Christianity's ideas on good and evil, as all three share much of the dualistic outlook of Western thought in general. All three religions could be said to be kinds of "qualified dualism." For followers of these Abrahamic faiths, the world is for the time being "dualistic"—it is sharply divided into the battling camps of good and evil. But unlike other kinds of dualism—for instance, Zoroastrianism and Manichaeism—this dualism is not ultimate and eternal; it is "qualified" by time. It is real, but it is only temporary. According to Jews, Christians, and Muslims alike, the one, true God will eventually and permanently defeat evil and imprison or confine it far away from his followers, who will live eternally with only goodness all around them, without any further threat from evil of any kind.

But Christianity has added the further idea that in this life, we are not merely tempted by evil and are able either to resist it or submit to it, but we are more fundamentally tainted by it; it is somehow a part of us, and it therefore does not just tempt us as an outside force but infects and perverts us from within. This is the fuller and more dire sense of original sin that is unique to Christianity and distinguishes it from all other world religions and philosophies, which tend to see human nature as more or less innately good, tending more toward eventual perfection than corruption. Although the doctrine of original sin is ultimately based on the story of Adam and Eve in the second and third chapters of Genesis, it is worth remembering that Jews share this same passage of scripture with Christians but do not interpret it the same way: for Jews, the story of Adam and Eve is the first among many similar stories throughout the Bible of people disobeying God and being punished for their sinful willfulness. As far as we can tell, the earliest Christians may have shared this Jewish interpretation of Genesis: the doctrine of original sin because of a primal "fall" in Genesis was not fully articulated and defended until Saint Augustine of Hippo (354–430 CE), who worked it out with help from Saint Paul's letters that mention a universal sinfulness (e.g., Rom. 3:9–20). We raise this interpretive issue not to minimize the importance or validity of the doctrine of original sin, but to maximize it: to be a Christian is to opt for an interpretation of scripture and of human nature that is either denied by or incomprehensible to billions of people of other faiths—even those faiths that share our monotheism and even our scriptures. Together with the idea of grace—which is the cure for original sin—belief in original sin is the defining doctrine of Christianity, for it distinguishes it from all other religions.

But as integral as original sin is to Christian belief, its implications are often so distasteful that we overlook it as much as possible, preferring to believe in the un-Christian idea that people are basically good—that left to their own devices, they will do the right thing and love and care for one another, at least most of the time. Probably nowhere is this tendency clearer and more overwhelming than in considering the horrible implications of original sin for our ideas about children's "innocence." It's one thing to say that adults are depraved: except in our own cases, we are usually quite willing to grant this possibility. But to say that children are somehow innately evil seems truly bizarre, almost demented or neurotic. Original sin notwithstanding, we will almost always insist that children are innocent, pure, loving, generous creatures who could ultimately harbor no wicked feelings or thoughts. They just get a little out of hand sometimes, but that's to be expected and is easily controlled anyway.

Saint Augustine will have none of this sentimental excuse making, and his probing analysis of original sin focuses on the idea that a child getting out of hand is exactly what proves its depravity. If there could be a five-hundred-pound baby like in the old Baby Huey cartoon, it would not be an object of mirth, but of complete terror, because it could not be controlled and would do whatever it felt like to get whatever it wanted. Worse than the most violent criminal, it would kill its own parents the first time they said "no" to anything. We only think that babies are "innocent"—the word in Latin means "harmless" as well as "blameless"—because they are physically incapable of pursuing their sinful desires, not because they don't have sinful desires: "Thus, the weakness of the baby's limbs is innocent, not its soul."[3] Augustine forces us to confront evil where we least expect or wish to see it, and generations of readers—from the German philosopher Friedrich Nietzsche (1844–1900) to almost every college student who is assigned *Confessions* in her literature, philosophy, or theology class—have reacted by calling him neurotic for saying such weird things about babies.

The Twilight Zone episode "It's a Good Life" takes Augustine's premise—that because of original sin, children are potentially even more evil and destructive than adults, because they have evil desires but have no self-restraint—and presents it in a way that is infinitely more compelling and frightening than Augustine's bald, prose statement of it. The story begins with a long narration by Serling standing in front of a map of the United States, explaining that everything except the town of Peaksville has disappeared. This destruction of the entire world—or Peaksville's removal from it—was effected by "a monster," a monster capable of using its mind to destroy anything or anyone; when the monster is feeling slightly more merciful, it only makes its enemies into imbeciles, as we see in the case of Aunt Amy, forced into a silent, vacant stupor for disobeying the monster's prohibition on singing. We are then introduced to the monster—an adorable six-year-old boy named Anthony Fremont (actor Billy Mumy, who appeared in several *Twilight Zone* episodes and went on to great fame playing the precocious and lovable Will Robinson on television's *Lost in Space* [1965–69]).

We see Anthony spending his day torturing animals by making them into grotesque combinations and setting them on one another. He then kills them by psychically wishing them into the cornfield, the dumping ground for all his failed experiments in cruelty. He has sent almost all the other children in the town into the cornfield, because they accidentally hurt or displeased him while playing with him. He has similarly killed almost all the adults. The few that remain are careful never to cross or disagree with Anthony, even if this means living a life of boredom and desperation, with no entertainment allowed except what a six-year-old would enjoy and with dwindling food supplies for which there is no replacement. Significantly, Anthony's powers do not extend to being able to create things with his mind, only to destroy them: his evil is sterile and self-enclosed. The episode terrifyingly spins out of control at a birthday party for one of the adults, where the man is given presents of brandy and a phonograph record, being solemnly reminded not to play it until he gets home, as there is singing on it. The man foolishly gets drunk, however, and lashes out at Anthony for his evil and destruction and at the other townspeople for their cowardice. He pleads with them to sneak up behind Anthony and bash his head in while he is temporarily distracted, but they are all too cowed to do so. Anthony kills the man and sticks his head on top of a huge, grotesque jack-in-the-box, then wishes the monstrosity into the cornfield. Sickened by the cruel murder and their own cowardice, the townspeople are then further shocked to see that it's snowing outside. Anthony's father cries out with anger and terror that this will kill their remaining crops but quickly reverses himself when he realizes that this might be taken as disapproval of the snow Anthony is bringing down, so he enthusiastically says, "It's good that you're making it snow, Anthony, it's real good!" With no exaggeration, I think this episode is one of the clearest and most convincing depictions of how original sin contaminates all human beings, even the most seemingly innocent.

A further implication of the Christian concept of evil is that in order to perpetuate itself, evil often relies on our misremembering or forgetting our past. We would not so adamantly reject Augustine's sinister description of childhood if we did not willfully forget all the nasty, selfish things that we did as children: for most of us this would include—at a bare minimum—stealing, lying, bullying and ostracizing other children, and torturing insects and dolls. Most of us usually take a further step and positively misremember our childhood—as well as our whole past life—sentimentalizing it into one of innocence and goodness; there is also the related tactic of exaggerating the insults and harms that others have done to us over the years, remembering ourselves as patient and long-suffering victims, when we were really more often the victimizers. All of these lull us into further sinfulness through bad habits of memory, habits that avoid guilt rather than accept it and lead to arrogance, self-righteousness, spite, and senselessly holding grudges and blaming others.

Such perverted misremembering of the past is depicted vividly in "Death's-Head Revisited," in which a Nazi S.S. captain, Gunther Lutze (actor Oscar Beregi), returns to the Dachau concentration camp to reminisce. Clearly, for him the place is not one of horror, but delight. It fills him with glee to remember the strutting, the barked commands, the absolute, arbitrary fear and authority he once exercised there; the gallows and the torture chamber hold especially fond memories for him, and he caresses them the way an alcoholic would a bottle, or the way a normal person would caress an heirloom that reminds her or him of a beloved person. But when he meets a mysterious man there and recognizes him as a former inmate, Captain Lutze retreats to a quite different kind of faulty memory that is always heard after every sin is revealed—bland, shrugging denial: it was a long time ago, no sense dwelling on the past, what's done is done, better now just to move on. The inmate, however, is there to make sure that this does not happen. He and the other murdered inmates are there as avenging ghosts. They force Captain Lutze to feel the pain he has inflicted on others, to accept finally what he has done. They belatedly force him, in effect, to remember things rightly and to have a conscience; but this newfound conscience—which would have kept him from committing the atrocities in the first place, if he had had it earlier—now only drives him mad. Captain Lutze is driven off at the end, as a doctor pronounces that something has suddenly rendered him permanently and irreversibly insane. Serling then gives the closing narration, driving home the absolute necessity of memory in combating evil:

> All the Dachaus must remain standing. The Dachaus, the Belsens, the Buchenwalds, the Auschwitzes—all of them. They must remain standing because they are a monument to a moment in time when some men decided to turn the Earth into a graveyard. Into it they shoveled all of their reason, their logic, their knowledge, but worst of all, their conscience. And the moment we forget this, the moment we cease to be haunted by its remembrance, then we become the grave-diggers. Something to dwell on and to remember, not only in the Twilight Zone, but wherever men walk God's earth.

Though the very similar anti-Nazi episode "He's Alive" is not nearly as compelling as "Death's-Head Revisited," here the heavy-handedness remains effective, because our tendency to excuse and overlook past sins is so strong that the exhortation to remember them has to be equally blatant and uncompromising. Also, although the original historical context of *The Twilight Zone* is noticeable and somewhat quaint throughout the series—its favorite examples of evil are from World War II and the cold war, everyone smokes cigarettes (not just the villains), the only gangs it depicts wear leather jackets and ride motorcycles, and the only physical addiction it knows of is alcoholism—it is as clear as ever that the moral lessons have not changed one bit "wherever men walk God's earth."

Faulty memory often leads to vindictiveness and spite, and few depictions show the self-destructiveness of these bad habits better than *The Twilight Zone* episode "One More Pallbearer." In it an independently wealthy man, Paul Radin (actor Joseph Wiseman), invites three people from his past—a teacher, a colonel, and a minister—to his state-of-the-art bomb shelter. Through an elaborate setup of sound effects and fake radio broadcasts, he makes it seem that nuclear war has begun and that the bombs will start to explode right above them in half an hour. The only way to survive will be to stay in his shelter, and to enjoy this privilege the three invited people only have to apologize to Radin for the wrongs that he feels they have done to him: his schoolteacher should apologize for failing him, his army commander for court-martialing him, his pastor for humiliating him. But they refuse, and they correct Radin's partial, self-serving memory of their supposed misdeeds: not only did he cheat in class, he tried to shift the blame for it onto an innocent student; not only was he cowardly in the army, he endangered others thereby; not only did he hurt someone, he drove a girlfriend to suicide. They reject Radin's offer and force him to let them out. Afterward, Radin hears an explosion, and when he ascends to the surface, he sees that the world has been destroyed by a real nuclear war. However, when we then see people picking up a quivering, demented Radin, we understand that the nuclear holocaust was only his delusion. Rather than accepting guilt and learning from it, Radin had played the martyr his whole life by falsifying his past; now when the people from his real past refuse to play their assigned parts in his revenge fantasy, his whole world crumbles and he becomes a real victim—of himself and the sinful memories that he let fester within him. He is a "pallbearer at a funeral that he manufactured himself," as Serling puts it in the closing narration. Similarly, in "A Piano in the House," a magical piano is able to dredge up embarrassing feelings and memories in people. After the main character cruelly uses it to humiliate others, he then has it turned against himself, showing him to be a sniveling coward, trapped in or by the past. The other characters, now not so embarrassed by their own revelations, happily leave him and go off to live and enjoy their lives.

Such bad habits of forgetting or misremembering the past can even—if indulged in long enough—ossify into stagnant repetition of it. The more we cease to notice our bad behavior, the less likely are we ever to change it. Ironically, although sin loses its tempting or seductive quality when it becomes a habit, it also becomes harder to break or resist, because it becomes just a boring, numbing, unnoticeable addiction. This facet of evil is made clear in the episode "Escape Clause." In it Walter Bedeker (actor David Wayne) is a hypochondriac who is an insufferable burden to himself and his wife. As Serling narrates, his only evil is his habitual and petty selfishness: "He has one interest in life, and that's Walter Bedeker. One preoccupation—the life and well-being of Walter Bedeker. One abiding concern about society: that if Walter Bedeker should die, how will it survive without him?" Bedeker is approached by Mr. Cadwallader (actor Thomas Gomez), who, as the devil, offers a typically devilish bargain: Bedeker's soul in exchange for complete imperviousness to all forms of bodily harm. There is in the bargain, however, an escape clause: Bedeker can die whenever he wants by summoning Cadwallader back. Bedeker agrees, and goes on to try all different ways to harm or kill himself, but nothing ever happens. After a very short time, however, this is no longer thrilling, it is just boring. Unlike the main character of the movie *Groundhog Day* (1993), who has a similar experience and even makes the same unsuccessful attempts at suicide, Bedeker does not take this opportunity to learn and grow but just falls back into moping and complaining. When he tries to jump off the top of his apartment building, his wife intervenes, the two struggle, and she falls to her death; if he did not actually push her off, he certainly is responsible for and viciously uncaring toward her fate. He sees it only as an opportunity to experience another form of failed death, by the electric chair, so he enthusiastically admits to the crime; the judge surprises and destroys him, however, by sentencing him to life in prison without the possibility of parole. In his cell, Bedeker summons Cadwallader, who gives him a fatal heart attack to end his evil, meaningless existence. Similar depictions that focus on repetitive boredom are seen in such episodes as "Shadow Play," "Judgment Night," and, perhaps most poignantly, in "A Game of Pool," in which a young Jack Klugman loses sight of what really matters in life—love, relationships, beauty—and obsesses over playing pool, condemning himself thereby to play the game for eternity.

Finally, *The Twilight Zone* is adamant that there is nothing powerful or even attractive in evil: it is impotent and empty, the shadow created by the light of goodness. This is another of Saint Augustine's surprising conclusions on evil: "Evil is nothing other than the absence of good, even to the point of complete nonexistence."[4] Such a banal emptiness of evil is shown in the episode "The Masks," which is similar in plot to "One More Pallbearer." This time, however, the man who summons others to his death really is dying, and there is no inaccuracy in his estimation of his visitors' evil. Jason Foster (actor Robert Keith) calls his daughter and her family to sit with him on Mardi Gras night as he is dying. There is, as usual, a catch: they must wear grotesque masks that he has had made by a local expert in the occult. As they sit, he accuses them of their pettiness and hypocrisy: while they pretend to be loving toward him and others, they really love only themselves and their petty desires—for money, prestige, looks, and cruelty. At midnight Jason finally breathes his last, and the accuracy of his accusations is obvious as his family members descend on his body like vultures, triumphant and exultant that he is dead and they now have his money. But their triumph is short-lived, as when they remove their masks, their faces now match the ugly masks, and more importantly, their outsides now reveal their hideous insides, as Serling summarizes in the closing narration: "They now wear the faces of all that was inside them—and they'll wear them for the rest of their lives, said lives now to be spent in the shadow." Ugliness and shadow are all that evil ever has to offer in *The Twilight Zone,* where evil is portrayed not so much as terrifying, but as disappointing and pathetic.

The utter, disappointing paltriness and ugliness of evil is depressingly depicted in other episodes as well, such as "A Most Unusual Camera" and "What You Need": in both tales, characters are presented with a device—in the first, a camera, in the latter, a fountain pen—that can tell the future, and the only use their pathetic minds can put it to is to use it to win at horse races. And when the device's magical abilities run out, rather than enjoy their ill-gotten gains, the characters turn on each other and kill themselves, senselessly and self-destructively grasping for more. Perhaps most strikingly, when the devil appears in the episode "The Howling Man," he also reveals how impotent evil really is. In this episode, a band of monks captures and imprisons the Prince of Darkness himself by using the symbol of their order—a shepherd's crook. (Apparently the script originally called for them to use a cross, but this was deemed too inflammatory; it is hard now to see how it would have offered offense to show the cross defeating evil.) Although Satan eventually escapes from his captors by tricking a gullible newcomer into lifting the shepherd's crook that is barring the door, the ease with which he is contained seems the more surprising part of the tale: the point is that the Devil is tricky, but that's the only power he has—his ability to trick or seduce people. Unlike God or even humans, Satan has no ability to accomplish or make anything on his own. If everyone ignored him, both evil and he really would be nothing at all. They would cease to exist, if they could not prey on the good.

Although it is a "text" that enjoys no canonical or authoritative status, *The Twilight Zone* repeatedly depicts evil in a uniquely and orthodoxly Christian way, and its creativity and artistry have made this message much more accessible to millions worldwide. While many readers have discounted the authoritative Saint Augustine as neurotic, millions of viewers of "It's a Good Life" have come away with at least a reduced estimation of human innocence and a greater unease at the reality of original sin. And by considering how the seductiveness of evil often relies on forgetfulness, misremembering, repetition, and pettiness, *The Twilight Zone*'s many cautionary tales against these aspects of sinfulness serve as nagging, persistent reminders to be on our guard against them and to be open to their life-giving opposites.

Grace and Preparedness for Grace

In opposition to the rather pessimistic doctrine of original sin, Christianity has set the hopeful doctrine of divine grace—the unmerited assistance that God grants to people to help them overcome original sin and grow closer to God. The exact human contribution to this process is variously interpreted—from full and willing cooperation to utter submission and surrender—but it seems clear that people can either harden their hearts against God's loving extension of grace to them or can be open and receptive to it. It is this receptiveness, and the loving acts that follow on it, that *The Twilight Zone* portrays so beautifully and so often.

One of the simplest and most easily overlooked experiences of grace is the experience that we have all had of being given an undeserved second chance. When we could have been punished or destroyed for our bad or foolish behavior, someone or some circumstance has unexpectedly arisen and allowed us to start over with a clean slate. Here again the level of our cooperation varies—sometimes it seems as though we are swept along by the new situation, and some other times we have to struggle very hard to follow through on the second chance. But either way, something beyond our control or merit changes our lives, sometimes in a radical and permanent way. *The Twilight Zone* being what it is, characters in it often get second chances that are quite beyond our experience—ones that include time travel, or communicating with the dead, or reversing the aging process—but they are still recognizable as human yearnings and recognizable as moments we too could reach for, if in more mundane, less supernatural circumstances.

A recurring kind of second chance in *The Twilight Zone* is the miraculous ability to return to one's childhood, to strip away all the grime of adult life that has accumulated over decades and relive a time of playfulness and openness. This happens in the episode "Walking Distance," in which an exhausted advertising executive, Martin Sloan (actor Gig Young), walks back to his hometown from a nearby service station where he has left his car to be repaired. He is surprised to see that nothing in the town has changed. His surprise increases as he realizes that he has stepped back in time. Martin then actually sees himself as a child, and tries to speak to the boy, but only succeeds in frightening his boyhood self into falling off a moving merry-go-round. The adult Martin collapses in pain at the same time as the boy Martin's leg is broken from the fall. Martin's father confronts him, now believing his incredible story of time travel, and asks him to go back to his time but leaves him with the kind of valuable advice that Martin had tried to give to his childhood self: "Maybe when you go back, Martin, you'll find that there are merry-go-rounds and band concerts where you are. Maybe you haven't been looking in the right place. You've been looking behind you. Try looking ahead." Martin limps back into the present, but there is hope that the chance that he's been given to see the past has done something more than just physically maim him: it has alerted him to the beauty that has been all around him all along, but which a sick combination of cynicism and nostalgia had dulled or obscured. Our reveries about the past may not be as literal and physical as Martin's, but if reminiscing about the past sensitizes us to the present's beauty and the infinite possibilities for happiness therein, then it is not too incredible to call it a graced moment; if it fills us with regret or despair, then it is just another of the kinds of unhealthy, sinful misremembering of the past we have already examined.

If "Walking Distance" showed that you cannot go back to your past but should appreciate the present, then "Kick the Can" went all the way to imagining that one's past could be reclaimed. Serling had ended "Walking Distance" with the somber rumination that a person might sometimes have "a little errant wish, that a man might not have to become old, never outgrow the parks and the merry-go-rounds of his youth. And he'll smile then too because he'll know it is just an errant wish." But "Kick the Can" shows that wish coming true. We are first shown an old man, Charles Whitley (actor Ernest Truex), being callously let down by his son, who refuses to take him in and condemns him to spend the remainder of his days at the Sunnyvale Rest Home, which Serling calls "a dying place" in both the opening and closing narrations. But Charles refuses to go quietly. Instead, like a grownup version of Peter Pan, or like the Jack Nicholson character in the movie *One Flew over the Cuckoo's Nest* (1975), he leads most of the other residents of Sunnyvale in a sort of rebellion, sneaking out late one night to play their favorite childhood game of kick-the-can. Charles's friend Ben (actor Russell Collins) thinks they are insane or foolish for doing so, and he goes to fetch help to get the other old people back under control. But when Ben and the doctor go outside, there are only children playing. Charles and the others have magically regressed and escaped back into childhood. Like any parable, the literal events of the story are not the point. Rather, "Kick the Can" reminds us that "acting one's age"—at the very least, doing so *all* the time—is a deadening, heartless existence, whether one is twenty-eight or seventy-eight. As Serling puts it in his subtly worded closing narration, "Childhood, maturity, and old age are curiously intertwined and not separate." Drinking from a garden hose, stepping over a crack lest one breaks Mother's back, letting the bubbles from ginger ale go up your nose, and however many more experiences one can think of—these are all things that we've supposedly outgrown, but if we refuse to do them still, we only make ourselves a little older and deader by refusing the constant grace that is innocence, simplicity, beauty, and joy in life.

A return to childhood is not the only kind of second chance available in *The Twilight Zone*. There are profound, painful second chances offered to cruel killers, not to return to childhood simplicity, but finally to have empathy and feel the pain of others, and thereby to stop their brutality and live virtuously. In "A Quality of Mercy" Lieutenant Katell (actor Dean Stockwell) leads a platoon of war-weary American soldiers in August 1945. They have cornered a small group of Japanese soldiers in a cave. The prudent as well as merciful thing to do is just to leave them there, as they pose no threat, but Katell is eager to prove himself and wants to assault the cave, thereby dooming many of his own men as well as the Japanese to futile deaths. But as they prepare their assault, Katell suddenly finds himself among Japanese soldiers. He is now Lieutenant Yamuri, and his unit has cornered a small group of Americans in a cave on Corregidor in

May 1942. He begs with his commanding officer not to attack the Americans, but his Japanese captain is as cold, insensitive, and brutal as he himself had just been, even using the exact same words to justify the senseless slaughter. Katell returns to the present, where the assault is thankfully called off because the atomic bomb has been dropped on Japan. Serling ends with the words of Shakespeare's *Merchant of Venice:* "The quality of mercy is not strained, it droppeth as the gentle rain from heaven upon the place beneath. It blesseth him that gives and him that takes." Lieutenant Katell has been blessed by a vision that taught him the quality of mercy; he will be a better soldier and person for it, as are we for having witnessed the difficult lesson.

Similarly, in "Mr. Denton on Doomsday" a man is turned from violence by the intervention of a mysterious force. The story is set in the Old West, where Al Denton (actor Dan Duryea) is first introduced to us as the town drunk, humiliatingly called "Rummy" and being made to sing "How Dry I Am" in order to get a drink. But we learn that he was once a deadly gunslinger, and when Mr. Henry J. Fate (actor Malcolm Atterbury) throws some magic his way, Denton is fast again, first shooting the gun arm of the bully who is tormenting him, then shooting the chain that holds a chandelier, thereby dropping it on the bully's head. But Fate's help is a mixed blessing at best, putting Denton back in the same situation that drove him to drink in the first place: now men once again foolishly challenge him to duels and he has to kill them. Worse, Denton's quick-draw ability was only a one-time event provided by the unpredictable Fate. But now Denton has been challenged by a young opponent and must fight, so he obtains a potion that Fate promises will make him fast again for exactly ten seconds. As he faces his opponent, Denton drinks the potion but suddenly notices that his opponent is drinking from an identical bottle. Both men fire and maim one another's gun hands, thereby making sure that neither will draw a gun ever again. Denton sees this as the blessing that it is, saying soothingly to his opponent, "You're blessed, son. We've both been blessed." Serling underlines the double blessing at the end: "Mr. Henry Fate . . . a fanciful little man in a black frock coat who can help a man climbing out of a pit—or another man from falling into one." This is, of course, a much better description of God's grace, which blesses and saves gratuitously and indiscriminately, than it is of some impersonal sense of "fate," which is as likely to harm as it is to help.

Appropriately enough, the series twice offered characters second chances in Christmas episodes. "Night of the Meek" presents us with a very bad Santa indeed: Henry Corwin (actor Art Carney), a drunk who plays a department-store Santa and who staggers into the department store so intoxicated that he's fired from even this modest position. But when he finds a bag that magically dispenses presents based on whatever the person really wants and needs, he takes nothing for himself but happily gives to everyone else. When the magical bag is empty, Corwin gets what he really wanted. It is not alcohol, though the bag readily supplied a bottle of brandy to the dour and unforgiving department-store manager, because in his case drinking some Christmas spirits was exactly what he needed. But for Corwin, what he wanted was the opportunity to go to the North Pole and work for Santa again next year, and a sleigh and reindeer appear at the end to take him there. Though perhaps sentimental and optimistic, the tale is still effective, for even the most cynical among us feel that Christmas is a time of second chances and miraculous reversals, as Serling—not himself a practicing Christian—describes it in his closing narration: "There's a wondrous magic to Christmas, and there's a special power for little people.

In short, there's nothing mightier than the meek, and a merry Christmas to each and all." Corwin was not made meek and generous by the magical bag—in fact, in the hands of other *Twilight Zone* characters such as we examined in the previous section, the bag would have been an awful curse that set them on a rampage of killing and destruction. Corwin was a good person to begin with, and the bag just gave him the opportunity to put down the bottle long enough to remember that and act upon that goodness.

In a much less sentimental way, the power of Christmas is just barely invoked in "Five Characters in Search of an Exit." The episode is one of the most surreal in a series that almost singlehandedly made the adjective applicable to television. Five people—an army major, a ballerina, a clown, a hobo, and a bagpiper—are trapped in a large cylindrical room with no windows or doors. The room is open at the top, with one enormous light shining down, wisps of smoke passing overhead, and occasionally a loud bell chiming. But that is all the characters know. They do not know how they got there, nor do they remember their names or any other aspect of their lives. The major (actor William Windom) encourages them to try to escape, which they attempt to do by standing on one another's shoulders. When the major reaches the top and climbs out, however, he falls over the side to whatever is outside the room, and the others are distraught at his loss. We then see that the room is really a sidewalk barrel for Christmas donations, into which people have thrown four dolls. A girl sees the major doll outside the barrel and puts him back in. Again, what literally happens is not the point. Throughout the episode, the dialogue is profoundly existentialist, as the major cries out, "What are we?! Who are we?!" to which the ballerina sadly replies, "None of us knows." One needn't live in a cylindrical prison to have had similar anguished doubts. The feelings between the characters are also some of the most touching and humane in the series: there is the barest hint of attraction or affection between the major and the ballerina, and there is a wonderful feeling of community between them all, as they all comfort one another, then all band together to escape their prison, and finally all mourn together the loss of their friend. (A similarly loving nonhuman community is shown in "The After Hours," this time made up of mannequins.) And Serling's closing narration ends with hope, if not downright assurance: "But this added, hopeful note: perhaps they are unloved only for the moment. In the arms of children there can be nothing but love." Love is once again affirmed as the essence of real human life, and we are sure that the five characters will again be graced by another chance for love.

Besides second chances, there is the grace of finally realizing that one's first chance was enough, that one's fears of failure and worthlessness were unfounded and that one has really lived a good and valuable life, despite one's self-doubt. This is part of the magic of the classic Christmas movie *It's a Wonderful Life* (1946), and it is the premise of *The Twilight Zone* episode "Changing of the Guard," which is also set at Christmastime. Ellis Fowler (played by the excellent character actor Donald Pleasence), an aging literature teacher at a private boys' high school, is dismissed from his position because he is so old. He plans on suicide, as he now believes his life has been a waste; he thinks that both he and the literature he taught have been utterly irrelevant to his students, forgotten the moment they left his class. But as he sits in his old classroom, loaded gun in hand, the ghosts of his former students appear. They identify themselves as students who have died since attending his class—most in war, one while conducting medical research using radiation—and each one testifies to how he carried with him the memory of one piece of literature, how it inspired him to courage and self-sacrifice. Seeing now that his teaching did make a difference, that it helped make other people's lives heroic and worthwhile, Fowler realizes his own worth and resolves against suicide. It is a simple, touching story of a person being miraculously pulled back from the brink of despair by finally seeing what was there all along—the enormous value of his life and his vocation. The episode is much more inspiring than other similar tales, such as *Dead Poets Society* (1989), which too often focus on the teacher, rather than on either the student or the subject being taught. In "Changing of the Guard," Fowler clearly feels awed before the tremendous heroism of his students and before the life-changing beauty and truth of the literature he has taught them. His is a humbling and uplifting story of a graced moment shedding light on a life that had been quietly and unexpectedly filled with grace all along.

If grace can turn a man from suicide, it can also help one to accept death, rather than futilely fighting against it. The peace and fulfillment that come from accepting rather than fighting against death are powerfully portrayed in episodes such as "Long Distance Call" and "Nothing in the Dark." It is also seen, together with other relevant ideas about grace, in the episode "The Obsolete Man." Like so many other *Twilight Zone* episodes, it is about the evils of totalitarian government, but it is also one of the most overtly religious. In a nightmarish, futuristic society, people are judged by the inhuman, all-powerful state as "obsolete" if they do not perform a function that the state recognizes as valuable; once so judged they are "liquidated." Their only privilege is that they may choose the place and method of their execution. Romney Wordsworth (actor Burgess Meredith, who appeared in four *Twilight Zone* episodes), a librarian who courageously shouts at his accusers, "There IS a God!" is judged at the beginning of the episode to be "obsolete" by a court led by the Chancellor of the state, because the state has banned books and declared that there is no God, and therefore a Christian librarian is doubly useless. Wordsworth schedules his execution for the following midnight in his apartment; only he and his executioner will know the means of death, however. Also, his final moments are to be televised. Wordsworth invites the Chancellor to his apartment in the final hour but locks him in to share his fate, after telling him that there is a bomb in the apartment set to explode at midnight. The television cameras broadcast to the world how Wordsworth calmly sits reading the Psalms out loud, while the Chancellor becomes increasingly nervous and frightened, finally crying out, "In the name of God, let me out!" Wordsworth mercifully lets him out, quietly saying, "Yes, Chancellor, in the name of God I'll let you out." As the Chancellor runs down the stairs, the apartment explodes. When the Chancellor shows up at his court the next day, however, he is the one who is declared obsolete. As he pleads for his life, a crowd of uniformed, automatonlike apparatchiks fall upon him, beating and tearing him apart. Wordsworth's final words were fearless ones from the Bible, and his final act was one of mercy, while the Chancellor lived and died in the fear and cruelty of his false idol, the state. The one entered eternal life after peacefully accepting his death and God's grace; the other denied God and died eternally after never really living.

Going beyond mercy, self-sacrifice is the ultimate and most Christlike expression of love for another. Self-sacrifice is a frequent theme in *The Twilight Zone,* guiding episodes such as "The Trade-Ins," "One for the Angels," and "The Fugitive." To bring our discussion full circle, let's look at the theme in the episode "In Praise of Pip," from the series' last season. This is especially apt, as actors who played evil or misguided characters in previous episodes reappear here: Billy Mumy, who played the demonic Anthony in "It's a Good Life," and Jack Klugman, who squandered his life away in "A Game of Pool," now appear as a father and son who save and redeem each other. Pip is first seen as a young soldier dying in a field hospital in Vietnam. Then his father is introduced—Max Phillips, a drunken bookie who mercifully lets a young gambler—who looks about the age of his son—out of a $300 debt. When Max's boss finds out, however, he simply has the gambler hunted down and beaten up, and then he takes back the money. As his boss confronts him with the beaten-up gambler and berates Max for this stupid lapse into kindness, Max gets a phone call that his son is dying. The news that he will not have a chance to undo or make up for his past failures as a father fills Max with self-loathing and rage against the waste that he has made of his life. He first lashes out at his criminal boss and another thug, stabbing them both to death, so as to retrieve the money and save the young gambler once again. Max is shot in the altercation, however, stumbling outside and staggering into the nearby amusement park where he used to take Pip as a boy. There he meets Pip, miraculously restored to ten years old again. The amusement park lights up and the two relive a happy outing from the past. But Pip suddenly says that he must leave now because he is dying. Max is alone, weeping, and he cries out to God, offering God his life for Pip's. Max dies, but when we see Pip as a young soldier returning to the amusement park, we know that the bargain was accepted by a forgiving and loving God. And in the grown-up Pip, we see a more complete redemption of his father, for at the amusement park Pip remembers only the fun that he had there with his father: there is no recollection of Max's drinking or other failures. Love truly conquers all in this episode—alcohol, crime, war, death—as Serling notes in his emotional closing narration: "The capacity to love is a vital, rich and all-consuming function of the human animal. . . . You can find nobility and sacrifice and love wherever you may seek them out—down the block, in the heart, or in the Twilight Zone." Max loved truly, if imperfectly, and that was enough for the God of love to redeem him, save his son, and transform their relationship into one of perfect and everlasting love. The clarity and purity of this episode's vision of grace and redemption are overwhelming.

Energized and transformed by God's grace intervening in their lives, the characters of *The Twilight Zone* go on to practice Christlike love for one another. Their experiences of grace make them forgiving, merciful, self-sacrificing, and gladly accepting of their own limitations and mortality. For all their strange circumstances, they are some of the noblest, most humane, and most Christian characters who have appeared on television.

Conclusion

The Twilight Zone offers much to a Christian viewer. It gives us some of the most compelling images of original sin, shocking us out of our sentimentality and wishful thinking much more forcefully even than Christian theologians could. It constantly shows us the futility and uselessness of sin, but also frightens us with how powerful and seductive it is. It frequently reminds us of how sin can work its way into our lives through laziness, addiction, and the kind of selective, self-serving memories in which we all indulge. Perhaps most importantly, over and over, *The Twilight Zone* uplifts and inspires us with stories of men and women who remain open to God's grace, who gladly let themselves be transformed by outrageous circumstances into what people were meant to be—a community of individuals loving and serving each other as they all grow closer to God. The series gives us some of the most beautiful, breathtaking moments of real, Christlike love to appear in any medium, flickering glimpses on the small screen of what eternal happiness and blessedness will be like.

V

The In-Breaking Bedazzlement of Truth

The X Files as Apocalypse

The truth of existence emerges from the theophanic events in history. . . . In its existential depth, a theophanic event is a turbulence in reality. The thinker who has become engulfed by it must try to rise, like the Aeschylean diver, from the depth to the surface of exegesis.

Eric Voegelin, *The Ecumenic Age*[1]

Then I turned to see whose voice it was that spoke to me, and on turning I saw seven golden lampstands, and in the midst of the lampstands I saw one like the Son of Man.

Revelation 1:12

Several aspects of this case remain unexplained, suggesting the possibility of paranormal phenomena. But I am

> convinced that to accept such conclusions is to abandon all hope of understanding the scientific events behind them. Many of the things I have seen have challenged my faith and my belief in an ordered universe, but this uncertainty has only strengthened my need to know, to understand, to apply reason to those things which seem to defy it.
>
> Agent Dana Scully, in *The X Files*[2]

Science Fiction, Apocalypse, and the Sensitive Spirit

This chapter explores the popular 1990s television show *The X Files,* produced and created by writer Chris Carter, in terms of its gospel-related implications. Despite the reluctance of Carter to say so, *The X Files* belongs more or less to science fiction; most of its fans think of it that way. Now the usual definition would cast science fiction as the genre of technological extrapolation, a kind of propaganda for the purely secular version of technical progress. Some science fiction does correspond to that idea: all the pulp-fiction planetary romances and battle-in-space movies that concern themselves with exotic and destructive hardware and with the conquest of nature through engineering. But we must seek the essence of the genre—thus also the central purport of *The X Files*—elsewhere.

The roots of science fiction in fact lie in the phenomenon of *apocalypse* or *revelation*.[3] Carter himself says as much in a spoken commentary on the sixth season of *The X Files* when he notes that the show's obsession with what might lie beyond the everyday world and its conventions is essentially a religious one. Carter even uses the word *apocalyptic.* The definitive entries in the science-fiction genre—both literarily and cinematically considered—suggest the same identification. Whether it is H. G. Wells's *The War of the Worlds* (1897) or Stanley Kubrick's *2001: A Space Odyssey* (1968), the well-wrought science-fiction story nearly always carries at least a tinge of what the philosopher of politics and history Eric Voegelin (1901–1985) calls the *theophanic event:* the in-breaking on everyday life of a sublime vision of things that says to its witness that *this* rather than the narrow everyday assumption about life and the world *is the truth,* and says so in such a way as to demand from the witness a total transformation of his or her existence. Science fiction, precisely because it takes an interest in first and last things, maintains an affiliation with every historical moment when someone, somewhere, gained a glimpse, wonted or unwonted, of an eternal order of things beyond the changeability of the merely mortal and therefore ever-perishing earthly scene.

Consider the case of Edgar Allan Poe (1809–1849), one of the innovators of the science-fiction genre and a writer whose work prefigures certain aspects of *The X Files.* Poe maintained a consistent interest in apocalyptic impingements on ordinary awareness and exploited them in a number of his key stories. Poe subscribed to a not-quite-materialistic view of the universe; according to Poe's cosmo-theology, the supernatural amounts to higher degrees of the natural misunderstood by badly informed, spiritually insensitive observers. While the biblical God, the God who is at once unfathomable and yet also personal, tends to go absent from this theory, a difference nevertheless remains in it, which distinguishes the errors of intellectual conformity and moral complacency from eruptive moments of overwhelming truth. These latter retain in them something of a conventionally divine character. Stories of *The X Files* often concern the limited horizon of the purely scientific view of life, just as they regularly underscore the need for openness to reality. Poe's work not only anticipates Carter's television series in a general way; it also provides specific motifs taken over by Carter and made part of the overall fabric of his saga.

Carter's idea of the relation of science and religion thus shows much in common with Poe's, which undoubtedly belongs in the *X Files* genealogy. Poe's *magnum opus,* the long prose poem called *Eureka!* (1848), purports to treat both the "material" *and* the "spiritual" aspects of existence; the former, asserts Poe, is inconceivable without the latter. *Eureka,* whose name in Greek means "I found it," deals with "the Volition of God . . . the Divine Will . . . an Intelligence greater than [our] own,"[4] and with the implications of these things for life as people habitually live it, a view implicit in *The X Files.* A Poe short story, "Mesmeric Revelation" (1844), tells of the soul's survival after death, another staple of *The X Files.* Poe's short story in dialogue form, "The Conversation of Eiros and Charmion" (1844), meanwhile tells of the catastrophic end of the world. When, in "The Conversation," Poe's narrator describes the final, fiery moments of the earth, he uses imagery whose source all literate people will recognize: "For a moment there was a wild lurid light alone, visiting and penetrating all things . . . then there came a shouting and pervading sound, as if from the mouth itself of HIM; while the whole incumbent mass of ether . . . burst at once into a species of intense flame."[5] This ensemble of portents and prodigies—combined, as Poe builds his story, with moral criticism of a society gone decadent, self-indulgent, and arrogant—takes its prototype in the last book of the New Testament, the Revelation or Apocalypse of Saint John the Divine, also called John of Patmos, whom nowadays scholars generally distinguish from John the author of the Fourth Gospel. Poe has recalled how John, in his vision, saw "hail and fire . . . and a third of the earth . . . burned up," and how "a great star fell from heaven, blazing like a torch," that struck dry the rivers and seas (Rev. 8:7, 10). While *The X Files* never represents the end of the world, cosmic violence always threatens existence in the stories that Carter's show tells. Metaphorically, much of life, as *The X Files* portrays it, has suffered drought and desiccation, particularly in the capacity of people for faith. *The X Files* suggests that a spiritual catastrophe has already occurred and that, in many ways, modern people live in the debris and demoralization left by a terrible disaster.

With its panorama of beasts and tyrants, its pageantry of angelic trumpet-calls and martyr-choruses, and its rectifying wrath and lake of fire, Revelation only barely made it into the New Testament. For a variety of reasons, most of Greek Christianity regarded it as troubling. Perhaps because official persecutions against the church had occurred largely in the West, Latin-speaking Christians better than their Hellenic counterparts could appreciate the vindictive anti-imperial strain in John's text, for Revelation is, among many other things, a sustained diatribe against Rome's abuse of its military and political power. Considered simply in its tone, judgmental and aggressive, with a hearty appetite for the direct punishment of the wicked, Revelation differs from the Gospels, with their morality of love. Revelation has always exercised a terrifying urgency over its readers, and here again one might justifiably refer to *The X Files* as an exemplary reflection of the tone and spirit of Revelation. The protagonists of Carter's drama find themselves in conflict with corrupt departments of the government and with power conspiracies at the highest level from the first episode of the first season.

When an *X Files* good guy starts opining, as occasionally happens, the rhetoric is likely to resemble that of an Old Testament prophet railing against the distortions of the age; anger can overtake the good guy and alienate him momentarily from his obligations under the rule of charity and love. In this, too, *The X Files* appears to draw on Revelation. While it differs from the four Gospel narratives, John's text resembles certain books of the Old Testament, such as those of Ezekiel or Daniel, which describe startling manifestations of the divine will and forecast an ultimate justice on a cosmic scale for all perpetrators of iniquity, Jew or Gentile, against the righteous. Yet Revelation, more than any other book of either Testament, also undoubtedly communicates with non-Christian apocalypse-literature of its period: its imagery corresponds as much with a Near Eastern, an Egyptian, an Olympian, or a Gnostic iconography as with anything purely biblical. The catchall nature of John's in-breaking vision experience should not surprise us however, as all people necessarily use the existing vocabulary even for the articulation of novel messages. The appeal might be God's, but the language is humanity's, so that items at hand in the cumulus of expression must adapt themselves as best they can in support of novel, redemptory discourse. In *The X Files,* Carter makes this type of religious eclecticism a technique, borrowing every imaginable weird strand of contemporary popular culture and spirituality into his on-going storyline, yet often showing how limited occultism and "New Age" religiosity can be. Our contemporary world resembles the world of late antiquity, for in it people suffer from a terrible loss of spiritual orientation. When confusion prevails, people grasp at spiritual straws, but not every straw entails genuine salvation.

Borrowing a phrase from the poet W. H. Auden, classicist E. R. Dodds famously characterized late antiquity, the period from the first to the fifth centuries CE, as an "age of anxiety" when Christian and pagan alike felt afflicted by "a growing contempt for all that can be done" in the earthly realm, disconcerted by "a sentiment of alienation" from the civic environment, and tugged at by a longing for "ultimate truth."[6] John, who comes at the beginning of late antiquity, knows the coercive might of imperial power, imprisoned as he is on Patmos by Roman authority for preaching the Word of God; and his community, that of the followers of Christ, is clearly *not* coincident with and thus may fairly be described as *alienated from* the larger civic environment of the Roman Empire, which rejects the new religion. John also longs for God's effulgent truth to clarify the murkiness, the confusion, and the tension of humanity's fallen estate, in which he grasps that he himself participates, willy-nilly, through the rebellion of Adam and Eve. The events of Christ's ministry, of his crucifixion and resurrection, far from easing the pathos of existence, have heightened it; this is so because, in the aftermath of the passion, the shortcomings of fallen humanity have asserted themselves to the faithful with redoubled adamancy, as has the abject senselessness of history comprised by the mere succession of imperial powers. Almost every episode of *The X Files* deals with a similar, contemporary heightening of pathos. The words of W. B. Yeats's oft-quoted poem not only fit our era, they also fit what *The X Files* show us about our era: "Things fall apart, the center cannot hold." When it happens that, in Yeats's words, "the ceremony of innocence is drowned" and "mere anarchy is loosed upon the land," then a people knows that an age of anxiety has arrived and with it the hour of decision.

The great moral rectification at the end of days envisioned by John answers the anguish that is given its rhetorical formulation by that other apocalyptic thinker of the New Testament, Paul of Tarsus. Settling his prophetic eye on Rome, which John, in Revelation, refers to as "Babylon," Paul sees a humanity "filled with every kind of wickedness, evil, covetousness, malice," its people "full of envy, murder, strife" who are "gossips, slanderers,

God-haters . . . inventors of evil" (Rom. 1:18). That this conviction about the injustice of the world corresponds by no means exclusively with the peculiar historical moment of the Roman Empire in Paul's day or John's, but rather with something ever present; that it exists always, everywhere; and that we may confirm it by a perusal of any big-city daily newspaper either today or tomorrow or the next day: these facts provide a key to the meaning of apocalypse, whether Paul's or John's or someone else's. Rome was the "center," in Yeats's sense, of the ancient world, as perhaps Washington D.C. is of the modern world. Nearly every *X Files* episode has a scene set in the Federal Bureau of Investigation headquarters in Washington D.C.

The FBI stands normatively for law and order, but *The X Files* depicts a condition in which the institutions of law and order no longer merit full trust. Another, perhaps a higher, law seems in tension with institutional law. Voegelin says of Paul in his study *The Ecumenic Age* (1974) that the bearer of revelation necessarily "lives in a state of existential unrest" because, having sensed the "divine reality," he is likewise profoundly acquainted with "the conflict between the divine law" on the one hand and "the weakness of the flesh"[7] on the other. Aware all at once of the promised perfection of forms at the end of historical time—a consummation vouchsafed to him in his vision in the form of the New Jerusalem or City of God—and of the imperfection of the prevailing anti-morality, the spiritual man commits himself morally to the former. He dedicates himself to the New Adam, purged of sin, and he maintains a heady skepticism for things earthly. The City of God thus functions for him as a deathless truth the preaching of which will help in salvaging the intolerable disorder of the City of Man from its own turbulent meaninglessness. "The philosophical and revelatory symbols," Voegelin writes, "are engendered by theophanic events" or, in another formula, "by the experience of divine presence in reality."[8]

It is important for modern people to remember that Jews and Christians were not the only "anxious" denizens of late antique society; pagans too, among whom we must number many morally good souls, could and did experience the same misgivings about circumstances as their Judeo-Christian neighbors. Historian Robin Lane Fox gives a wide-ranging account of late-antique theophanic events (to borrow Voegelin's term) based on hundreds of documented apparitions in his remarkable *Pagans and Christians* (1986); Fox links them to "times of strain and anxiety,"[9] much in the manner of Dodds. Writes Fox: "In times of collective tension, whole cities claimed sightings of their god."[10]

In an allusion to a popular science-fiction film of the 1970s directed by Stephen Spielberg, Fox refers to the late-antique rash of divinity-apparitions and heavenly displays as "close encounters."[11] The second half of the twentieth century also constituted a time of collective tension—related, in part, to the cold war, with its threat of nuclear annihilation—in which the "close encounter" with alien beings bearing revelatory if enigmatic messages became a prominent theme, an item in the prevailing folklore of ordinary people. Is the UFO phenomenon essentially religious, a kind of subspecies of apocalypse? More than one commentator has so concluded, beginning with the Swiss psychologist Carl Jung (1879–1961), who detected spiritual motifs, such as conversion, in the bizarre stories of the so-called contactees, or people who claim to have been contacted by extraterrestrials. Jung's study, *Flying Saucers: The Myth of Things Seen in the Sky,* appeared in 1957. More recently in *Alien Agenda* (1997), an open-minded study of all aspects of the UFO phenomenon, writer Jim Marrs concludes that the persistent myth of aerial peculiarities and of beings associated with them might well function as "a wake-up call" to our civilization, "a not-so-subtle message that human intellectual knowledge is not the end-all of existence or any assurance of peace and tranquility."[12] In *The X Files,* the symptoms of anxiety affect not only those who yearn to believe and to make sense of their condition through faith; they also affect purely secular people, who, however, are less able than the others to interpret their disorientation.

"The Truth Is Out There"

Flying saucers and alien beings constitute the two most recurrent topics of *The X Files*, but Carter's conception always wraps them in a metaphysical aura and always endows them with a moral meaning. Carter's version of the UFO phenomenon also invariably suggests extraconstitutional abuses by government, social distortion, and a pervasive alienation of modern humanity from all things spiritual.

According to Ted Edwards, in *X-Files Confidential,* Carter has acknowledged the work of John E. Mack, a Pulitzer Prize–winning Harvard psychiatrist who studies the abductees (people who claim to have been abducted by extraterrestrials), as having influenced much of the matter of the series.[13] Mack speculates, in *Abduction* (1994), that the UFO phenomenon, or myth or rumor, takes its context in the pronounced recalcitrance of the modern "Western worldview" to acknowledge truths beyond those of a narrow materialism; Mack writes of "a core belief in our culture that is violated by the alien abduction phenomenon, namely the total separation of the spirit and the physical world."[14] Poe held this same view about the limitations of the dominant outlook in the 1830s and '40s, when he was writing his grotesque and disturbing tales, which his contemporaries received as mere titillating ghost or horror stories. What rational person could take such things seriously? Poe, the visionary misfit, sought solace in drink; he died penniless and near friendless in Baltimore. It took half a century for scholars to admit timidly and grudgingly that his contribution might have been valuable, that he had been a social critic, a psychologist, and a genuine thinker.

Carter's series takes its name from a fictional subdepartment of the Federal Bureau of Investigation. Special Agent Fox Mulder (actor David Duchovny), who studied psychology at Oxford and who later gained a reputation in the FBI academy as a brilliant profiler of criminal perpetrators, single-handedly pursues cases that conventional investigative techniques have failed to resolve. Here we detect one of Poe's contributions to *The X Files,* as Mulder's unconventional approach to forensics resembles that of Poe's intellectual crime solver, C. Auguste Dupin, in "The Murders in the Rue Morgue"; but joined to this Poe-like resemblance is an insight about faith and knowledge conditioned by the New Testament, particularly by certain statements of Paul, but also some of John's.

In the series' pilot episode, when viewers get their first glimpse of Mulder's basement office in the J. Edgar Hoover Building in Washington D.C., they see a poster displayed prominently on the wall opposite the door that, in addition to its representation of a hovering spaceship, carries the capital-letter phrase: "I WANT TO BELIEVE."

In the second-season episode "Colony," Mulder introduces the story with an offscreen voice-over, saying: "I have lived with a fragile faith built on the ether of vague memories from an experience that I can neither prove nor explain. When I was twelve, my sister was taken from me, taken from our home by a force that I came to believe was extraterrestrial. This belief sustained me, fuelling a quest for truths that were as elusive as the memory itself. To believe as passionately as I did was not without sacrifice, but I always accepted the risks . . . to my career, my reputation, my relationships . . . to life itself."[15] The confession of a personal—an experiential—bond with the odd phenomena that interest and indeed obsess him signifies much for the tenor of *The X Files*. Mulder's character-history suggests an originally success-driven modern individual whose complacency about life has shattered against the impingement of the weird. The individual understands this radical insecurity with its concomitant yearning for faith as a new nearness to, although not yet the possession of, truth.

This feeling of nearness concerns something different, however, from the paltry truth of the logic choppers or evidence weighers or other people who have never questioned their deepest assumptions; it concerns something that transcends mundane life, for which the classic flying saucer functions as an adequate symbol in abeyance of better ones. Mulder's *second* motto (the first being "I WANT TO BELIEVE") is, "The truth is out there," and these words also operate as the overarching declaration for the whole *X Files* series.

Psychology and forensics belong, then, to the domain of science; but once the rationally inexplicable weirdness has taken place, the person committed to rationality all by itself finds himself or herself alone and adrift. In an unexpected way, dislocation, alienation, or even shock can entail productive sequels; they can induce, although not invariably, a spiritual reorientation of the positive sort. At the beginning of Revelation, John stresses that on the occasion of the great signs in the sky and the unsealing of the seals, having previously endured the Roman persecution of Jesus and the subsequent scattering of the apostles, he felt himself "in the spirit" (Rev. 1:10).

The phrase suggests a powerful tension in daily life and a heightened receptivity to the theophanic event; such a phrase might also apply to Moses, exiled in Midian, at the moment of the meeting with the burning bush, out of which speaks the voice of God. That, too, was revelation. Mystics of all sorts report that visionary liftings of the veil arise in the framework of what, in clinical terms, we would call "despondency" or "depression," or the proverbial "dark night of the soul." Despondency and depression, however, are precisely too clinical, too much the vocabulary of a paltry materialism, whereas "dark night of the soul" suggests the richer character-drama of revelatory embroilment. Mystics also report that the visions alter their liaison with the world, a fact that Mulder acknowledges when he talks about the "sacrifice" of his "career . . . reputation . . . relationships . . . life itself."

In *Abduction,* author-researcher Mack speculates that the strange events surounding the UFOs might indicate how "our consciousness has become so atrophied that we are simply unable, on our own, to be open to the spirit world."[16] In our skepticism and materialism, writes Mack, we might well "have created the spiritual conditions" that make necessary "the dramatic reopening to the world from which we have distanced ourselves."[17] So the collective unconscious, so to speak, addresses us through the existing vocabulary.

Yet openness to signs and a dissatisfaction with the world, while necessary for faith, are not sufficient for it. An unqualified receptivity can mean the abandonment of critical intuition, even of decorum and decency. Jacques Vallée, another interpreter of the UFO myth who rejects the notion that such things have any physical (let alone any extraterrestrial) reality, has accused Mack of excessive literalism in his dealings with the abductees. In an interview, Vallée says of Mack and others: "They are hypnotizing everybody who's ever had a strange experience and telling them they are abductees by suggestion. . . . [While] they are doing that in good faith . . . to my way of thinking, that's unethical."[18] Mulder leans towards Mack's type of UFO fundamentalism rather than to Vallée's less literalistic, rather more anthropological view. Mulder's superiors fear that he has grown obsessive and unskeptical. Other agents refer to Carter's protagonist out of his earshot as "Spooky Mulder." An ongoing structural element of the series is that these superiors have given Mulder a partner, whether he wants one or not, to rein him in: she is the rational, medically qualified Dana Scully (actress Gillian Anderson), also a special agent of the Bureau, in every way the characterological opposite of Mulder.

A devotee of the essential scientific principle of the simplest possible explanation, Scully provides the skeptical-empirical counterweight to Mulder's visionary eccentricity. In 1 Corinthians, Paul admonishes his co-religionists in that Greek city about the ecstatic forms of their worship, especially their devotion to speaking in tongues and their pretension to esoteric knowledge. Christians require inspiration, Paul agrees, but inspiration without rational judgment ceases to have its proper value. "Brothers and sisters," Paul writes, "do not be children in your thinking; rather be infants in evil, but in thinking be adults" (1 Cor. 14:20). Paul, who enjoys the benefits of a Greek education, adds: "I would rather speak five words with my mind, in order to instruct others also, than ten thousand words in a tongue" (1 Cor. 14:19).

Near the end of the first season, in the episode "EBE," after a noticeably ambiguous and tense case, Scully tells Mulder: "I have never met anyone so passionate and dedicated to a belief as you. It's so *intense* that sometimes it's blinding. But there are others who are watching you, who know what I know, and whereas I can respect and admire your passion, they will use it against you. Mulder, the truth is out there, but so are lies."[19] The Mulder-Scully dialogue will lend its tensile strength to almost every *X Files* story, with occasional ironic exchanges of position.

Scully's chastening influence on Mulder combines with Mulder's interest in the UFO phenomenon in several first-season episodes that define their respect for each other and delimit the terms of their cooperation. Other themes—such as the disintegration of basic social structures, like the family, or the coercive intrusion of government into private life—also emerge in these flying-saucer-oriented episodes. *The X Files* develops arcane lore of unseen layers of government and of secretive power grabs, as terrifying by implication as any outright onslaught of bug-eyed monsters from Mars. In "Deep Throat," named proximately after the shadowy figure in President Richard M. Nixon's Watergate scandal who leaked incriminating information about the chief executive to investigating reporters, Mulder becomes aware of an extraconstitutional shadow government with its own armed enforcers, whose focus seems to be the shielding of the public from all disturbing knowledge related to alien activity on earth. Mulder himself as an FBI agent belongs to the federal government, but this *other, secret government* seems to be waging a steady, stealthy war against the elected government.

The plot concerns the disappearance of an Air Force officer, Colonel Budahas, who works in a classified project at the fictional Ellens Air Force Base in Idaho. Scully says to Mulder: "Want to see something weird. . . . Ellens Air Base isn't even on my USGS quadrant map,"[20] a fact that already hints at a campaign of misdirection and denial. Midwestern or northern plains settings seem *de rigeur* for flying-saucer stories, as in Spielberg's *Close Encounters*. Budahas (actor Andrew Johnson) behaved oddly before he went missing, according to his wife; at a dinner party, for example, he calmly sprinkled fish food on his steak. He has comported himself in a withdrawn and uncharacteristic manner for several weeks leading up to his disappearance. Peculiarly, the Air Force has not spoken of the colonel's absconded status and has stonewalled his wife's inquiries as to his whereabouts. That is why she has contacted the FBI.

Director Daniel Sackheim drenches the mise-en-scène with angst. The region of the Great Plains appears in American art and literature traditionally as an agricultural paradise resistant to modern corruptions—as the home of good, Protestant farming stock, of intact families, and of children disciplined by Sunday school and their daily chores. The propinquity of the military base, however, has thrown a morbid shadow over the local community. The townspeople are either kooky or surly; Mrs. Budahas greets Scully and Mulder into a house gone preternaturally quiet, and she herself gives the impression of someone living with abject puzzlement ratcheted up by gnawing terror. Local teenagers assure Mulder that strange lights, originating at the base, flicker in the local sky at night; he shows them a photo of a UFO, and they claim to have seen a similar object. Scully notices that the same kids have obviously been smoking leafy intoxicants, and she criticizes her partner for taking them at their word: "Mulder, you could have shown that kid a picture of a flying hamburger and he would have told you that's exactly what he saw."[21]

The two agents eventually ascertain that Ellens Air Force Base serves as a repository for foreign—and, Mulder argues, *alien*—technology; they surmise that test pilots assigned to the facility fly hybrid aircraft incorporating advanced systems. More than one flyer has first gone missing and then turned up, only to turn odd. Mulder, but not Scully, further supposes that the nonhuman technology affects the pilots deleteriously. When Colonel Budahas returns, he has no memory of what might have happened to him; he behaves childishly and strikes viewers as helpless and autistic. His wife now treats Scully and Mulder with hostility. Aggressive "Men in Black" apprehend Mulder when he sneaks into a restricted area; they subject him to the same amnesia-inducing treatment that has rendered Budahas so passive, although the process affects Mulder less severely than it does the colonel. Scully remains skeptical: "Just because I can't explain it, doesn't mean I'm going to believe [that the weird lights] were UFOs."[22]

"We see in a mirror dimly" (1 Cor. 13:12), Paul told the Corinthians reprovingly, an attitude not uncongenial to Scully in her role as cautioner and skeptic. Never be too sure about what you only think you see. Test everything. Apply Occam's Razor to all puzzles. These things Scully might say. Scully, although doctrinally independent, grew up in a Catholic household; she always wears a small golden cross, a gift from her mother on her fifteenth birthday. Carter's teleplays often subtly remind viewers of this token of childhood religiosity perhaps not entirely outgrown.

At the end of the episode named after him, the highly placed informant whom Mulder calls "Deep Throat" asks him, "Why are those like yourself, who believe in the existence of extraterrestrial life on Earth, not entirely persuaded by all the evidence to the contrary?" Mulder answers: "Because all the evidence to the contrary is not entirely dissuasive." "Deep Throat" (actor Jerry Hardin) then affirms, speaking of the extraterrestrials, that, "*they've* been here for a long, long time."[23] The assertion hardly qualifies as evidence, however, so that really Mulder *knows* no more than before in any provable way; it is a mere verbalism aimed at his desire to believe. Yet events have revealed facets of existence, which Mulder in his obsessive state has overlooked: the increasing *alienness* of North American life, the fatalism with which people submit to police coercion, governmental mendacity, unneighborliness, the self-destructive fatuity of unparented adolescents, and the corrosion of traditional values. A theme of John's Revelation, the deadness of the living to their fellow humans, underlies the "Deep Throat" episode. Even the title, deriving as it does ultimately from a notorious pornographic film of the 1970s, contributes to the atmosphere of crassness and cynicism. The Lord tells John to tell those who call themselves followers of Christ, "You have abandoned the love you had at first" (Rev. 2:4); the Lord tells John to say to them, "You have a name of being alive but you are dead" (Rev. 3:2). The last phrase in particular describes the blighted Budahas family, which will never be the same again.

The script of "Conduit" returns the action, again UFO-related, to farming country, where a Sioux City, Iowa, family headed by a divorced mother has a two-generation history of abduction experiences. Darlene Morris (actress Carrie Snodgrass) has a daughter, Ruby, who has vanished in bizarre circumstances while camping at Lake Okobogee: a bright light stabs through the night while anything metal, including Darlene's camper, shakes and vibrates as though caught up in a fluctuating magnetic field. A younger child remains untouched, except that he undergoes behavioral changes, staring absentmindedly at a television screen showing nothing but static, while he draws rows of ones and zeros on page after page of lined paper. Mulder submits the scribbling to a fellow agent, who discovers that it is binary code broadcast from a secret military satellite. The boy is the *conduit* of the episode's title; yet the message that, as unwilling medium, he *conducts* presents no decipherable meaning. The armed security people take the child for examination, but release him when they can establish no evidence of a threat to the nation. Mulder wants to believe, but once her children return Morris wants only to forget; she refuses to talk about her own abduction and forbids Mulder to submit either the girl or the boy to hypnotic regression.

The final scene takes place in a church, where Mulder sits in silence, remembering his sister, who, according to his story, disappeared before his eyes in a classic abduction scenario. Carter has delivered another portrait of fractured community. Teenaged sexual promiscuity belongs to the pattern, as does divorce, the single-parent household, public surliness, jealous murder, and forms of petty outlawry, such as a motorcycle gang with characteristics of a flying-saucer cult. In an earlier scene, set in a bar, a burly, tattooed specimen says to Mulder: "You should ride with us sometime. You might see some things that would change your mind. Get a killer sunburn in the middle of the night."[24] But change his mind how? In context, the promise is ambiguous; it belongs to the prevalent half-understanding about their troubles exhibited by the townspeople.

The crisis in the community might stem from the turbulence of bizarre events, or the turbulence of bizarre events might be a projection of the crisis in the community; or perhaps they are one and the same, inseparable. Mulder's love for his vanished sister has twisted into his preoccupations. In the third-season episode "Quagmire," Scully compares Mulder, in his obsessiveness, with Herman Melville's fanatical captain from the novel *Moby Dick* (1851). "You're like Ahab. You're so . . . *consumed* by your personal vengeance against life, whether it be its inherent cruelties or its mysteries, that everything takes on a warped significance to your megalomaniacal cosmology."[25] A bit later she asks: "The truth or a white whale? What difference does it make?"[26] Mulder's seeking sanctuary in a house of God at the end of "Conduit" suggests that he, like the unfortunate test pilots, has become deadened and therefore stands in need of healing and redemption.

The Four Horsemen, the Beasts, and Justice

The final book of the New Testament deals in images of enormity, none more famous than that of the Four Horsemen—those galloping figures of War, Famine, Pestilence, and Death—set upon the world by the unsealing of the first four seals. Revelation names only the fourth, Death, but John implies the character of the other three.

The Horsemen loom large in Western art, nowhere more graphically than in the *Apocalypsis cum Figuris* (1498), a suite of engravings by the Nuremberg artist Albrecht Dürer (1471–1528); Revelation also supplied themes for the painterly work of Hieronymous Bosch (1450–1516) and Matthias Grünewald (1500–1530), contemporaries of Dürer. The fifteenth and sixteenth centuries indeed constituted a time of crisis for Christendom, with early signs of protest against Rome and the stirrings of sectarian warfare; indeed, some people at the time predicted that the year 1500 would see the end of days and the last judgment. In *The X Files,* too, as the seasons follow one another and the greater patterns impress themselves ever more indelibly on Scully and Mulder, their awareness increases that they live in a world—and in a time—when the dreadful cavalry is once again charging about and stirring up the melee of confusion and crisis. The cumulus of his experience convinces Mulder, for example, that his positive hopes about alien contact lack a basis and that something far more sinister glowers from the shadows. He perceives that alien impingement in the human realm—insofar as that is what it really is—actually threatens humanity, that it is demonic, and that unscrupulous human powers are using it as an opportunity for aggrandizement and imperium.

The fact that one lives in civic turbulence, amidst the disintegrations of justice, creates both a need and a danger: in crisis, people yearn for the authoritative word that will quell conflict and restore order to the community; but in crisis, it becomes hard to differentiate genuine from spurious authority. When the crisis reaches a pitch of incertitude, people incline desperately to *any* promise of deliverance. The Revelation of Saint John the Divine warns against false prophecy, admonishing the faithful, when the hour is nigh, not to heed the Beast's beastly servant, the one who "performs great signs, even making fire come down from heaven to earth in sight of all" (Rev. 13:13). Revelation says of this second Beast, whom we should probably take as identical with the antichrist, that "it deceives the inhabitants of earth" (Rev. 13:14), who venerate its many images and agree to subjugate themselves to its will.

By manipulating the people into following him, the imperial deceiver also, in John's words, is able to "make war on the saints and to conquer them" (Rev. 13:7). Falsehood can achieve power only by a direct assault on the truth, as the bloody chapters of twentieth-century history have taught us. Even people of goodwill run the risk of investing their trust in dazzling untruths.

Although it is a difficult thought, myriads of idealistic people in the twentieth century threw in with the messianic schemes declared by unscrupulous would-be saviors of the people. Lenin and Stalin said that a Communist utopia lay in the immediate future after the revolution; Hitler, too, held out the picture of a renewed community free from internal scandals and liberated from all external threats. The Bolshevik and National Socialist regimes used the language of justice, while at the same time perverting the Jewish and Christian notions of justice. They promised that *this world* could be perfected through the rigorous application of one or another ideological formula.

Believers in alien visitation often say that the extraterrestrials come as teachers of social, political, religious, or scientific perfection or as the immediate architects of paradise—that they have an angelic function. Mack quotes one of his hypnotic-regression subjects as relaying the outlines of the alien agenda vouchsafed him by his adbuctors. Human interbreeding with the aliens, the subject tells Mack, will create a "hybrid tribe," that is to say, a *superior humanity* that will resettle our world after the extraterrestrials effect "the destruction of the populations of the earth."[27] The subject says, "If the world comes to an end as we know it and another . . . human consciousness . . . inhabits the earth then we've progressed."[28] In the symbols deployed by this particular UFO believer, we see a startling combination of the flying-saucer cult in its classic form with a political utopianism according to which the end justifies the means—as in the twentieth-century exterminations. We see also the spiritual confusion that John and the other New Testament writers so inveterately depict. In the second-season opener, "Little Green Men," Mulder participates in just that type of yearning confusion, which, for John, typifies the perpetual crisis of a fallen humanity. Mulder makes his way to the Arecibo radio telescope in Puerto Rico.

The Arecibo antenna, the largest in the world, has remained in active service since its establishment in the 1960s, but for the purposes of the episode it serves for a SETI ("Search for Extra-Terrestrial Intelligence") facility that the government—or some other agency—has forced to shut down. In *The X Files,* hidden commissioners are always acting to suppress legitimate research.

Radically strange events befall Mulder as he ferrets among the gadgetry. He believes himself to have discovered the hoped for "Wow!" signal, as radio-astronomers call it. This would be a signal of unmistakably artificial rather than of merely natural origin coming from a planetary system associated with a known star. In context, SETI represents the fruitless attempt of post-Christian civilization to address the problem of *Homo sapiens'* transcendental urge, whose truth a purely materialistic mentality denies, but which persists despite the denial. One might recall the odd religiosity that imbues nonbeliever Carl Sagan's novel *Contact* (1985) and director Robert Zemeckis's 1997 film adaptation of it. In his *Dimensions,* Jacques Vallée notes sourly that, "we are developing a great thirst for contact with superior minds that will provide guidance for our poor, harassed, hectic planet"; Vallée sees this thirst as gulling us into a "trap" of our own device.[29] Vallée's words might well be a comment on Sagan's displacement of traditional faith; it also applies to the chilling insouciance that informs the vision of Mack's psychiatric patient, as previously cited. In "Little Green Men," Mulder does possibly see an alien entity surrounded by a halo of blinding light, but his mental state, monomaniacal, throws his perceptions into doubt. He wonders to Scully, "Is this just some elaborate joke played on those who want to believe?"[30] Such skepticism about his own enthusiasm as Mulder can muster will serve him well in subsequent situations.

When the "Men in Black" show up, they prove real enough. Mulder just barely escapes with life and limb. He has retrieved a digital tape spool, which he believes to contain positive evidence of human-alien communication, whatever problems this would solve. But a strong magnetic pulse, of unknown origin, has wiped the tape clean, leaving the agent once again with no evidence save his own word that anomalies have occurred. Mulder takes away from his Puerto Rican foray a heightened sense that the UFO phenomenon belongs to a larger, intimidating picture of tyranny on the one hand and chaos on the other. The *X Files* aliens *menace* those who encounter them, unlike the benign entities of *Close Encounters* (1977) or *ET* (1982); no less so do the "Men in Black" (also the "Blue Retrieval Team"), the ubiquitous armed squad of the secretive, nondemocratic shadow government. At the end of the first season, the "Men in Black" or their kindred had assassinated Mulder's informant, "Deep Throat." These helmeted soldiers manifest themselves often, as in the important sequence of episodes—comprising "Anasazi," "The Blessing Way," and "Paper Clip"—which spans the end of the second and the beginning of the third seasons.

In Revelation, John the Divine predicts that in the waves of panic at the end of days, the people will allow the servitor Beast, who is the antichrist, "to exercise authority" (Rev. 13:5). The masses will respond to power for its own sake, sacrificing justice for the purely secular redemption of Caesarean politics. In "The Blessing Way," speaking of the shadow government, FBI assistant director Walter Skinner (actor Mitch Pileggi) says, "There isn't a federal judge they couldn't persuade."[31] Skinner's pronouncement implies an illusion of living in a republic of laws, when in fact people live in an arbitrary regime of tyrants. Who are "they"? As a recurring character named "The Well-Manicured Man" (actor John Neville) will tell Scully in "The Blessing Way," *they* constitute "a consortium representing global interests," who "act impulsively."[32] "Paper Clip" next reveals this Consortium (or "Syndicate") to have roots in mid-twentieth-century totalitarianism, particularly but not exclusively in the Nazi regime. At the end of World War II, as the story would have it, American politicians cynically extended amnesty to Axis scientists in exchange for their existing results and for their continued cooperation in the cold war arms race. So far the tale has a basis in fact (think of the German rocket scientists), but Carter is a speculator and a fabulist, so the extrapolated details diverge into the purely fictional.

In Revelation, John projects images of terrific rectification because his historical context is the injustice of Roman rule. The Four Horsemen come "to conquer," "to take peace from the earth," and "to kill with sword, famine, and pestilence" (Rev. 6:1, 4, 8). The Beast and his servitor Beast also lust for power and work to gain it through acts of impressive, hence charismatic, violence. *The X Files'* Consortium—its bland name disguising its wickedness and reminding us of what Hannah Arendt called *the banality of evil*—comports itself along the lines of a classic power conspiracy. Thus did Victor Klemper (actor Walter Gotell) perform medical experiments in the Nazi concentration camps alleged by the story to have aimed at the creation of biological weapons and an alien-human hybrid.[33] The sinister alliance consisting of a dictatorial-ideological cabal on the one hand and of alien interlopers on the other reaches back, in Carter's myth, to the years of World War II, the greatest of overt sociopolitical disruptions of the twentieth century. The human element of the pact has put itself beyond good and evil, in the classic pattern of modern ideologues; the alien element, being demonic and nonhuman, acts entirely without sympathy but rather with malice toward people, treating them as we treat laboratory rats. Carter's indirect assertion that ideology inevitably conflicts with received morality is an important one; the hostility of the Nazis not only to the Jews but also to Christians, and of the Bolsheviks to the same, attests to it.

When Mulder and Scully confront Klemper, he says that he committed all his acts "in the name of science" and urges that "progress demands sacrifice."[34] In another third-season episode, "Talitha Cumi," the recurrent "Smoking Man" or "Cancer Man" character (actor William B. Davis) describes the modern mentality as believing only in "authority," by which he means power; modern people have "grown tired of waiting for miracle and mystery," the Cancer Man says, and nowadays "science is their religion."[35] Here the term *science* means technological and political power, specifically the Cancer Man's own power as a hierarch of the Consortium, for he is a megalomaniac who has sacrificed his own family in his climb up the ladder of the secret order. As for Klemper's genetic experiments, he took inspiration from the Nietzschean-Hitlerian idea of an Aryan superrace. Klemper's justifications resemble those of actual war criminals, and they correspond to the prevailing, incipient twenty-first-century moral relativism.

Cover-ups having stymied Mulder's investigation, and his frustration having filled him with a spirit of rage, Scully accuses her partner of forfeiting "the very notion of justice."[36] It is justice that, as an agent, he has sworn to uphold. In two subsequent third-season episodes, "Nisei" and "731," we learn that a Japanese counterpart of Klemper's research existed. Writer Frank Spotnitz ascribes the fictional Dr. Ishimaru's pseudoscientific atrocities to the Japanese army's actual biological warfare laboratory in Manchuria, the infamous Unit 731 (hence, the episode's title). Japanese military researchers exposed Chinese peasants and American POWs to disease germs and other pathogens in hellish experiments. The Consortium has long sustained Klemper's program and that of his Japanese opposite number, hoping that the results will grant them sway over the world.

Mulder has a congressional protector, Sen. Richard Matheson (actor Raymond J. Barry),[37] who speaks to him knowingly of "past deeds, which might illuminate present treacheries" and of "monsters begetting monsters."[38]

In "731," we see the "Men in Black" in action again, this time as a brutal killing squad that machine-guns to death a group of disease victims, whose sickness has the hallmarks of a genetically altered plague-germ. Director Rob Bowman stages the scene to resemble newsreels of the German "Special Action Units" in action in World War II. This cluster of third-season stories suggests that the assorted plagues and mutations in other first- and second-season episodes—such as "Fire Walker" and "Emasculata"—also belong to the Consortium's sinister agenda.

During the sequence in Revelation where John of Patmos witnesses the unsealing of the seals, the following passage occurs: "When [the Angel] opened the fifth seal, I saw under the altar the souls of those who had been slaughtered for the Word of God and for the testimony they had given; they cried out with a loud voice, 'Sovereign Lord, holy and true, how long will it be before you judge and avenge our blood on the inhabitants of the earth?'" (Rev. 6:9–10). In yet another *X Files* third-season episode, "Piper Maru," the guilt-stricken survivor of a particularly grisly Consortium scheme tells Scully of those who did not survive: "We hear them every day, they talk to us, they haunt us, they beg us for meaning. Conscience is just the voices of the dead trying to save us from our own damnation."[39]

While Saint John of Patmos can help viewers to make sense of the often confusing *X Files,* Carter's series can also help thoughtful people understand something about Revelation. The terrific events depicted in John's visions as happening at the end of days *had already happened* many times in history; such events have continued to happen in the two thousand years of history since the time of Jesus Christ. Christianity, like Judaism, is a religion of justice; and justice, for its sake, demands the two faculties of memory and conscience. The real object of

Christian revelation is thus the innocence of all victims of malicious power. The function of Christian revelation is to make people aware of the urgent need to rectify the civic scene. Those who sense injustice should strive to make daily life as decent as it can be, but they should not invest in impossible-to-achieve utopian schemes such as those offered by the political ideologies. As Paul writes to the Romans, "The wrath of God is revealed from heaven against all ungodliness and wickedness of those who by their wickedness suppress the truth" (Rom. 1:18).

From the Perversion of the Symbols to Comic Relief

The willingness of the *X Files* creators to admit serious religious and philosophical discussions into their fantastic stories undoubtedly accounts for the nine-year life of the series. *The X Files* frequently satirizes its own genre—prime-time television entertainment—but the empty diversions that its writers justifiably mock tend to disappear swiftly, after a season or two. Viewers of the Mulder-Scully saga sustained their interest because, although uneven, the show never avoided disturbing moral questions and only rarely yielded to the demands of political correctness. *The X Files* was subversive precisely in treating genuine spiritual experience with respect and in showing the two agents now and then actually taking solace in an ecclesiastical setting.

In the third-season episode "Revelations," Scully, after learning of disturbing truths about events that have befallen her, seeks advice from a Catholic priest. In the fourth season, her illness causes her to return yet more openly to her childhood Catholicism. Mulder's "I WANT TO BELIEVE" poster turns up in almost every episode, even when we glimpse it only fuzzily (but recognizably) in the fleeting background. An uncritical desire to believe, however, can distort perception and thinking, as Paul reminds the Corinthians, who lean toward the mystic shenanigans of the Gnostics. Whereas Paul and Saint John the Divine had described spiritual fulfillment as something that would occur in the next, but not in the present, world, the Gnostics fervently believed that *this world* could be transformed into the promised City of God, or the New Jerusalem. When this happened, humans themselves might become gods.

We have previously mentioned the name of Eric Voegelin; we have also noted the interest of the *X Files* writers in political ideology. We have further commented on episodes that explore critically the German National Socialist ideology and the wartime Japanese imperialist ideology. Several fourth-season episodes—"Musings of a Cigarette-Smoking Man," "Tunguska," and "Terma"—make reference to the Marxist-Leninist ideology of the Soviet Union and Communist China. *The X Files* at last also contains much commentary on middle-class North American life, with its uncritical belief in material progress as the be-all and end-all of existence. In *The Ecumenic Age,* Voegelin reminds us that the twentieth-century ideologies resemble dogmatic religion in their demand for absolute adherence and in their hostility to rival positions; Voegelin indeed understands ideology as *political religion.* He notes what we have earlier noted, following his lead: that the major symbols of those first and last things against which people find their bearings in existence are, for Western people and especially for Christians, the symbols of the New Testament; they are particularly those of the Gospel writers and Saint Paul, but necessarily also those of Saint John the Divine.

Paul's foremost symbol of the important relation of existence to eternity and of injustice to justice is the resurrection of the dead, a symbol that Paul elaborates everywhere in his writings and that John rehearses in vivid imagery in Revelation. As Voegelin reminds us, however, for Paul and John, the resurrection of the dead, the destruction of the powers, and the advent of the New Jerusalem, or City of God, are events, not *in time,* but at the juncture between time and eternity. Yet, Voegelin argues, persistently in modern Western culture frustrated thinkers, enraged at the fact of injustice, have perverted the gospel symbols, claiming them not as allegories of eternity, but as schemes for realization *in time* or in history.

Voegelin cites as an example Karl Marx, who "has been quite explicit on this point." Voegelin summarizes Marx this way: "Revolutionary killing will induce a *Blutrausch,* a 'blood-intoxication'; and from this *Blutrausch* 'man' will emerge as 'superman' into the 'realm of freedom.'"[40] The magic of the *Blutrausch* is the ideological equivalent to the promise of the Pauline vision of the resurrected. Voegelin notes again how Marx and the other prophets of revolutionary (hence ideological) transformation-within-history have all invariably and necessarily presented themselves as saviors-of-humankind who insist that the savior of the received tradition—and for the inheritors of Christendom, this means Jesus—was himself false and that he is no longer a useful or even a *permissible* reference. Jesus has become for the tyrants an obstacle, just as he was for the philosophical apologists for the Roman emperors. The religion-hatred of the Marxists and the National Socialists bears out Voegelin's assessment. Voegelin describes the ideological tyrants as egomaniacal rivals of the real prophets, and he writes of their regimes as altogether a "deformation of humanity and divinity"[41] through bloody, utopian projects.

We referred, in our chapter on *Doctor Who,* to the Russian nineteenth-century writer Fyodor Dostoyevsky, whose novel *The Demons* deals with a textbook case of ideologue-revolutionaries trying to transform reality by stirring up insurrectionary turbulence so that they can capture the authority hitherto granted to a divine redeemer. In the case of *The X Files,* another Dostoyevsky reference is appropriate, this time to *The Brothers Karamazov* (1880), or more particularly to its inset story of "The Grand Inquisitor." Dostoyevsky's Grand Inquisitor anticipates the Lenin- or Hitler-type demagogue from a full generation before its appearance on the political scene. This sinister figure claims that freedom, as conceived under Christianity, makes people unhappy, because they secretly but powerfully loathe self-responsibility; he proposes therefore to make people happy, under his terms, by depriving them of freedom. Should Christ come again to redeem humanity by setting people free, the Grand Inquisitor says, it would be obligatory to kill Christ before he could complete his mission. He, the Grand Inquisitor, would be happy to do the job.

In the *X Files* third-season episode "Talitha Cumi," Cancer Man functions as Carter's version of the Grand Inquisitor. Speaking candidly of the Consortium's schemes for world domination, Cancer Man remarks the willingness with which people yield their freedom: "We give them happiness and they give us authority. . . . Men can never be free, because they're weak, corrupt, worthless and restless. The people believe in authority. They've grown tired of waiting for miracle and mystery. Science is their religion. No greater explanation exists for them."[42]

Mulder and Scully stand in opposition to Cancer Man and his Consortium, because they remain committed to truth; they keep themselves open to reality and sustain themselves as moral agents. Mulder and Scully notice that many people, in fact, willingly surrender their freedom in exchange for a degraded "happiness." They notice a pandemic resistance to acknowledge what cannot be seen so that, when no obvious miracles occur, people give up their faith and put their trust entirely in a shrunken "science" of appliances and goods. Paul tells the Romans: "Now hope that is seen is not hope. For who hopes for what is seen? But if we hope for what we do not see, we wait for it with patience" (Rom. 8:24–25). A characteristic of utopian thinking is *impatience.* Patience is a virtue; its opposite is not. Yet impatience *marks* the modern world, with its addiction to petty gratifications *now* and its hostility to all deferrals of satisfaction. The moral perversion of all utopian schemes lies in their subordination of living individuals—those whom scripture calls on us *to love*—to an unrealizable abstraction that the utopians nevertheless insist will be realized shortly if only all of those who will not comply with the program can be gotten out of the way.

By contrast, Mulder and Scully act to each other devotionally, the more so as the seasons unfold. Carter wisely never let them tumble into bed with each other, as routinely happens in television dramas, but kept their *eros* platonic. It is perhaps true that, in its sixth through ninth seasons, *The X Files* began to treat its own transcendental symbols literally, as in Scully's Immaculate Conception, and that it inclined toward childishness in Paul's sense. The first five seasons, however, consistently upheld a mature view of existence that incorporated a morality congenial to because informed by a Judeo-Christian attitude toward life.

The X Files occasionally descends from its unexpected (for television) seriousness to make fun of itself. Given that ideologues never make fun of themselves, because they are constitutionally incapable of humor, the ability of the *X Files* writers to make light of their own preoccupations should reassure us of their basic honesty. No episode does this as well as writer Don Morgan's third-season episode "Jose Chung's 'From Outer Space.'" The

Christian polemicist Tertullian (160–230) boasted, *Credo quia absurdum,* "I believe because it is absurd."

One might adapt Tertullian's formula to "Jose Chung's 'From Outer Space'": *Gaudeo quia absurdum,* "I enjoy it because it is absurd." What can one say of a teleplay that casts, among others, wrestling's Jesse Ventura and *Jeopardy*'s Alex Trebek in supporting roles as, so it seems, aliens? What can one say of an *X Files* episode in which the first thing to happen is that aliens get abducted *by other aliens?* The episode features two characters—Major Vallee (actor Terry Arrowsmith) and Sergeant Hynek (actor Michael Dobson)—named after prominent UFO writers. Jacques Vallée we have quoted several times in the present chapter; Spielberg acknowledges that the character of Monsieur Lacombe in *Close Encounters,* played by the French film-director François Truffaut, was based on Vallée. J. Allen Hynek, who coined the term "close encounter," appears as himself at the climax of the same film. Morgan's script appropriates elements from one of the weirdest UFO books ever written, John Keel's *The Mothman Prophecies* (1971), later (2002) adapted to the silver screen, and he appropriates them also from certain classic B-grade science-fiction movies of the 1950s—most prominently from Ray Harryhausen's *Twenty Million Miles to Earth* (1956).

As in the opening chapter of Keel's book, small-town Americans mistake regular human beings, in this case Mulder and Scully, for aliens, or for "Men in Black." An all-too-certain respondent says: "One of them was disguised as a woman, but wasn't pulling it off. Like, her hair was red . . . but it was a little *too* red, you know. And the other one, the tall lanky one, his face was so blank and expressionless. He didn't seem human."[43] The script reveals the real nature of the persistent crisis that provokes revelation-as-flying-saucer: "I hate this town. I hate people. I just want to be taken away to some place where I don't have to worry about . . . finding a job."[44]

Some *X Files* episodes will be too intense and frightening, or a bit too heady in other ways, for youngish viewers. Carter's series inspired a number of cinematic imitations, such as Mark Pellington's *The Mothman Prophecies* and M. Night Shyamalan's *Signs* (2001), which copy and also somewhat intensify its mixture of science-fiction, Gothic, and theological speculation. As entertaining as these might be, one can hardly avoid thinking of Carter's series while watching them; without the adventures of Scully and Mulder, these other metaphysical thrillers would never have been made. On the whole, the first five seasons of *The X Files* will retain their high rank as exmples of first-rate science fiction with a serious religious and theological slant. "The truth is out there."

VI

Preaching the Word

Babylon 5 and the Universal Gospel

In the beginning was the Word, and the Word was with God, and the Word was God. He was in the beginning with God.

John 1:1–2

The Originary word . . . is given to all human beings as a guarantee of their access to the scene of human language, which is the primary characteristic of their humanity.

Eric Gans, *Science and Faith*[1]

The Babylon Project was a dream, given form. Its goal: to prevent another war, by creating a place where humans and aliens can work out their differences peacefully. It's a port of call—home away from home—for diplomats, hustlers, entrepreneurs, and wanderers.

Main-title overdub, *Babylon 5,* season 1

Anthropology, Theology, and Language

Because the remarkable television epic *Babylon 5,* which began its five-year run in 1992, not only can but must be described as a story about the way in which palaver—*talk*—is preferable to war, the way in which talk is indeed tantamount to *peace,* it seems natural to frame the treatment of it in a single recurrent gospel term: *the Word.*

It is speech that provides much of screenwriter J. Michael Straczynski's *Babylon 5* saga. His well-drawn protagonists talk, talk, and talk; and so they must, for they aim by inveterate conviction at justice, fair exchange, and peace. Speech, the basis of fellowship and common sense, provides the medium of these other things. The *Babylon 5* "good guys" defend their principles by main force when needs they must and as every people may. Otherwise they talk in the languages of Earth, and they talk in the languages of other planets: Narn, Centauri, Minbari, and Drazi. In an ongoing parliament of dialects they bargain and cajole in order to find a common meaning; they try to restore to unity, for the benefit of all, the persistent and dangerous confusion of tongues—that unpleasant fact of mutual hostility and misunderstanding made vivid in the Old Testament by the story of the Tower of Babel that has immemorially bedeviled humankind. In the tower, humanity vainly proposed to storm heaven and to rival God. By way of instinctive imitation, however, everyone became everyone else's rival; mayhem ensued and the tower fell. Humans could no longer understand one another; as siblings became strangers, they dispersed into mutually unintelligible bellicose nations. The story's moral is clear: the covetousness of the power seeker tends inevitably to the chaos of everyone for himself or herself. In this way, the biblical discussion of the Word goes intimately with its discussion of power, an intimacy as integral to *Babylon 5* as to the Gospels, where Jesus wields always the disarming parable. Hardly an episode of *Babylon 5* passes without one of the series' many parable tellers making his or her persuasive allusion at the critical moment.

The idea of the Word—in Greek, *Logos*—plays a central role in gospel theology. The idea of the Word is related in turn to the ideas of breath and spirit; the Latin *spiritus* indeed means "breath." In Genesis, Yahweh's "spirit" or breath (in Hebrew, *ruach*) originally brings the world into existence by "moving," as Genesis says, on the formless chaos, so separating the waters into those above and those below and so demarcating the night from the day.

Prebiblical creation stories, such as the Mesopotamian *Enuma Elish,* depict the origin of the world in warlike, catastrophic imagery. *Enuma Elish*'s chief god, Marduk, slays the giantess Tiamat in a prolonged and gruesome battle and builds the familiar world out of her corpse; Zeus, in the Greek poet Hesiod's *Theogony* (eighth century BCE), must subdue the monstrous Titans violently before he can enforce his calm, Olympian rule-of-law. To call forth existence by breath or word, therefore, already represents a significant change in the conception of how the universe finds its settled form. The Old Testament understands that being and speaking exist in a specific relation to each other, perhaps because speech implies consciousness and because consciousness makes the world available, recognizable, and understandable to a subject. After creating the world, God *sees* that it is good, where the verb implies a process of consciousness and a gesture of rational assessment. An important Hebrew term relating to speech is *dabar,* which translation renders either as "word," "judgment," "news," or "event," depending on the context. The gospel, as the epochal "Good News," is rooted in this ancient Hebrew concept.

In Exodus, for example, *dabar* refers to the *law* that God settles on the exiled people. Similarly, the Time Lord society in *Doctor Who* and Star Fleet in *Star Trek* are both governed by explicit laws that prohibit exploitative interference by one party in another's affairs. We shall see the same motif at work in *Babylon 5*.

In their commentaries on the Gospels, the early Christian exegetes accepted an equivalency between the Semitic-language words for *breath/speech/word*, on the one hand, and the Greek term *Logos* on the other. Greek-speaking Alexandrian Jews, such as Philo (first century CE), had shown them the way; they selected the word *Logos* for their translation of Genesis. This was a natural choice: for it is the breath, signifying life, which makes possible the word. In so doing, these earliest writers of scripture assimilated the Hebrew notion of God's life-giving breath with the Hellenic idea of speech or language not merely as the means by which people communicate, rather than fight, but as a structuring principle behind God's creation *implicit as well* in the conspicuously nonfortuitous realm of human order. Language gives life: it gives life to humanity by being the trait that distinguishes human beings from all other creatures and by enabling them, by explicit law and by usage, consciously to order their lives. Self-determination under objective moral guidance is another theme that resonates continuously in *Babylon 5*.

Order always strikes people as nonfortuitous and conscious, the result of some intelligent effort. If the universe appeared to make sense to observers, it would necessarily draw its comprehensibility from the fact that a deliberating creator-spirit had spoken it forth out of nothing, endowing it in the act with a *logic* resembling that with which human beings endow their utterances when they make plain their own ideas and perceptions. In the same way, as thoughtful people once said, a pocket watch logically implies a watchmaker, as no mechanical contrivance can have assembled itself randomly. Human behavior also exhibits patterns that are subject to analysis; it is never random and is therefore broadly predictable. While the idea of *logic* takes its place in the context of Greek thought, one ought to remember that, in the Old Testament, one of the most often iterated motifs is the related idea of "*prophecy*." Prophecy is not entirely separate from logic. But who or what is a "prophet"? A prophet, or in Hebrew a *nabi,* is someone who *speaks;* the *nabi* characteristically pronounces his *dabar,* or "word," as, for example, in Amos (2:1; 4:1; 5:1), on behalf of God. More specifically, the prophet is someone who speaks to a crisis in the community, to social disorder, whose cause he sees and whose continuance he wishes to curtail by informing those who have made the emergency how to end it. The *nabi,* in other words, is a logical analyst of behavior. So can anyone be who examines himself or herself. As Paul says, "For you can all prophesy one by one, so that all may learn and all be encouraged" (1 Cor. 14:31). Prophecy maintains its affiliation with reason or common sense, both of which it refines and intensifies.

The prophet thus *foresees* trends, not magically, but through the eye of experience and wisdom, detecting patterns in past events and projecting their likely repetition on the basis of present behavior. The prototypical instance occurs in Exodus, when Moses has ascended Mount Sinai to await God. In Moses's absence, the wanderers suffer a relapse into cultic frenzy—the infamous orgy around the golden calf—of the type on which they had presumably turned their backs when they left Egypt. Moses confronts this outbreak of destructive disorder when he comes down from the mountaintop; significantly he brings with him the stone tablets incised with the commandments of Yahweh.

The commandments—the prescriptive particular variations on "thou shalt not . . ."—*are* the veritable Word of God, which proposes as its goal nothing less than to quell, not just this crisis, but, preemptively, all future crises as well by establishing a clear communal sense of what will constitute orderly—and disorderly—conduct. At the moment of creation, the breath or word of God established the cosmic order; when Moses reveals God's commandments, called in Greek the *Decalogue* or "Ten Words," the verbal intention of God reestablishes communal *form* in a violently *de*formed social setting. The commandments or laws define the rules whereby Moses and his lieutenants subdue the irruption of sacrificial violence and restore order among the people; they also endow the reformed people with a new and stable identity, as adherents of the law. God's Word, expressed as a code of behavior that everyone follows, becomes the peaceful background for the proverbial pursuit (if not the attainment) of happiness.

Of course, the person who testifies for divine law runs a risk: one should remember that the Greek word for a witness is *martyr,* and that the fate of a prophet usually coincides with that of a *martyr,* in that term's secondary and brutal sense of one who incurs the wrath of his or her audience and perishes at their hands for speaking critically of them. Our earlier discussion of Doctor Who and the Powers mentioned the ambiguity of Moses's disappearance toward the end of Exodus; but many of the Old Testament prophets end the same way, done in by the irate people, who chafe at rules. In John's Gospel, Jesus often recalls Moses and the commandments, indicating that he, Jesus, has come to fulfill an ancient tradition of pitting language against violence and that he will probably suffer the usual prophetic fate. Popular obtuseness remains an obstacle: "He testifies to what he has seen and heard, yet no one accepts his testimony" (John 3:32). Difficulty always accompanies keen perception; the act of critical self-examination likewise cuts against the grain of habit. Coming to grips with the gospel *Logos* means enduring the pangs of what doctors of the soul call conversion.

One of the earliest of Greek philosophers, Heraclitus of Ephesus lived a thousand years after Moses and nearly five hundred years before the birth of Christ in cultural and historical circumstances quite different from those faced by the Israelites in their desert exile, before they settled in Canaan and become the Jews. Yet Heraclitus, like Moses, appears as a stern advocate of order against disorder, of law against lawlessness, and so he appears also as a prophet bearing the distinct mien of a martyr. Heraclitus figures in the history of Western thought as the one who founded the "*Logos* tradition" as such in philosophy and who, in so doing, gave the notion of *Logos* its subsequent, more or less fixed definition. Emancipated commentary since the eighteenth century has typically tried its best to distinguish the philosophical "Word" from its religious counterpart, emphasizing the differences and eliding the similarities, usually in favor of the Greek rather than the Christian version. From a gospel perspective, however, we might well say that it is the Greek version that strikes us as slightly defective; but the defect might also be capable of redemption and assimilation.

Consider the characteristics of the *Logos,* as Heraclitus develops that notion in his aphorisms. Heraclitus says, "The word proves those first hearing it as numb to understanding as the ones who have not heard." He says, "The habit of knowledge is not human but divine." He says, "Wisdom is the oneness of mind that guides and permeates all things." The philosophical *Logos,* like the Christian *Logos,* concerns what "truly is," and how effects are related to causes not only in physics but also and most especially in ethics. Yet because habit gets in the way of perceiving the truth, the philosophical *Logos* requires its devotee to change his or her usual perspective and to adopt a stance of humility. Heraclitus notes prophetically that "many fail to grasp what they have seen and cannot judge what they have learned."[2] The legends surrounding Heraclitus suggest that he met his death violently at the hands of the Ephesians, who took offense at his criticisms of their usages and behaviors.

The one element that does sharply distinguish the Gospel *Logos* from Heraclitus's *Logos* is the Gospels' insistence that participating in God's Word entails love, as Jesus announces in the Sermon on the Mount. This is no small difference. Even so, it is difficult to grasp the full import of the gospel *Logos* without first seeing how much of the Greek *Logos* goes into it. The early Christian writers knew this. Saint Augustine even declared that the Platonists—the inheritors and developers of the original Heraclitean *Logos* philosophy—had shared in revelation and that their works formed an independent witness to scripture. The apostle John's metaphor of God's Word as *light* reflects Heraclitus in many ways, as when he records how although "the light has come into the world," people nevertheless "loved darkness rather than light" (John 8:19), or when he avers that, "if we walk in the light as he himself is the light, we have fellowship with one another" (1 John 1:7). Love and fellowship together constitute the Gospels' revolutionary minimal morality, where elsewhere at the time complicated incompatible codes of ethics ruled life in different communities. It is ever the case in *Doctor Who,* and often the case in *Star Trek,* that differing parties must discover what minimal agreements they can make to resolve a conflict between them. This is also the case in *Babylon 5.*

The anthropological thinker Eric L. Gans writes that, in Christianity, morality succeeds ethics: "It was Christianity—specifically the ethical vision of the Gospels—that first proposed the moral model not merely as a standard for the private sphere but as the sole basis of human action."[3] The word *ethos,* from which comes the English "ethics," is related to the word *ethnos,* meaning a particular people with its peculiar ways, hence to "ethnicity" in the restrictive sense. Where Jews had one code of behavior and Romans another, where Greek differed from Persian, and every tribal people from every other, the Gospels declare a *universal humanity* and propose a single, embracing principle, namely, the reciprocity of the loving fellowship, as the deliverance from hoary rites that divide one group from another and pitch whole kingdoms into implacable conflict. The moral is the universal as distinct from the merely ethnic.

John sums it up this way: "Whoever loves a brother or a sister lives in the light, and in such a person there is no cause for stumbling" (1 John 2:10). The evangelism of the Gospels consists in testifying for this minimal yet radical moral principle. Through the testimony of their lives, the followers of the Gospels inaugurate a new type of creation, abolishing the old order of the pagan nations, of the interminable war of differences, and beginning a new order based on faith in a God unlike all previous gods because he is identical with the Word.

Healing the Fractious Stars

The fractious ecumenical space of the competitive starfaring worlds provides the background of all action in *Babylon 5.* Like most science fiction that concerns itself with planetary empires, *Babylon 5* projects the politics of the historical Roman Empire on a galactic stage. Earlier, literary examples of the same gesture are A. E. van Vogt's *Empire of the Atom* series (1946–47) and Isaac Asimov's *Foundation* trilogy (1942–52). Critics have written that both van Vogt and Asimov profited by their reading of Robert Graves's *I, Claudius* (1934) and *Claudius the God* (1935), novels with a Roman imperial setting; van Vogt and Asimov also undoubtedly knew General Lew Wallace's *Ben Hur* (1880) and Henryk Sienkiewicz's *Quo Vadis* (1896), which detail the struggle of Christian fellowship in the context of dictatorial cruelty and official persecution. Significantly, both *Empire of the Atom* and *Foundation* include a religious subplot; in both, monastic communities ensure the survival of civilization past the inevitable collapse of mismanaged large-scale political structures, as the pious brotherhoods did in the actual post-Roman centuries until the consolidation of medieval Christendom. Walter M. Miller's *A Canticle for Leibowitz* (1960) sets a similar story in a terrestrial postnuclear milieu. The religious communities in *Empire of the Atom, Foundation,* and *Canticle for Leibowitz* preserve the best in the afflicted culture by reinterpreting it in the light of newer, simpler, *re*-visionary insights; they replace physical infrastructure with the wisdom of essential verbal formulas.

That *Babylon* writer-creator Straczynski thought in such terms while working out the major arcs of his five-year story becomes plausible in light of the final fourth-season episode, entitled "The Deconstruction of Falling Stars." The penultimate sequence of "Deconstruction" happens 1,000 years after the main plotlines of the series have found their culmination. After a warlike cataclysm called "the Great Burning," terrestrial society has become isolated from the stars and has fallen back to a pretechnological level. Brother Alwyn supervises an order of monks who take inspiration from the ancient heroes legendarily associated with the "Babylon Project" and related campaigns and endeavors and who try, subtly, to rebuild the fallen civilization. An earlier fourth-season episode, "Late Delivery from Avalon," had featured a man (actor Michael York) who believed that he was King Arthur, the legendary savior of the British during the sixth-century CE barbarian invasions.

Scholars think that the Arthur legend grew around a real person, whose character and deeds assumed a fabulous form over the ages. This has happened again, it appears, in the case of people from before the *Babylon 5* saga's "Great Burning." Brother Alwyn's order conforms partly to a Christian (specifically Catholic, as references to "Rome" indicate), but also partly to a distinctly alien spiritual orientation, that of the race known as Minbari, who play a key role in the five-year story. Alwyn tells an acolyte-brother whose faith has faltered not to despair: "The prophecies of Delenn III said that the *An'la'shok*—the Rangers—would come again to the Earth in her greatest hour of need, and rebuild what was once the cradle of Sheridan and the Alliance."[4]

In the context provided by the series, these words imply a great deal. Sheridan is John Sheridan (actor Bruce Boxleitner), second commander of the Babylon 5 station, first president of the League of Non-Aligned Worlds, and first president of the Interstellar Alliance. Delenn III is a descendant of the original Delenn (actress Mira Furlan), the Minbari ambassador to the Babylon 5 station in those old (to Alwyn) centuries. Ambassador Delenn altered herself genetically to become human and married Sheridan, twin acts of conviction and devotion. The marriage carried great symbolic weight, because fifteen years earlier Earth and Minbar had fought a terrific war, the mistrust of which never fully dissipated, not even after humanity and the Minbari had fought together and with others in a defensive campaign against the sinister threat of "the Shadows." The Alliance arose on the minimally, morally self-evident proposition that, while "the Universe speaks in many languages," it nevertheless speaks "in only one voice." The Alliance's "Declaration of Principles"—a topic in the fifth season's first episode,

"No Compromises"—states that this voice speaks in a language "not Narn or Human or Centauri or Gaim or Minbari" but, rather, that of "hope . . . trust . . . strength, and . . . compassion." This voice belongs to "the heart and . . . the soul." It is, finally, as the "Declaration of Principles" puts it: "Always . . . the same voice . . . the voice of our ancestors speaking through us . . . the voice of our inheritors waiting to be born. It is the small, still voice that says we are One. No matter the blood, no matter the skin, no matter the world, no matter the star, we are One."[5]

This "Declaration of Principles" nicely articulates the irreducible insights that contribute to the overlapping Greek and Christian ideas of the Word. Identifying *Logos* with wisdom, Heraclitus had, as we have seen, then proceeded to identify wisdom with God. Heraclitus affirmed that, "we need the word to keep things known in common,"[6] as when the common observance of explicit laws binds citizen to citizen in a town or state, or as when people acknowledge the same God and assemble in the unity of worship. The wise man of Ephesus also understood his verbal Principle-of-all-Things to exercise an illuminating power, comparable to a flash of lightning. A current expression among the nonhuman denizens of the Babylon 5 station is "Great Maker!"—an expostulation that hints at the convergence of their deepest intuitions, as though, in moments of stress, they all sensed the supervisory clairvoyance of the same transcendent being. For the Gospels, too, God's Word battles as light against the darkness of sin and evil. John writes that "God is light and in him there is no darkness at all" (1 John 1:5). As God is also "the Word," language and light must be the same thing, a conclusion reached concurrently by many in the ancient Greek-speaking world, not only by Christians. Words and names constitute the intellectual and moral forum where people find constructive agreement and where they find truth. Matthew quotes Jesus as saying, "For where two or three are gathered in my name, I am there among them" (Matt. 18:20).

Jesus's saying includes an explicitly linguistic element. The binding word must be spoken—and so remembered—by a self-consciously devoted community, although the community itself need consist of no more than two or three. The Hebrew phrase *"Sh'ma Yisroel,"* which begins an important prayer, means "Listen, O Israel" and serves to call attention to the liturgical message. Speaking and listening *are* remembering, and remembering, that greatest of all faculties of awareness, is light. Gans, writing of Christianity's "minimal ethic," notes how "moral reciprocity," the basic law of the Gospels, "is implicit in the symmetrical interaction of participants [in any activity] in their use of language."[7]

The passion of Christ intensifies this fundamental insight, and the Gospels crystallize it in the deeds and parables of Jesus. As the gospel spreads, says John, "The darkness is passing away and the true light is already shining" (1 John 2:8). When Sheridan establishes the Alliance, he turns to the Narn ambassador G'Kar (actor Andreas Katsulas) to write the "Declaration of Principles." G'Kar, having endured torture and tribulation and having forgiven one of his tormenters, qualifies as a *nabi,* a prophet, in the biblical sense. A follower of G'Quon, a Narn spiritual leader of the earliest civilized period on his home planet, G'Kar spends much of season three and part of season four copying out *The Book of G'Quon* and adding his own commentary to it. In the final third-season episode, "Z'ha'dum," when conquest of the sentient races by the genocidal Shadows looms and when Commander Sheridan has gone missing, G'Kar cites the great Narn teacher: "G'Quon wrote, *'There is a greater darkness than the one we fight. It is the darkness of the soul that has lost its way.'*"[8] Losing one's way signifies forgetting one's moral bond with others; it signifies perverse obliviousness to the *voice,* as G'Kar says, that speaks of the unity—as in the term "One" in his "Declaration of Principles"—of sentient creatures.

In "The Deconstruction of Falling Stars," the desperate Stephen, whom Brother Alwyn consoles, has been copying a sacred text recounting the legends of the Rangers, the spiritual-martial arm of the Alliance. The parallelism with G'Kar's copying activity and with the medieval scribes is obvious. Viewers get a glimpse of a page where Stephen has written the Latin phrase *"Rangers eis nomen est."* This translates as, "Their name shall be called Rangers." After calming Stephen and sending him away, Brother Alwyn turns to the camera, as though to a communication device, and says in an officious way that the younger man, although troubled, will one day make a good Ranger. Brother Alwyn is submitting his periodic report; he is *himself* a Ranger, proving that the old "Declaration of Principles" has survived the cataclysm and that those who want to build on decency see themselves as following in the footsteps, not only of the fictional characters of the drama, but of the main biblical figures as well.

The "Declaration of Principles" exists only as far as persons of determination have put them consistently into practice. The names recall such persons, and they thus also recall the "Declaration of Principles" as deeds of faith. A Catholic order, led by Brother Theo, had taken up residence on the Babylon 5 Station in the third-season episode "Convictions." Theo's order must have merged with the Rangers. The moniker "Theo" is probably short for *Theodore,* a Greek cognomen that translates as "Given to God." The *Babylon 5* saga treats Christianity with knowledge and sympathy rare in commercial art.

Straczynski admits to reading with enthusiasm in the Bible and in other theological and philosophical texts. "I have always enjoyed Socrates, Aristotle, and Plato," he says, "but I will confess to having a soft spot for Zeno, because he was *such* a pain in the ass." He sets store by *The Meditations of Marcus Aurelius,* the philosophical diaries of a spiritually inclined Roman emperor of the second century CE. Straczynski adds, "I actually managed to plow through the *Enneads* by Plotinus, which is a bit dry, but interesting."[9] All of these interests, yet especially the biblical and Plotinian ones, find expression in aspects of the *Babylon 5* saga. Plotinus (204–70 CE) adapted the theology of Plato (427–347 BCE), who in his day had been one of the elaborators of Heraclitus's *Logos* doctrine, to the conditions of imperial society. Plotinus, like Plato, leaned decisively in the direction of monotheism and, while not a Christian, nevertheless has much in common with Christian thinkers of the same time. The same is often the case with modern, spiritually inclined thinkers, who, while not adherents of Christian doctrine per se, nevertheless assume a good many essentially New Testament principles. The *Babylon 5* writers, especially the main writer, Straczynski, fall into this category.

More remains to be said about the relevance of late antique theology, Christian and otherwise, to *Babylon 5*. Saint Augustine (354–430 CE), a Platonist before he converted to Christianity, takes pains in his *Confessions* to assimilate Platonic theology to Christian doctrine. He writes of his providential encounter with "certain books of the Platonists," declaring that God must have arranged for him to make acquaintance with them. "And therein I found," he says, "not indeed in the same words, but to the selfsame effect . . . that 'in the beginning was the Word, and the Word was with God, and the Word was God.'"[10] In addition to the *Logos* idea put forth in the first sentence of the Fourth Gospel, Augustine found many other Christian ideas in Platonism. Among Augustine's "books of the Platonists," Latin translations of Plotinus must have figured.

In his *Nature, Contemplation, and the One,* Plotinus asserts, "All things are striving after Contemplation, looking to Vision."[11] To be open to existence is, for Plotinus as for Augustine, to sense the transcendent ground of all creation in the benevolent orderliness of the "Maker."[12] Gazing into the heavens, Plotinus writes, the seer "sees the splendor of the stars [and] thinks of the Maker," for whom another name is "the Good."[13] In *On the Good,* Plotinus refers to the Supreme Being as "the One": "Thus the Supreme as containing no otherness is ever present with us [and] we with it when we put otherness away."[14] Many times a *Babylon 5* episode will either begin or end with one or more of the main characters gazing out through the observation galleries of the large orbiting structure into the Van Gogh–like splendor of the starry night.

The Good Is Also the Beautiful

G'Kar's "Declaration of Principles" draws on Plotinian monotheistic mysticism as much as on Jewish and Christian insights about the universality of humankind and the oneness of divinity. An incident in a second-season episode of *Babylon 5* called "There All Honor Lies" illustrates another way in which Straczynski's protagonists remain open both to the philosophical intuition of cosmic orderliness and to the moral intuition that peaceable communion with their fellow creatures—the highest form of which is love—is both an existential imperative and its own precious reward. In the phrase of Paul to the Corinthians, "God is a god not of disorder but of peace" (1 Cor. 14:33). The story of "There All Honor Lies" concerns a plot by recidivist Minbari to frame Sheridan for murder and thereby to displace him as commander of the Babylon 5 station. During the Earth-Minbar War,

Sheridan made himself notorious among the enemy for destroying one of their supposedly indestructible star-cruisers. The resentment against him has lingered sorely among die-hard factions of the Minbari. Mike Laurence Vejar directs one of the few scripts in the series written by someone other than Straczynski, the author in this case being Peter David. The story, basically a "whodunit," runs on a charge of considerable tension, relieved by a comic subplot involving dolls based on station notables and by a brief but impressive sequence concerning "one moment of perfect beauty." As a diplomat, Sheridan must get to know the alien ambassadors. The toughest nut to crack among these is the Vorlon ambassador, Kosh (actor Ardwright Chamberlain), whose enigmatic utterances resound from within his bulky "encounter-suit," so that his real appearance remains mysterious.

Sheridan has accepted Kosh's offer to tutor him in Vorlon ways. Despite the harassment of seeking to vindicate his innocence against the false charge, Sheridan accedes to an unexpected summons from Kosh. The two go to a remote and seemingly uninhabited part of the station. Kosh indicates a door. Sheridan enters. A low ceiling and large unidentifiable bundles create a close environment where, in a corner, sits a hooded figure, possibly other than human. Sheridan sits, cross-legged; the creature proffers a bowl, obviously asking for a donation. Sheridan carries no hard currency, but after much embarrassed talk he drops his insignia in the cup. Voices suddenly sing out unseen, their quality enhanced by a cathedral-like echo. The shapeless bundles arise as graceful dancers in somberly colored robes. Director Vejar manages a dazzling chiaroscuro, with many disorienting but delightful shifts of camera angle. The voices sing a Gregorian hymn, *Puer natus est,* or "A Boy Is Born." In English, the hymn says in part: "To us a Boy Is born, to us a Son is given, whose shoulders will bear the world's dominion."

The striking concert-and-service, which lasts less than a minute, injects a Christian message of hope, just when Sheridan feels some measure of despondency, into an otherwise alien yet thoroughly beguiling encounter. The word *communion* springs to mind. Writer David supplies the scene, but creator Straczynski presides as ubiquitous supervising agency. One suspects the presence of Plotinian or Augustinian motifs. In *On the Intellectual Beauty,* Plotinus argues that the divine "One" is not only the Good and the True, but also in steadfast Platonic fashion, the Beautiful: "We ourselves have beauty when we are true to our own being; our ugliness is in going over to another order; our self-knowledge, that is to say, is our beauty; in self-ignorance we are ugly. . . . Thus beauty is of the Divine and comes Thence only."[15] Shortly before his conversion from Platonism to Christianity, Saint Augustine experienced a pronouncedly Plotinian ecstasy. He describes it in his *Confessions,* addressing his remarks to God, as his having been "transported to thee by thy beauty" and as a discovery of "the unchangeable and true eternity of truth above my changeable mind."[16] Augustine would assimilate this Platonic vision of the ineffable to Christian doctrine by an allusion to Romans, where Paul urges the congregation: "Ever since the creation of the world [God's] eternal power and divine nature, invisible though they are, have been understood and seen through the things he has made" (Rom. 1:20).

Matters of aesthetics figure but little in the Gospels, which tackle *moral* issues, but Paul's comment serves as a reminder that the Gospels never deny, but everywhere affirm, the beauty of creation, through which the limited mortal awareness becomes cognizant of supernal wonders.[17] Jesus justifies the action of the woman who anoints him with expensive oil because, as he says, it is "beautiful" (Greek *kalos*; Mark 14:6; Matt. 26:10). Early Christianity fought an internal battle, moreover, between the iconoclasts, who wanted to forbid images and ornament, and their opponents, who thought that artistic beauty could enhance worship and bolster faith. In both the Greek East and the Franco-German West, iconoclasm faded. Medieval Christianity thus expresses itself not only in monasticism and the *Imitatio Christi*, but also in Gothic architecture, stained glass, passion drama, poetry, narrative, religious painting and sculpture, and the elaboration of sacred music.

Not particularly religious, Sheridan nevertheless once spent time studying meditation techniques in a Tibetan Buddhist Lamasery, as viewers learn in "Deconstruction." That Kosh has set Sheridan up to witness "one moment of perfect beauty" with a surprising Christian content cannot be accidental or meaningless, for the Vorlon, while cautious, always acts according to a long-range plan. Before Sheridan became commander of Babylon 5, Jeffrey Sinclair (actor Michael O'Hare) filled that office. In the first-season episode "Babylon Squared," Sinclair himself explains that before joining Earth Force (the spacefaring terrestrial military), he trained for three years under the Jesuits, intending to pursue a religious life. In the two-part second-season episode "War without End," Sinclair returns 1,000 years through time, transformed into a Minbari, to become Valen, the Moses-Socrates-and-Jesus of that planetary culture. Valen not only established the dominant religious creed of the Minbari, but also founded the Rangers, or *An'la'shok*. These warrior-monks took as their sworn purpose to defend the civilized worlds in the first Shadow War, which occurred during Valen's lifetime, and to be unobtrusively on guard thereafter. Just before Sinclair slips through the time rift to his strange retro-destiny, the being called Zathras (actor Tim Choate) identifies him as "the One," another name for Valen. Valen famously prophesied concerning a *second* Shadow War, which would befall the galaxy 1,000 years in *his* future, at which time the Minbari would need to unite with another race, namely, the human race, in order to prevail against the forces of darkness. This second war is about to happen in the *Babylon 5* saga's present.

The Vorlons are involved in these temporal paradoxes in a mysterious fashion, perhaps as supervisors of their weird involutions—all of which suggests that when Sheridan witnesses the "one moment of perfect beauty," the display signifies his own election to fight in the immemorial *moral struggle* of good against evil, of light against darkness. The moral content remains wedded indissolubly to the aesthetic form. The performance takes place in the context of a reciprocal exchange between Sheridan and the hooded alien. Reciprocity, as we have argued, is at the heart of gospel morality. It is to be remarked, finally, that while the alien stays silent, Sheridan *talks*. The Word makes itself felt. Given that Valen is Sinclair and that Sinclair is a Catholic, it would seem that the Minbari, in their way, are Christians! "If we walk in the light," as John says, "as he himself is in the light, we have fellowship with one another" (1 John 1:7). As Barnabus (first century CE), one of the earliest organizers of monastic life, puts it: "There are two ways of teaching, and two wielders of power; one of light and the other of darkness. Between these two ways there is a vast difference, because over the one are posted the light-bearing angels of God, and over the other the angels of Satan; and one of these is the Lord from all eternity to all eternity, while the other stands paramount over this present age of iniquity."[18] We note also that "the one moment of perfect beauty" is a conversion experience, a redirection of awareness, of the kind intrinsic not only to the Christian, but also to the Greek *Logos,* as in Heraclitus.

Plurality, Passion, and Love

Once upon a time, Christian theologians engaged in what historians of religion and of science together refer to as the plurality debate. The origins of the plurality debate lie in pagan antiquity; they relate to developments in ancient science. In the introduction, the names of Democritus (born ca. 460 BCE) and Epicurus (341–270 BCE) appear in reference to the doctrine known as *atomism*. This doctrine argues boldly that the cause of all natural phenomena is the movement and combination and disintegration and recombination of tiny particles, too small for the senses to detect, which belong to distinct kinds and are indivisible. The word *atom* translates as "indivisible." Democritus invented the idea—one long-term result of which, nuclear explosives, influenced all late-twentieth-century lives—but Epicurus elaborated it; among the latter's elaborations we find the idea that if the behavior of the atoms was consistent (as it appears to be), then one would expect them to do elsewhere in the universe what they have done in "our" corner of it: form suns and worlds and give rise to all the species of life, including *Homo sapiens*. Says Epicurus's Latin follower Lucretius, in his long poem *On the Nature of Things:* "So you must admit that sky, earth, sun, moon, sea and the rest are not solitary, but rather numberless."[19]

While they coined the idea of a plurality of worlds, the atomists never maintained a monopoly on it; other schools of philosophy speculated on the topic. Plutarch of Chaeronaea (46–120 CE) thought that the moon probably supported intelligent life; he guesses about the Lunarians in his dialogue *On the Face in the Moon*. Lucian of Samosata (115–200 CE), to whose name we have also made reference in the introduction, wrote the first planetary romance, *The True History;* he sent intrepid explorers to the moon and recorded, for the first time in any prose narrative, a war between competing stellar empires. Followers of Aristotle, on the other hand, argued for the finitude of the cosmos and the uniqueness of the earthly world.

The plurality debate lay dormant for a long time, surfacing again in the context of Christian theology in the sixteenth and seventeenth centuries. Johannes Kepler (1571–1630) espoused the pluralist position explicitly; Galileo Galilei (1564–1642) probably sympathized with it but reserved commitment because of the example of Giordano Bruno (born 1548), burned at the stake by the Papal Inquisition in 1600—partly because of his exhortations on behalf of the "many worlds" doctrine. By the end of the seventeenth century, the debate had revived and had found exponents among Protestant and Catholic thinkers. A best seller of the late seventeenth century was Bernard le Bovier de Fontenelle's *Conversations on the Plurality of Worlds* (1686). Fontenelle (1657–1757) popularized, although he did not invent, the major logical—or rather *theological*—proposition in support of plurality, the argument from *plenitude*. Based on the new astronomy of the day, which had shown the planets to be worlds and the stars to be distant suns, probably possessing worlds, plenitude asks whether God, supposing him to have created the universe, would have made all those millions of worlds without putting them to a use. "No," is plenitude's answer. But what use, then? The same use as the earth's, to be the home for *other* humanities, plenitude answers.

The counterargument also exploited the motifs of God's goodness and of his consistency. It asked whether God would have made innumerable *other* planetary humanities, when they, because of their remoteness from the earth, could not have received the gospel, so that they would, therefore, remain out of reach of redemption. "No," is the counterargument's answer: God would not create and then abandon—from which the antipluralist infers that humanity has no alien neighbors. But plenitude reserves an arrow in its quiver: why should God not have arranged for Christ to appear everywhere to all the humanities? Why should the Word not have been preached on those other worlds in tongues appropriate to them? That would indeed be the logical extension of God's infinite creative capacity and his infinite mercy.

The general optimism of the eighteenth century made plurality a widely current opinion at the time. Alexander Pope (1688–1744), the British Catholic poet, endorses it in his *Essay on Man* (1733), with the qualification that *we* can know only *our* world. Nevertheless, it must be the case that "worlds on worlds compose one universe," where "system into system runs" and "other planets circle other suns," and a "varied being *peoples* every star." Pope also wrote *Universal Prayer* (1738), suitable for utterance (so he supposed) by *any* sentient being, terrestrial or otherwise. Invoking God as "Father of All" and "Great First Cause," Pope concludes with this dedication:

> To Thee Whose temple is of space,—
> Whose altar earth, sea, skies,—
> One chorus let all beings raise!
> All Nature's incense rise.

Pope's phrase "Great First Cause" anticipates the oft-repeated oath of the *Babylon 5* aliens: *"Great Maker!"* The whole of Pope's *Universal Prayer* anticipates G'Kar's "Declaration of Principles" for the "Interstellar Alliance." Between Pope's *Prayer* and *Babylon 5,* however, stands another appreciable item in the genre constituted by the crossroads of theology and science fiction. The remarkable novel *Star Maker* (1937) by William Olaf Stapledon (1886–1950) exerts considerable influence on the *Babylon 5* saga, as it does on virtually all science fiction subsequent to it. Stapledon intends *Star Maker* to supply—as fiction, of course—nothing less than the history of all sentient species in the universe, from its beginning to its end; it also deals with the intuition of sentience that it bears a relation, as creature to creator, to a supernal Being whom Stapledon, taking a cue from Plotinus, calls the Star Maker.

The disembodied consciousness who serves Stapledon for a narrator and who joins with many other telepathic minds says of this intuition and its related quest: "The sustaining motivation of our pilgrimage [was] the hunger which formerly drove men on Earth in search of God."[20] Whatever the nature of the Star Maker, whether it is "Power" or "Reason" or "Love," the keenest awareness always responds to it with profound yearning. Sometimes this puts the respondent at odds with the majority and transforms him or her into a moral reformer or a prophet. Thus, Stapledon's narrator, in a poignant conceit, refers in the plural to "the Christs of all the worlds."[21] In the course of his epic, *Babylon 5* writer Straczynski gives us at least one such religious martyr around whose passion others experience a powerful moral conversion. This is the Narn ambassador, G'Kar, who, more than even Captain Sheridan, functions as the moral fulcrum of Straczynski's extended tale.

Some details of exposition are necessary. Of the several arcs that define the five seasons of *Babylon 5,* two bear importantly on the passion of G'Kar: the first of these is the Narn-Centauri war, and the second is the (second) Shadow War. The two are closely related. The Centauri, more technically advanced than the Narn, once colonized them and claim haughtily to have raised them from barbarism to civilization. Once the Narn become a spacefaring people who assert their equality with their former masters, the Centauri, a society in domestic political disarray, react with offense and resentment. The idea of reestablishing control of the Narn home world becomes a cynical motif of Centauri internal politics; the Centauri threat leads to Narn preemption.

The first episode of season one of *Babylon 5,* "Midnight on the Firing Line," explores the immediate consequences of the Narn attack on a Centauri agricultural colony. The Centauri retaliate. As they possess better weapons than the Narn, they emerge victorious. The Narn now turn more disgruntled than ever. G'Kar becomes the implacable foe of Centauri ambassador Londo Mollari (actor Peter Jurasik), and vice versa. The war draws Mollari deeper into Centauri politics, at which time an agent of the Shadows approaches him in the person of their oily proxy Ethan Morden (actor Ed Wasser), who proposes to solve the problem of Narn aggression in a way that will raise Mollari's status on Centauri Prime. It is the old satanic bargain, mitigated only by the fact that when he enters it Mollari neither guesses who his new allies really are nor foresees how brutally they will act.

When Mollari finally disdains the Shadows' demonic assistance, other Centauri endorse it, until Narn lies defeated, with millions of its people dead, the survivors now being slaves of the conquerors. G'Kar, a member of the Narn planetary government or *Kha'Ri*, begins to sustain himself on pure distillate of hatred. Almost the whole of season three prolongs G'Kar's humiliation and anger until, jailed for a violent outburst, he experiences a religious vision linked to *The Book of G'Quon.* On his release from penal lockup, G'Kar prevents an anti-Centauri uprising among the other Narn on the Babylon 5 station, where Sheridan has extended them asylum; G'Kar becomes increasingly convinced that revenge for its own sake against the Centauri will neither assuage his sorrow nor break the cycle of violence that is devouring both peoples. A new principle is required. Meanwhile, a troubling emperor-usurper has seized power through assassination on Centauri Prime: Cartagia, as he is called, is as mad as the Roman emperor Caligula and has entered into a secret pact with the Shadows. Like a *Doctor Who* bad guy, Cartagia suffers delusions of grandeur and believes that a mass sacrifice of his fellow Centauri will promote him to godhood.

Mollari begins a long rapprochement with G'Kar. For both parties this is initially entirely pragmatic; and here the G'Kar-Mollari plot begins to shade into the Shadow War plot. Through twists and turns, G'Kar ends up a prisoner of the mad Cartagia, but it is by design, with the end of ridding Centauri of its psychopathic ruler, ending the occupation of Narn (hence G'Kar's desperate cooperation), and helping the good guys against the devilish Shadows. Nevertheless, G'Kar's peril deepens, and he must withstand terrific torments.

In the fourth-season episode "The Summoning," which takes place in the Centauri redoubt on Narn, Cartagia orders G'Kar scourged while Mollari, who must not betray his new relation to the victim, witnesses the spectacle without being able to protest. John McPherson directs Straczynski's script with many overt allusions to the passion narrative as related in the Gospels, even making the sadistic servitors of Cartagia begin by crowning G'Kar with a circlet of thorns. In *The Babylon File* (1997), Andy Lane suggests Deuteronomy 25, a prescription for corporal punishments, as the main biblical reference in the scourging scene; but the imagery belongs to the Gospels. Mollari visits G'Kar in the dungeon where Cartagia has had him thrown, only to discover that the emperor has perpetrated the additional outrage of plucking out one of the Narn's eyes. The next morning, guards bring G'Kar before the emperor to be executed; the battered fellow limps in his chains, and he carries around his neck a heavy yoke giving the impression of a cross. The parallelism is not complete, as G'Kar breaks his chains, creating a distraction during which Mollari—or rather, Mollari's aide-de-camp Vir Cotto (actor Stephen Furst)—dispatches the tyrant-madman. The Centauri now depart from the Narn home world, but the bloodthirsty celebrations of the liberated Narn so disgust G'Kar that he prefers to return to Babylon 5.

Mollari will say to G'Kar many episodes later that, in the moment when he looked on the savaged Narn in the bloody cell, he felt a surge of pity greater than any he had experienced before and so began to reform his life, as far as he could. Something of G'Kar's own suffering and something of the effect that his trial had on Mollari go into the "Declaration of Principles." "Here," G'Kar's document states, "gathered together in common cause, we agree to recognize this singular truth and this singular rule: that we *must* be kind to one another because each voice enriches and ennobles us, and each voice lost diminishes us."[22] Actor Katsulas brings a great pathos to G'Kar, apprehensible despite the complicated prosthetics and make-up entailed by the role. Not only Straczynski's lines, but also Katsulas's thespian ardor call to mind a passage in John's Gospel: "The words that I have spoken to you are spirit and life" (John 6:63).

G'Kar is a preacher of the Word. Sometimes his meditations assume the form of subtle analyses of behavior from a moral point of view. Sometimes they sound like parables or aphorisms. In the fifth-season episode "Meditations on the Abyss," this bit of dialogue between G'Kar and another Narn occurs, with the speaker in an aphoristic mood:

> **Narn:** What is truth? And what is God?
> **G'Kar:** Truth is . . . a river.
> **Narn:** And what is God?
> **G'Kar:** God is the mouth of the river.[23]

The Supreme Being of the *Babylon 5* saga appears to be the God who is also the Word. A river figures in the Gospels—the Jordan, in whose waters the followers of the Baptist experience rebirth. G'Kar's comment might also reach back to Heraclitus, originator of the Greek *Logos* philosophy; Heraclitus most famously stated, "The river where you set your foot just now is gone—those waters giving way to this, now this."[24] Modern thinkers have always interpreted this saying as an expression of moral and epistemological relativism, as a claim that, in the flux of existence, we can never certainly know anything. A more likely interpretation is that the aphorism articulates the tension between those things that are eternal and those that, in the mortal realm, fall subject to change. As such, the assertion is by no means incompatible with gospel morality.

Jesus urges us, for example, to render unto Caesar what is Caesar's and unto God what is God's. Caesar changes every few years; God, being eternal, does not. At the end of the fifth (and last) season of the series, G'Kar leaves the station in company with Lyta Alexander (actress Patricia Tallman), another tragic character who has suffered for her convictions and has endured the ordeals of an outcast. They depart into unknown space, much as pilgrims searching for the source of truth in the unfathomable mercy of the divine.

G'Kar finds his way to a life motivated at last solely by love. Indeed, G'Kar and Lyta's bond seems but to reflect another bond, also equally unlikely. The two other characters who cleave to each other in the same cause are Ambassador Delenn, the Minbari representative to the Babylon 5 station, and Captain Sheridan. Delenn descends from the Minbari line started 1,000 years before her own generation by Valen, who, as the series reveals, is none other than Commander Sinclair; Delenn has human ancestry by way of the time paradox. At the end of season two, as we recall, Delenn transforms herself into a human being. She has respected Sheridan since he first came to the Babylon 5 station to take up his office, just as he has respected her. A deeper bond slowly but surely draws them closer, until neither can deny the love that burns in each for the other. As chaos disrupts the order of things around them, Sheridan and Delenn find a kind of salvation in each other: through Delenn, who belongs to the religious caste on Minbar, a new element of spirituality enters Sheridan's life. Minbari have many ceremonies to mark the stages of life, including those that signify betrothal and marriage, and Sheridan must submit—sometimes reluctantly and often with comic results—to them. Sheridan dies before Delenn, disappearing mysteriously in a region of the galaxy known as Coriana Space. In "Deconstruction," Delenn says three times to the ideological fanatics who have tried to distort Sheridan's biography that he was a good man. She does not but she might have cited scripture: "He was a burning and shining lamp, and you were willing to rejoice for a while in his light" (John 5:35).

While *Babylon 5* is intentionally ecumenical, incorporating theological and spiritual motifs from a wide variety of sources, it is nevertheless culturally biblical, as expressions of Western culture tend to be even despite themselves. The ecumenicist position is, after all, a Western, largely Christian one, mediated by the gospel tenet that God the Creator makes all human beings in his image. The earliest Christians thought of themselves as Jews and were Jews by birth and custom; in seeking converts, the evangelists never made ethnicity a criterion. God's Word was meant for *all,* as the preachers saw it.

We have earlier referred to the ecclesiastical debate about the status of art in Christian worship: images were important to evangelism because they conveyed ideas in a world where only a minority were literate.

Another important debate of the formative centuries of Christianity was the contest between a puritanical conception of the church according to which only the absolutely uncompromised and untainted would be allowed into the congregation and a liberal conception that understood the need to readmit those who had lapsed and to admit those who might also participate in civic paganism. Bishop Donatus of Carthage, for example, held a narrow conception of the church; he argued that participation in civic paganism disbarred a person from receiving communion. Bishop Augustine—Saint Augustine—of Hippo held a broad conception, having himself wandered widely from the orbit of orthodoxy during a peregrine youth. Saint Augustine argued that Christians needed to welcome as many as possible to share in their creed and that a too puritanical attitude would, in fact, be an abrogation of the gospel imperative. Yet another important debate, in the generation after Augustine, pitted those who wanted to abolish all pagan learning from Christian education against those who, like Saint Basil of Caesarea (fourth century CE), believed that Christians could learn much from their pagan ancestors. Augustine had made much the same case in his discussions of the Platonists.

In celebrating the ecumenical principle, *Babylon 5* demonstrates that it lies along a line of Western thinking that stretches from the Old Testament and the earliest Greek thought through the Gospels and the earliest commentaries on them right down to the present. This conscious continuity with the intellectual and spiritual past would qualify as remarkable in any context: that it is the case in a science-fiction serial designed for television makes it something extraordinary.

Toward a Conclusion

Science Fiction, Contemporary Popular Culture, and Gospel Theology

We may say, furthermore, that Christianity is the "religion" of modern man and historical man, of the man who simultaneously discovered personal freedom and continuous time (in place of cyclical time). It is even interesting to note that the existence of God forced itself far more urgently upon modern man, for whom history exists as such, as history and not as repetition, than upon the man of the archaic and traditional cultures.

Mircea Eliade, *The Myth of the Eternal Return*[1]

In the course of his acquisition of knowledge man rises by degrees to a higher level, and he also sinks below it. These two movements from below upwards and from above downwards are inevitable, and without them man cannot get his bearings in the world. Man should be ready to sacrifice everything for the sake of Truth, but Truth is often bitter to taste and he frequently prefers some deceitful illusion, which he finds elevating.

Nicolas Berdyaev, *Truth and Revelation*[2]

Television and the Promise of Technical Innovation

The commandments of Moses enjoin humanity from (among other things) making or venerating *sacred images*. The biblical conscience sees in idols and totems—as in any other specimen of what, in the Victorian lexicon, would have been called a mumbo jumbo—a derailment of genuine piety and a morbid shrinking-down of awareness. God is transcendent; the statue or fetish is a mere dead thing. To confuse the latter with the former would be tantamount, therefore, to forgetting our status as moral people who participate in reason as well as in devotion. Now modernity, in its spasms of technical conjuration, has tossed forth no device quite so idol-like or quite so idolized as television. Were the hypothetical Martian ethnologist secretly to observe the behavior of modern people—in, say, North America—he or she might justifiably draw the conclusion that the household television set really is an idol of some sort and that, in their daily attendance on the weird glow of the cathode-ray tube, the tens of millions of people devoted to it constitute a case of exemplary, indeed of unparalleled, cultic piety. Few people born after 1945 can imagine daily life without its admixture of broadcast imagery, information, and paltry drama. With the atomic bomb and penicillin, the one an actual enormity and the other a genuine boon, television indeed betokens the new age of technological excellence that had supposedly dawned with the end of hostilities and which held out to the rising middle class a life of splendid affluence and leisure. The lower type of literary science fiction, concerned with "predicting" new gadgets, had speculated abundantly about television, predicting its advent as early as the 1890s. Illustrator Harry Grant Dart's cartoon for a 1911 issue of *Life* thus depicts a bourgeois living room crowded with conveniences, including a projection-television apparatus with a menu for changing the channel: "Golf," "Aeroplane Races," and "Theater" figure among the programmatic choices.[3] That menu would be familiar to any cable TV-service or satellite subscriber; they can receive the Golf Channel, the Speed Channel, and the Arts and Entertainment Channel. Only the range—not the character—of televised fare has been enlarged.

The famous New York World's Fair of 1939 featured television with eager promises in its World of Tomorrow pavilion, sponsored by General Electric. Homes of the future would boast every sort of automated ease, and television would obviate the annoyance of going out to see a movie. Television had gotten an abortive trial, in fact, in the 1930s, when the United States, Great Britain, France, and Germany all developed limited television schedules in major metropolitan areas. None of it displayed any great merit. A 1999 German documentary, *Television under the Swastika,* shows clips of minor-league sports events, mediocre variety acts, and primitive cooking shows that look a good deal like early, locally originating American television. The Parisian television station transmitted through a mast on the Eiffel Tower, itself a symbol of technological progress. The war interrupted these developments, such as they were. Television resurrected itself rapidly, however, in the late 1940s, surpassing radio and cinema as the primary entertainment venue for a majority of Americans by the mid-1950s. Other nations soon caught up with the United States, often importing American programs and dubbing them in the local language. Always the receptive audience regarded television as a technical advance, which it was, if we take radio as the benchmark, for now the broadcasters could send pictures along with the audio signal. But, as in Nicolas Berdyaev's formula quoted in our epigraph, the ascent of technical know-how corresponded with the descent of wisdom, as a new lower standard imposed itself on the mind-at-large among the affected people.

Early television included some more or less science-fictional fare, such as *Space Patrol* (1950–55), *Captain Video* (1949–53), and the Dumont Network adaptation of *Flash Gordon* (1951), filmed in a Berlin television studio, no less, left intact after the Allied bombing campaigns of 1944–45. Producers aimed these serial programs at children or, as it might be, at adults with exceedingly childlike and therefore malleable minds—the sponsor's ideal television watcher. Crass mercantilism drove television from the moment of its revival. Despite occasional literary assistance by a real writer (a refugee, say, from radio drama), the cardboard teleplays of these early outer-space melodramas were invariably trivial, a fact more or less dictated by the commercial character of the medium and reaffirmed in most of the later science-fictional entries in the prime-time lineup. We need only recall *Voyage to the Bottom of the Sea* (1964–68), or *Lost in Space* (1965–68), or the other Irwin Allen–produced series that proliferated in the same decade, to form the apposite judgment. Ideas of any kind, not to mention religious or spiritual ideas, would have gotten in the way of the simple story and distracted attention from the advertisements. Religion, always controversial, frightened producers and sponsors like almost nothing else. The BBC's early-1950s *Quatermass* series, with scripts by Nigel Kneale, later of *Doctor Who* fame, excelled the American shows in technical sophistication and in acting but remained on the level of a monster thriller. Science fiction could reliably predict the advent of the technical device called television, but it could predict neither the degrading insipidity of televised programming nor the sociological consequences of the mass dissemination of the same degrading insipidity.

In the Dart cartoon, for example, the television set merely takes its place among the other mechanical wonders, forming an item in the ambient material prodigality of the times. The owner of the room and of its devices looks safely cultivated and stuffily Episcopalian. He little suspects that the television set is a demonic presence ready to corrode everything that he takes for granted in terms of habit and custom and likely to transform his children into neobarbarians. By the time science fiction began to see television as a destructively transformative power—as Cyril M. Kornbluth (1923–58) does in "The Marching Morons" (1951) or as Ray Bradbury (born 1928) does in "The Veldt" (1952)—video broadcasting had already been in existence for some time. It was not going away.

If the science-fiction writers could not exactly predict television, they could nevertheless assess it when it appeared. It seemed patent to a Kornbluth or to a Bradbury that the phenomena of the spiritual and of the religious, out of which civilization grows, could not reliably descend into the sphere of this most leveling of all mass media, except in a perverse form; nor could the medium itself, in its normative (low-level) mode, readily rise to the altitude of the spiritual or the religious. Television was therefore *not* going to be much in the way of a boon to civilized society. It seemed patent indeed to a Kornbluth or to a Bradbury that the cathode-ray tube portended what we now call *the dumbing-down of culture*—and portended it with a vengeance. A culture centered on twenty-four-hour-a-day broadcasting of anything and nothing would find itself infantilized and stupefied. Inanity would crowd out all the painfully acquired higher values of the Western Judeo-Christian tradition. Fifty additional years of experience has established a large *Q.E.D.* under their original critique. Insofar as television has undermined literacy, which any college teacher can testify to be the case; insofar as it has coarsened both conscience and decorum; insofar as it has reduced the attention span of the average person: insofar as it has done these things, it has moreover also undermined the faith of the scriptural religions, thereby contributing to the moral confusion of the day. What passes for "religious broadcasting" mostly only parodies and distorts what educated people think of as faith; mainstream television meanwhile remains obsessively and meanly antireligious, particularly antibiblical, and promulgates a kind of crude paganism, typified by MTV. Network television's anti-Christian bias is intimately related to its antiliterate ethos and its pandering to the natural resentfulness of youth.

The Gospels constitute a *scripture,* not an orally mediated *myth,* and they must, *as such,* be in some tension with any mass recursion to a purely *oral-demonstrative* mentality. Bradbury saw television as swiftly alienating children from their parents and driving a wedge between the generations; Kornbluth saw it as the focus of a new type of celebrity cult, which would fascinate people and dissolve their allegiance to all other dispensations—custom, religion, and the state alike. Kornbluth also saw television as the catalyst of a universal lowering of taste and mental capacity.

It is something of an anomaly, then, that television, not cinema, is the medium that engendered the six remarkable science-fiction series that we have addressed in the foregoing chapters. It is enough of an anomaly that it demands an explanation. We would argue, however, that a television series such as *The Twilight Zone, Doctor Who,* or *Star Trek* is potentially more serious—precisely because it sustains its meditation on human nature at greater length—than the typical science-fiction movie, as superior as the latter might be in its scale of theatrical mounting and technical refinements. This superiority of the television program, although only potential, derives from the serial story's capacity for steady representation of character and of situation, with a prolongation of attention that cannot so easily happen in a ninety-minute or two-hour movie. This is despite the truth that a good movie is still better than a bad television-show. The case of

Doctor Who provides an object lesson. We have seen how literate and meditative the *Doctor Who*-writers could be; we have sampled the earnestness and skill of the various camera directors and art directors. They were students of archeology and painting, readers of Shakespeare and Dostoyevsky—intelligent and cultivated people.

In the mid-1960s, an American producer, Milton Subotsky, traveled to London to make two exploitative *Doctor Who* films, both based on the "Dalek" premise. The Daleks, whom we have mentioned in passing in our chapter on *Doctor Who,* are a race of robots, incapable of emotion or love, which attempts habitually to subdue all other races in the galaxy; once the Daleks were human, but nuclear warfare disfigured them physically and spiritually, and they retreated into their armored "traveling machines." Gradually they became altogether mechanical and heartless. The telling motto of their technocratic-*cum*-racial jihad is: "*Seek! Locate! Exterminate!*" In their numerous appearances the Daleks symbolize the willingness of modern humanity to sacrifice its distinguishing—its redeeming—qualities on the altar of *libido dominandi,* to banish emotion for the sake of efficiency, and to eliminate all supposedly unnecessary functions. The idea behind them, while not terrifically original—it appears in Mary Shelley's *Frankenstein* (1822) and reappears in Karel Capek's *Rossum's Universal Robots* (1922)—resonates with actual dehumanizing events and tendencies of the last one hundred years.

Doctor Who and the Daleks (1965) and *Daleks: Invasion Earth, 2150 A.D.* (1966), both starring Peter Cushing as the redoubtable Time Lord, offer ninety minutes or so each of cliff-hanging action on colorful sets; and they boast production values much in excess of those associated with the jerry-built television series. Both are bereft of ideas, however, and both take the characters down several notches from their serial development, simplifying and denaturing them. Cushing's Doctor becomes a doddering eccentric of a grandfather, who tinkers with his time machine in the disused stable. Without a meaningful story to give them context, the Daleks themselves become risible, ineffective wheeled boxes. The focus on a precocious child actress (ten-year-old Roberta Tovey) likewise dispels any possibility of a serious story, because it demotes the grown-ups to so much background. Of course, Subotsky cared not a farthing whether *adults* would respond to his movies; he wanted to pull in the bubble-gum crowd, which he apparently did. Both entries ranked among British box-office smashes in the tandem years of their back-to-back release; they did well in North America, too, and they have reappeared in the DVD format. But we should admonish ourselves that massive appeal never automatically implies significance. It is rather the opposite, if anything. The massive appeal of something usually only means that a slick advertising campaign has succeeded.

Why is it that *Doctor Who* achieved sagacity and tapped into wonder as a low-budget television program yet scored a philosophical and theological "zero" when transferred to the big screen? The question has a meaning for *The Twilight Zone* and *Star Trek,* both of which also migrated to cinema and largely ceased to be contemplative or edifying when they did so. Stephen Spielberg's *Twilight Zone: The Movie* (1983), during the filming of which actor Vic Morrow needlessly lost his life, is a garish embarrassment; it is ugly, bathetic, sentimental, and deservedly forgotten. The *Star Trek* film franchise, beginning with *Star Trek: The Motion Picture* (1979), reliably excited and amused audiences, mining nostalgia for the aging actors, but these movies, no matter how impressively mounted, never challenged the imagination, as "Classic Trek" regularly did.

A connection exists between the notion of the *serial* and the notion of the *serious.* The root concept is that of a *series:* the recurrence of an event or a pattern according to some perceptible regularity on which awareness can fix so that the mind is drawn into the sustained contemplation of its object's intrinsic orderliness, which awareness comes to recognize and cherish as an instance of a larger cosmic orderliness. Such sustained contemplation is thus, as the philosophers have said, the beginning of all wisdom and indeed of all genuine devotion. When the object of contemplation by humans are humans themselves, then this seriousness of attitude becomes the starting point of knowledge and freedom—and of the type of life that rises above mere primitive satisfactions and absorption in the present. The story of the Old Testament is the emancipation of the Hebrews from cosmic polytheism and sacrificial cults; the story of the New Testament is the extension of the Hebrew spiritual achievement to all of humanity. New Testament *follows* Old Testament: the Gospels constantly quote from the prophets and psalmists. The relation of the two parts of scripture already hints at the character of seriousness. It must have something to do with the active maintenance of the past and a deliberate orientation to the future; it must in some manner be attentive to itself and generally studious of the external world, including other people. But what, then, is the precise structure or character of seriousness?

Let us stay close to the notion of scripture, which we have already introduced, and which implies the ability of a person to decipher the graphic marks on a page or other surface into their intended significance. In reading, whether it is scripture or a newspaper, the alphabetically literate scan from left to right and down the page, assimilating individual words to larger grammatical structures and finally into lengthy narrative sequences (stories) or profound analysis. There is a finite number of letters, but there are many thousands of words; ultimately, there is a finite number of words, but a potentially infinite number of sentences—of arguments or of tales. At each recurrence, the letter or word is the same as before, but it is also altered by its new context. Thus the reader *reconstitutes* the more or less complex thinking that the written text records; he or she reconstitutes it by noticing not only the recurrent patterns but also the subtle progressive variations on the recurrent patterns. Intrusions and distractions interrupt the reader's mental focus—always a consciously sustained act—and prevent him or her from putting the whole into coherent order. As long as the mind continues to focus, however, it can "translate" the alphabetic marks on the page into a sonnet by William Shakespeare, a short story by Guy de Maupassant, a gospel chapter, or an analysis of ethics by Plato, Aristotle, Saint Paul, or Saint Augustine. Reading is slow rather than fast; it requires effort rather than affording ease, which is why pampered undergraduates rebel against it. On the other hand, reading takes its context in the undistracted leisure provided characteristically by the type of organized life that we call civilization. Literacy and civic life go together. In coming to grips with the great texts, the educated citizen continuously reconstitutes, privately, the historical chain of causality that has generated the public condition called civilization. Augustine's remarks on reading in his *Confessions* bear on the point.

In book 1, Augustine remarks on the fundamental relation of basic literacy to all subsequent and higher learning. The written language is, Augustine says, a type of "conventional understanding [that] men have agreed upon," which permits a people to establish a steady record of experience to which all who have studied that same "conventional understanding" will have access.[4] Augustine also notes that "reading and writing" embody a basic discipline for literate people, in which even young children begin to grasp that spiritual accomplishment requires one "to restrain the excesses of freedom."[5] Finally, as in the case of Holy Scripture, the written word embodies and makes permanent the experience and wisdom of the generations. In the written word, people participate in a collective memory that transcends individual memory, for which, as Mircea Eliade reminds us, the word is *history.* The idea of history is another generically *serial* and therefore also *serious* idea. Those people exist *historically* who succeed in seeing beyond the horizon of immediate and petty concerns; to be concerned on a daily basis with issues beyond the merely existential or personal is one of the marks of a civilized, as opposed to a barbaric, mentality. When we live consciously as civilized people we live also *in* history—and the history *in which* we live includes religious revelation and the totality of revelation's consequences. The constitution of a *historical* people—a people characterized by its awareness of living in a continuum of persons and customs and events—is thus intimately linked, as Eliade opines, with the Bible, for Judaism and Christianity are the religions that originally establish a notion of open linear history by interrupting the old, closed notion of ritually mediated cyclical time.

Like the biblical religion that it assimilates, our civilization makes heavy demands; it confers a boon but sets an obligation. Quite possibly at any given time not everyone who enjoys the benefits conferred by religion or by civilization fully participates in either. Not all are literate, for example; not many have a sense of history. Whereas in past centuries, Eliade argues, Christian civilization enabled "millions of men . . . to endure great historical pressures," in modernity, by contrast, a significant fraction of people have relapsed into "traditional, 'anti-historic'" modes of being.[6] The terrific *ease* and affluence of a society like the modern Western society tempts people into relaxation and insouciance. Why trouble oneself with seriousness when so much alluring diversion lies so ready to hand? One frequently used name for this flight from civilized seriousness is *popular culture,* with its emphasis on immediate gratification rather than on prudence or deferral and on the body rather than on the soul or the mind.

The invocation of *popular culture,* so called, brings us back to the topic of *television,* the technological innovation that, more than radio or the movies, has eroded the seriousness of the average person. This in turn brings us back to the anomaly of our six television series, each one of which engaged itself in the critique of existence by which civilization conserves its gains and maintains its transcendental orientation; each one of which also incorporated gospel motifs, thereby demonstrating a real affiliation to the continuity of the Western, Judeo-Christian tradition. What factors permitted the creators of these six programs to ensconce them, for a time, in the medium least conducive to the curatorial maintenance of higher values, intellectual and moral? What does their existence tell us about our cultural and spiritual condition at the beginning of a new century? And what value do they have, in sum, that they deserve our custodial attention?

Popular Culture, Mass Culture, and the Integral Society

Classic outsiders, the originators of all six series stood askew to the dominant trends of the times; a prophetic cantankerousness clung to all of them, even when a given individual was not churched or otherwise specifically religious in a conventional way. Born in Syracuse, New York, to Jewish parents, *The Twilight Zone*'s Rod Serling (1924–75) had served in the paratroops in World War II, in the Pacific theater; after the war he went to Antioch University in Ohio, where he converted to Unitarianism. The driven Serling wrote for radio in the years just after the war, much influenced by radio dramatist Norman Corwin, who also influenced Ray Bradbury, and always in Corwin's moralistic style. Sensing an opportunity in the newly revived television medium, Serling produced effective Corwin-like dramas for a Cincinnati station before moving up to the New York–based networks. Serling almost certainly would not have found entry into the television world as it formed itself in the 1960s; he could have done so only when television was still new, experimental, pliable, and not yet rigidly institutionalized.

According to biographer Gordon F. Sander, Serling looked to television because he "had become dismayed—and angered—with what he saw as the increasing trashiness of radio."[7] Sander quotes Serling: "Radio, in terms of drama . . . dug its own grave. It had aimed downward, had become cheap and unbelievable, and had willingly settled for second best."[8] Sander indeed characterizes the Serling who conceived and realized *The Twilight Zone* as a "prophet-outcast" of the late-1950s television industry, a man who wanted to use fantasy as "a prism through which to view America's soul."[9] Serling told CBS's Mike Wallace in a 1959 interview:

> I stay in TV because I think it performs the function of providing adult, meaningful, exciting, challenging drama without dealing in controversy. I think it's criminal that we are not permitted to make dramatic note of social evils that exist, of controversial themes, as they are inherent in our society. I think it's ridiculous that drama, which by its very nature should make a comment on those things which affect our daily lives, is in a position, at least in terms of television, of not being able to take that stand.[10]

The twin notions that (a) radio has descended into "trashiness" and that (b) television now performs the critical social function formerly undertaken by radio suggest that Serling had an insight into the connectedness of so-called technical progress, popular culture, and conscience: industry offers its technological innovations to the market on the promise that they will improve the quality of life; the promises seem plausible, but events rarely fulfill them, and the net effect of the innovation is to degrade life in some unforeseen way. A new innovation now appears, which critics see as redeeming the betrayal of the previous innovation, which at first it does, in some compromised way, only to lapse into the inevitable desuetude soon after its advent.

A lazy, popular pressure, the infamous lowest common denominator of taste, often coerces the custodians of the innovation to compromise its higher potential for the sake of immediate return, disregarding the net cultural consequences. Throughout *Doctor Who*'s long and recently revived life, its creators and producers have had to battle with the BBC's Audience Research department, which systematically surveys viewer response to current programming. David J. Howe and Stephen J. Walker reprise some of these responses in their *Unofficial and Unauthorised Guide to Doctor Who* (2003); they reveal a constant theme of audience complaints that the ideas and stories of the series were difficult to understand. "Too far fetched to be anything but childish" is a typical and rather self-contradictory remark,[11] given that what the respondent really seems in reaction against is the complexity, rather than the simplicity, of the story. The more intellectually and morally complicated a story was (the less the producers actually aimed it at children), the more likely the disgruntled watchers were to say that it was *too far-fetched.* Howe and Walker report of the quite intelligent twelfth-season story "Genesis of the Daleks" that, "with its themes of warfare, racial hatred and genetic experimentation, [it] had provoked complaints from viewers and from the self-appointed moral watchdogs of the National Viewers and Listeners Association, headed by Mary Whitehouse."[12] The *Doctor Who* production crew, to their credit, mostly resisted.

Although their language is irritatingly that of 1980s academic criticism, John Tulloch and Manuel Alvarado properly note in their *Unfolding Text* (1983) that, at its best,

Doctor Who has always made intelligent use of "intertextuality."[13] This admittedly jargonlike term nevertheless denotes something both real and sophisticated, namely, an audience's recognition of wide-ranging cultural allusions of a more or less *literary or artistic* order. Tulloch and Alvarado write:

> Even at the most simplistic level—recognition of references to Greek myth, Shakespeare, the Bible, history, Lang's *Metropolis,* "specialised" sciences etc—[*Doctor Who*] seeks to establish a "complicit" relation with its audience. . . . In the case of the . . . educated audience—a significant target group for *Doctor Who*—these "double meanings" (where the "allegorical" reference is in fact to another "high art" text or to an entire mode, such as melodrama) can have as much to do with the pleasure derived from the text as its "scary" dramatic qualities have for a younger audience.[14]

Interviewed by Tulloch and Alvarado, *Doctor Who* producer (in the 1970s) Graham Williams said:

> We discovered that very much the largest single sector of our audience was between 26 and 36, and almost as large a segment was between 36 and 46. So the adult audience very much outnumbered the children—which was our gut reaction to start with. We thought it was *terribly* dangerous to start playing down to what we would imagine kids would want. . . . I reckoned that [*Doctor Who*] was being made for the aware and hopefully imaginative sixteen-year-olds who could really latch on to the possibilities. We never tried to take a theme to its logical conclusion. We almost always would stop somewhere and say, "You work out the rest of it." I think spoon-feeding is a dreadful cliché-ridden operation.[15]

The struggle between art and trash is also the struggle between adult acuity and childish obtuseness. Given the title of the present study, we ought to be reminded of Paul's frequent admonitions to the early Christian congregations to act like responsible, adult representatives of humanity and not to wander off into childish or otherwise self-centered fantasies.

Christ is not a magician like Apollonius of Tyana, and God is not a thunder hurler like Zeus who chooses sides in a battle; the devil is not an ogre under a bridge who can be banished with an incantation to let travelers cross. Jedi Master Obi-Wan Kenobi does not offer us salvation, nor does Darth Vader tempt us into sin, as iconic and ever present as those characters might be. Such things were and are myth, which in the new faith, people must outgrow. Paul emphasizes the relation of reason to Christian life, which means that genuine Christians must be more than dogmatic adherents of a sectarian agenda spoon-fed them by leaders; the prophets said the same to the Hebrews. We note that Tulloch and Alvarado include *history* in their list of "intertextual" allusions in *Doctor Who.* History, as we have argued, belongs to the type of consciousness that accompanies civilized life; history, as Eliade argues, belongs particularly to Western, *Judeo-Christian* consciousness, shaped by the linear, open idea of time inaugurated in biblical apocalyptic writing and worked out (among others) by Augustine.

Perhaps the term *popular culture,* used pejoratively, misnames its object. Consider the Christianity that marked Europe up until the Reformation: the universal piety, the institutional almsgiving, the proliferating cults of the saints, and indeed the *ideas* of piety, of almsgiving, and of sainthood added up, after all, to a "popular culture," because it belonged to and endowed with an intelligible form *the people* at large. It assimilated French, Italians, Spaniards, Scandinavians, Germans, and English people to a single moral-cultural dispensation that transcended as well as absorbed local peculiarities. It had a moniker of its own: *Christendom.*

To venerate a saint meant to know something about the individual saint, which meant in turn (given that a particular sainthood was a *local* phenomenon) to know something about the history of one's native ground, the genius loci. To venerate a saint meant, at the same time, to understand that sainthood stemmed from and belonged to something beyond the local—something universal. Thus, the cults of the saints were, in the context of Christendom, elements in a type of popular history for the unlettered, which helped them understand how the *parts* of their world were integrated spiritually into a whole. To give alms meant, in the context of Christendom, to participate in a generosity that was valid and honored everywhere; to observe a social form that *other people* also observed. Even a custom such as the pre-Lenten carnival, with its granting of license during a special interregnum of the law, had a form and served a healthy function, allowing people to discharge pent-up resentments in a nondestructive, channeled way. The Teutonic carnival in Munich had its Italian-flavored counterpart in Venice; the Gallic carnival in Brussels had its Swedish-flavored counterpart in Stockholm. Christendom created universality in one sense while permitting great diversity in another, and so it avoided the pervasive conformism of modern, large-scale societies.

Modern popular culture, with its culmination in television, might better bear the name of *mass* or *commercial culture.* As Berdyaev puts it in his study *Slavery and Freedom* (1943): "The word 'people' [the root of the term *popular*] does not mean the same thing as the word 'masses.' The people is to be defined qualitatively in terms of its labor, its religious beliefs, and the plastic forms of its existence."[16] Berdyaev died forty years before MTV came into being but he might be writing about it nevertheless. The "mass," as distinguished from the "people," consists of "the irruption of vast numbers of people in whom personality is not expressed, and with whom there is no qualitative definition," but rather only "great excitability" and a readiness to be fascinated in the basest sense of that term.[17] In mass culture, as Berdyaev argues, "the making of idols is still going on."[18] As though to affirm Berdyaev's charge, a current wildly successful television program bears the title *American Idol,* and it supposedly creates a stream of newly minted celebrities—every one of whom swiftly fades from memory after receiving his or her dose of hysterical adulation. In reference to *Doctor Who,* Tulloch and Alvarado note that science fiction is past-oriented or historical, as well as being futural, but that it carefully differentiates *two* pasts. One of these is the past of ritual repetition, as in the exemplary *Doctor Who* story "The Aztecs." The other is the past in which an epochal event frees people from enslavement to ritual cycles and grants them the possibility of meaningful development beyond a parochial horizon. *Star Trek,* too, recognizes these two pasts, confronting the ritual past critically and intelligently in "Who Mourns for Adonais" and "Plato's Stepchildren," among other stories.

Science fiction has an anomalous place in television, but this misplacement merely reflects its eccentricity in popular culture widely construed. Science fiction sets its roots in metaphysics, theology, anthropology, and philosophy, as we have indicated in our introduction. Speculation about the "plurality of worlds," for example, begins with the Greek atomist philosophers five hundred years before Christ; the earliest plausible candidate for a science-fiction story, Lucian of Samosata's *True History* (200 CE), functions both as a popular entertainment (a fantastic story designed to appeal to a wide audience) and as a satire on empire and war. *True History* features an interplanetary conflict complete with the equivalent of the Death Star—the ultimate anticipation of *Star Wars*—and a subtle criticism of inhuman bureaucratic structures of the kind that characterized the Roman Empire; the impelling urge of the protagonist is a desire to break free from the meaninglessness of existence in a vast, imperial state where the citizen is reduced to a cipher. Rather like Rod Serling twenty centuries later, as reported by Sander in his book, Lucian's hero feels *dismayed and angered* by the tawdriness of a too-settled life, by complacency, and by a pervasive laziness of the mind.

The science-fiction-like texts of the sixteenth and seventeenth centuries similarly mix the themes of the heroic exploit and Viking-like exploration with philosophical and, more particularly, with *theological* discussion, as in Johannes Kepler's *Somnium* (1620–30) or Christian Huygens's *Cosmotheoros* (1698). Kepler and Huygens are also deliberate participants in the religious debates of their times, addressing the Catholic-Protestant split. Thus, science fiction at its best has been a philosophical and even a theological genre since its appearance. This thoughtful element, so essential to the genre, is what led British writer Colin Wilson (born 1931) to declare science fiction to be "quite simply . . . the most important form of literary creation that man [has] ever discovered."[19] This is because science fiction "is an attempt to stimulate the earth-bound imagination of man to grasp the immensity around him" and to engage in anthropological "self-discovery."[20]

Science fiction's determination to take a lofty view distinguishes it from other popular genres, which tend to be preoccupied with various forms of adolescent resentment. In the 1950s and '60s, it is true, westerns and crime dramas could embody a moral structure, feature adult actors, and maintain a serious tone. One remembers the Michael Ansarra series, *The Law of the Plainsman* (1959–62), in which the protagonist, a Harvard-educated full-blooded Apache, exercises justice as United States Marshal in the New Mexico Territory in the 1880s while being on friendly terms with the territory's governor, General Lew Wallace, the author of *Ben Hur*. Richard Boone's *Have Gun Will Travel* (1957–63) also benefited from excellent, culturally informed writing and an adult attitude. Like *Doctor Who,* the Ansarra and Boone series were full of literary allusions and high-cultural references. *Naked City* (1958–63) and *The Untouchables* (1959–63) likewise exhibited a thoughtful moral structure and intellectual maturity. After the demise of *The Twilight Zone,* Serling tried his hand at a western, with Lloyd Bridges in the lead, but the project met with network resistance and failed. The mid-1960s seems to have marked the demise of serious television in the United States. What is serious after the 1960s is invariably a short-lived exception.

If we look at the types of programming that have dominated American television in recent decades, we find ourselves in the midst, precisely, of youth culture. In *Beverly Hills 90210* (1990–2000) or *Dawson's Creek* (1998–2003), two immensely highly rated series, the producers focus on a world purged of adult presence, in which adolescent viewers are invited to experience the forms of petty resentment vicariously: the resentment, for example, of one foregrounded member of an erotic adolescent triangle against another; the resentment of the teenaged group against adult strictures, such as the ones restricting sexual contact; the resentment of the less affluent against the more affluent or of the athletically unsuccessful against the athletically successful.

When the producers of *Star Trek: The Next Generation* (1987–94) introduced the teenaged Wesley Crusher character (actor Will Wheaton) and thrust him to the fore, the audience reacted negatively, forcing a redirection of the story line back into the adult realm and a gradual relegation to the décor of the young ensign. Viewers of serious science-fiction programming have different criteria from other television-watching groups, as suggested by the remarks of Graham Williams, the *Doctor Who* executive quoted earlier. Putatively mature television dramas, like *NYPD Blue* or *ER,* qualify as "adult" by virtue of their profane language, sexual content, and overt violence, but they really merely exchange the high-school setting for a law-enforcement or a medical one; they retain the resentment-saturated—hence, extraordinarily dramatically limited—story lines. They seek not to edify but to titillate.

The commandments of Moses not only enjoin us from idolatry; they also enjoin us, twice no less, from *covetousness,* and covetousness is but another word for resentment. Far from liberating us from our pettiest concerns, as art is supposed to do, and as our six science-fiction series did consistently, mass-culture television programming immerses us in and goads our basest impulses. Since the world of mass-culture television programming is exclusively, vehemently, a preliterate and youth-oriented world, where a combination of narcissism and eroticism trumps everything else and where *time* does not really exist, such programming also cuts us off from any serious contact with the moral-cultural continuum.

Moral Fiction and Spiritual Life

If Rod Serling and the *Doctor Who* creators were forceful outsiders determined to disseminate their moral-critical insight, then so too were Gene Roddenberry of *Star Trek,* Patrick McGoohan of *The Prisoner,* J. Michael Straczynski of *Babylon 5,* and Chris Carter of *The X Files.* Men of persistence, each carried out a genuine struggle to bring his vision to a recalcitrant medium. Roddenberry's struggle to realize *Star Trek* is itself an epic story of visionary determination, going all the way back to the 1950s, but Straczynski's is hardly less so. Another common fact about five of the six series—we exclude *Doctor Who,* which proved exceptionally long-lived—is that, after achieving a place in the programming schedule, they seem to have inspired corporate unease, as though the medium simply could not digest them, despite the formation of a nucleus of devoted viewers. CBS, always nervous about Serling, struck *The Twilight Zone* from its schedule in 1964. NBC abandoned *Star Trek* after three seasons. The Fox Network jettisoned *Babylon 5* after four seasons. The Sci-Fi Channel then picked up the series, yet without much enthusiasm; nevertheless, *Babylon 5* did fulfill its planned five-year story line. The Sci-Fi Channel stopped production of Straczynski's sequel, *Crusade,* after thirteen episodes, however, because they discovered that people would tune in for it but leave off watching when it was over, an implied critical judgment about the Sci-Fi Channel's adjacent programming, which the executives could not stomach. The fact that *Crusade* took up serially where *Babylon 5* ended probably also told against it. In the history-less world of mass entertainment, seriality far too much resembles seriousness, and the medium must therefore discourage it. *Crusade* showed much promise and likely would have rivaled *Babylon 5* for intelligence and inventiveness, but this was not to be.

We have noted, borrowing precepts from Eliade and Berdyaev, how technical innovation has tended to betray its moral promises. Serling thought that radio had betrayed its obligations, and he looked to television to redeem the debt, which it did fitfully for a short time, only to fall into the same degraded rut as the technology that it had superseded. Even Serling's own later attempts to reprise the type of moral storytelling that made *The Twilight Zone* meritorious, as in *Night Gallery* (1969–72), could not rise to their creator's own original example. Commercial television thrives on a shallow novelty that comparison with the best would undermine—so, for many years, *The Twilight Zone* or *Star Trek* found itself banished to syndication, even more weighted down by commercial interruption than it was when in first run; the prints began to fade, and repetition in an unfit context dulled the first luster of the phenomenon. But a technical innovation would occur in the 1990s that heralded a change both in the proprietorship and in the manner of exhibition of archival television. As long as broadcasters—including cable broadcasters—decided what viewers could or would see, based on demographic sampling, the viewing market (so to speak) was not truly free in that it never really conformed to the preferences of the individual consumer. It remained mass-oriented. Videotape began to alter this, but most people found tape clumsy, bulky, and perishable, all of which it is.

The digital videodisc, or DVD, solved the technical problems associated with videotape: it is more permanent and, having no moving parts, is cheaper to manufacture than videotape; it is incapable of mechanical failure. As producers reissued the huge reservoir of archival material, even niche programming became profitable again in the new format. As long as *only* a million people will tune in to see *Babylon 5,* the program fails to justify the sponsor's investment; when a million people buy or at least regularly rent *Babylon 5,* the proposition becomes a sweeter one for the producer-distributors. Direct marketing bypasses sponsorship, which, as we have argued, always advocates for the lowest common denominator of taste. With DVD, for the first time, a genuine viewer discretion became possible and has already altered the way in which discerning people *use* the television set. As Paul Cantor, author of *Gilligan Unbound* (2002), has put it, DVD comes close to being a scholarly medium, especially where unusual or quality material is concerned—not only motion pictures but television as well. The DVD sets of *The Twilight Zone* or *Babylon 5* are richly annotated with commentary from writers, directors, and actors; viewers may watch at their discretion without submitting to the antidrama of sponsor interruptions. When the object of scrutiny possesses real merit, *watching* becomes more like *reading,* although the latter will always be a more refined activity than the former. In acts of discretion sensitive people respond most healthily and with the greatest justifiable wariness to the toxicity of contemporary mass culture; this is as it should be for those who take the gospel position (or even the Platonic or Stoic or Confucian position) that resentment and concupiscence—the main ingredients of the mass-entertainment formula—corrupt the dignity of human beings.

Once we can sift, acquire, and control our sampling of television fare, however, a qualitative change has occurred that favors critical viewing and, among other things, makes life easier for parents who would like to buffer their children, as far as possible, from the worst of commercial mass entertainment. We refer to people who, not objecting to entertainment, nevertheless think that entertainment should have some edifying justification beyond a paltry time-killing diversion and some relation to mores and to art.

It is anomalous, as we have argued, that our six series found their context, however tensely, in television; it is also anomalous, even paradoxical, that, although belonging to the science-fiction genre and dealing with planetary and other exotic settings, these six series are *more realistic* than the usual television fare. How could this be so? Roger Scruton distinguishes, in his *Intelligent Person's Guide to Modern Culture* (2000), between popular culture and high culture on the one hand and fantasy and imagination on the other. Popular (or rather mass-oriented) culture specializes in fantasy and high culture in imagination:

> The ennobling power of imagination lies in this: that it re-orders the world, and re-orders our feelings in response to it. Fantasy, by contrast, is frequently degrading, for it begins with the premise of a given emotion, which it can neither improve nor criticize but only feed. [Fantasy] is a slave of the actual, and deals in forbidden goods. Where

imagination offers glimpses of the sacred, fantasy offers sacrilege and profanation.[21]

Scruton adds that, while a civilization "may survive the religion that gave rise to it . . . it cannot survive the triumph of fantasy, cynicism and sentimentality," because these "cheapen our endeavors by directing them away from what is serious, long-term and committed, towards what is immediate, effortless and for sale."[22] Erotic melodramas, such as *Dawson's Creek,* pretend to be realistic while pandering to an adolescent desire never to grow up or face responsibility, always to have appetite (especially sexual appetite) assuaged without consequence, and automatically to be accorded status without having to pass through any of the rites or ordeals that confer it. The pretense of realism lies in the high-school setting, which is familiar and therefore seems plausible, but because the stories put no real obstacles between desire and fulfillment, and never present anyone who fails to conform to the Hollywood notions of "cool" and "pretty," they will not support the claim of verisimilitude. On the contrary, in convincing the inexperienced that they are as sophisticated as the experienced, the *Dawson's Creek* type of programming badly misleads those who naively invest in it. The cheapness is just as Scruton indicates—a cheapness of cynicism and sentimentality trapped in paltry emotions.

Removing us from the familiar, all-too-often insipid, world of our petty resentments and thwarted consumer desires, a *Star Trek* or a *Babylon 5* elevates us from the realm of easy but restricted references upward to the realm of metaphor and allegory; in leaving the familiar behind, good science-fiction stories, literary or cinematic, foreground our awareness of essential anthropological truths. What we say of *Star Trek* or *Babylon 5* we could also say of *The Twilight Zone,* with its explorations of radical contingency. We note how in the typical *Twilight Zone* story, weirdness bursts in on the familiar scene, thereby once again making the familiar provocatively unfamiliar, throwing baseless assumptions into relief, and testing our commitment to fundamental principles. A representative *Twilight Zone* episode resembles a medieval mystery play, like the well-known *Everyman*. Serling did all that he could to necessitate active, as opposed to passive, involvement in his stories.

The prototype of all radically contingent situations is the passion, in which the followers of Christ confront their human, all-too-human stature and see into those base inclinations of humanity from which Jesus, as redeemer, comes to salvage them. Peter, the most loyal, denies his master thrice; all scatter themselves into the crowd, demoralized, as the murder of the innocent victim, under official aegis, occurs. The gospel story became the basic story of the postclassical world, as the Odysseus or Oedipus story had been the basic story of the ancient world. The gospel story gives structure to the tales of King Arthur and the famous Quest for the Holy Grail; it makes itself felt in the Viking sagas, many of which directly concern the Christianization of the heathen, warrior-based society of northern Europe. The institution of chivalry stems from the assimilation of the Germanic warrior code to a specifically Christian conception of piety and decency. A knight, like Sir Lancelot, must always confront the possibility that his moral failures will disqualify him from his privileged status. Lancelot, in betraying Arthur, loses his privilege of participating in the great quest; he falls out of grace. A knight retains his status only insofar as he consistently puts Christian precepts into practice and helps others to lift themselves up from their fallen condition. Since our defects are *real,* the medieval romances, whether of Arthur and his knights or of others, were also *real,* or rather *realistic,* despite their imaginary settings and situations.

It is not at all implausible to compare *The Twilight* Zone to a medieval mystery play. Neither is it far-fetched to speak of the *Star Trek* or *Babylon 5* characters as translations of medieval knighthood, on the Arthurian model, into the only untrammeled field left open to modern people—the unknown country of planetary or galactic space. In this way, science fiction, like medieval legend, is a genre that seeks *to transfigure* the baseness of a fallen world into something ideal and so provide its audience with a transcendental criterion to guide its development, whether individual or social. Berdyaev writes in *Slavery and Freedom,* in words that correspond with those of Scruton on fantasy and imagination, that

> the liberating significance of art lies . . . in its unlikeness to this repellent and ugly life of ours, this life fettered by necessity. . . . Art in its way reveals the truth about life, the most grievous and torturing truth. . . . We find in [art] a passing over to another world, to another plane of existence, [and a type of] idealism, which, as it were, anticipates a new reality. . . . Art is [thus] creative transfiguration, not yet real transfiguration, but an anticipation of that transfiguration. . . . Art is not passive but active, and in this sense theurgic.[23]

Berdyaev's words address art generically, while we are writing of science fiction, a more particular topic, as it manifests itself in our six television programs. In contrasting *Doctor Who* or *The Prisoner* to the run of mass-entertainment television, however, we find ourselves making a point that is central to Berdyaev's larger critique and that we therefore gladly adopt.

When, as Berdyaev argues, an art permits itself to pander to an audience comprised of "consumers" rather than "creators"—to the mass of *passive* people, that is, rather than to the nucleus of *active* ones—then a noxious atmosphere of "snobbery," or what we have called petty resentment, begins to corrode "freedom of spirit."[24] Science fiction at its best has always aimed at the same integral standards as high art taken as a whole and has therefore always sought to engage its audience in the great imaginative thought-experiment whereby we contemplate anthropology and theology in the form of poetic figures engaged in moral struggle on an unfamiliar stage that throws actions into relief. In their willingness to join in the continuum of the Western tradition—especially in their willingness to engage topics that come to light in the Gospels—our six series constitute severally an attempt to bring to the fallen medium of television a lofty narration that will elevate rather than debase those who turn their steady attention to it. *Babylon 5, Doctor Who, The Prisoner, Star Trek, The Twilight Zone,* and *The X Files* show that, despite the failures of our age, the influence of the gospel story is still active, still fecund, still conducive to what Berdyaev calls the "co-operation" and "joint action of man and God"[25] in morally based works of art. We see in *The Twilight Zone* or *Babylon 5* the questing spirit reaching upward from the plane of everyday life into the realms of revelation and redemption.

Notes

Chapter 1: Grappling with the "Powers"

1. J. Douglas, ed., *The New Greek-English Interlinear New Testament,* trans. Robert K. Brown and Philip W. Comfort (Wheaton, IL: Tyndale House, 1990).

2. René Girard, *I See Satan Fall like Lightning,* trans. James G. Williams (Maryknoll, NY: Orbis Books, 2001), 96.

3. Ibid., 96.

4. Ibid., 97.

5. David J. Howe and Stephen James Walker, *The Unofficial and Unauthorised Guide to* Doctor Who (Tolworth, Surrey: Telos Books, 2003), 450.

6. Barry Letts (after Guy Leopold), *Doctor Who and the Daemons* (Tiptree, Essex: Target Books, 1971), 9.

7. Also translated as *The Devils* or *The Possessed.*

8. Stalin began life as a seminarian of the Georgian Orthodox Church but got himself expelled from his novitiate, after which he pursued revolutionary politics and bank robbery. His hostility to religion—to Christianity and Judaism alike—in the later, political phases of his career, takes on a suspicious coloring against this background. Stalin's notorious "cult of personality" indeed shows all the hallmarks of the primitive cult of the god-king, as in Egypt. To refer to this cult as "religious" is, therefore, not to blaspheme but simply to make an anthropological observation: Stalin, like Hitler (with his carefully cultivated reversion to Germanic paganism), is a throwback to primitive forms.

9. Letts, *Doctor Who and the Daemons,* 62.

10. Ibid.

11. Ibid., 84.

12. Girard has pointed out that, by a rigorous reading of Genesis, Cain is the founder of the first actual society, a society founded on Cain's sacrificial murder of his brother Abel; Genesis tells how Cain founded a people, who took his name, after he was driven into the wilderness in punishment for his fratricide. The

Canaanites, who possess the promised land prior to the arrival of the Hebrews (who, on settling down there, become the Jews), are linked by their name to the establisher of human sacrifice; the Canaanites themselves practice sacrificial infanticide, which, taking the prophets seriously, exercised great allure over the Jews, who regularly lapsed from their Mosaic religion.

13. Letts, *Doctor Who and the Daemons,* 102.

14. René Girard , *Violence and the Sacred,* trans. P. Gregory (Baltimore: Johns Hopkins University Press, 1977), 133.

15. Letts, *Doctor Who and the Daemons,* 78.

16. Ibid., 79.

17. Ibid., 28.

18. Ibid., 88.

19. Ibid., 92.

20. Ibid., 170.

21. Ibid.

22. Terrance Dicks (after David Fisher), *Doctor Who and the Stones of Blood* (Tiptree, Essex: Target Books, 1980), 33.

23. Ibid., 23.

24. René Girard, *The Scapegoat,* trans. Y. Freccero (Baltimore: Johns Hopkins University Press, 1986), 156.

25. Ibid.

26. Dicks, *Doctor Who and the Stones of Blood,* 35.

27. Terrance Dicks (after Chris Boucher), *Doctor Who and the Image of the Fendahl* (Tiptree, Essex: Target Books, 1979), 65.

Chapter 2: Christian Virtues and Human Nature

1. These are *Star Trek: The Motion Picture* (1979), *Star Trek II: The Wrath of Khan* (1982), *Star Trek III: The Search for Spock* (1984), *Star Trek IV: The Voyage Home* (1986), *Star Trek V: The Final Frontier* (1989), *Star Trek VI: The Undiscovered Country* (1991), *Star Trek: Generations* (1994), *Star Trek: First Contact* (1996), *Star Trek: Insurrection* (1998), and *Star Trek: Nemesis* (2002).

2. Cf. Jeffrey Scott Lamp, "Biblical Interpretation in the *Star Trek* Universe: Going Where Some Have Gone Before," in Star Trek *and Sacred Ground: Explorations of* Star Trek, *Religion, and American Culture*, ed. J. E. Porter and D. L. McLaren (Albany: State University of New York Press, 2000), 193–214, esp. 193 (quoting Okuda): "*Star Trek* has indeed become an icon of 20th-century popular culture."

3. Ibid.

4. Cf. Robert Asa, "Classic *Star Trek* and the Death of God: A Case Study of 'Who Mourns for Adonais?'" in Star Trek *and Sacred Ground: Explorations of* Star Trek, *Religion, and American Culture,* ed. J. E. Porter and D. L. McLaren (Albany: State University of New York Press, 2000), 33–59, esp. 33: "It [*Star Trek*] was a generally well-written, well-acted, serious attempt to comment on current social issues in the guise of science fiction. Previously, only *The Twilight Zone* had used the genre for so lofty a purpose."

5. On *Star Trek* as a "morality play," see Ina Rae Hark, "*Star Trek* and Television's Moral Universe," *Extrapolation* 20 (1979), 20–37, esp. 21; and Jon Wagner and Jan Lundeen, *Deep Space and Sacred Time:* Star Trek *in the American Mythos* (Westport and London: Praeger, 1998), 31: "These are, after all, morality plays, and much of the morality they champion has its parallels in religious tradition. In these and other *Trek* stories, people must resist the temptation to give in to their basic animal impulses—fear, lust, aggression, the desire for security—in favor of such higher motives as duty, loyalty, compassion, and sacrificial love." On Roddenberry's hostility toward religion, see Anne Mackenzie Pearson, "From Thwarted Gods to Reclaimed Mystery? An Overview of the Depiction of Religion in *Star Trek,*" in Star Trek *and Sacred Ground: Explorations of* Star Trek, *Religion, and American Culture,* ed. J. E. Porter and D. L. McLaren (Albany: State University of New York Press, 2000), 13–31, esp. 15; Wagner and Lundeen, *Deep Space and Sacred Time,* 32, with bibliography.

6. E.g., Kenneth Marsalek, "*Star Trek*: Humanism of the Future," *Free Inquiry* 12.4 (1992), 53–56; Pearson, "From Thwarted Gods to Reclaimed Mystery?" 14: "In *Star Trek*, organized religion tends to be portrayed as the product of a pre-rational age, antithetical to science and reason, and God is depicted as a category mistake—an advanced alien life-form mistaken for a god."

7. Cf. Wagner and Lundeen, *Deep Space and Sacred Time,* 33: "Indeed, the 'human' virtues that *Trek* explicitly upholds, such as self-control, sobriety, knowledge, courage, friendship and attention to duty, are parallel to many of the ideals that Americans can associate with their moral upbringing as Christians, Muslims, Jews, and so on." The compatibility of *Star Trek* with Christianity is taken to an extreme in an early commentary on the series: Betsy Caprio, Star Trek*: Good News in Modern Images* (Kansas City: Sheed Andrews and McMeel, 1978).

8. This is most often done by Spock touching the other being's head, but when the plot requires it, it can also be accomplished without physical contact (e.g., "The Omega Glory").

9. See esp. Asa, "Classic *Star Trek* and the Death of God." Pearson ("From Thwarted Gods to Reclaimed Mystery?") does note more sympathy for religion in the later series and movies.

10. Cf. Wagner and Lundeen, *Deep Space and Sacred Time,* 32: "The denunciation of false gods is not in itself antireligious; on the contrary, it appears in the Bible."

11. Ibid., 30.

12. The *Twilight Zone* episode "Stopover in a Quiet Town" uses exactly the same plot twist, though more sinisterly.

13. Kirk's quotation in the episode; Milton's original is "Better to reign in Hell, than serve in Heav'n" (*Paradise Lost,* 1.263). Khan will return in the second *Star Trek* movie to wreak much more havoc.

14. Cf. Hark, "*Star Trek* and Television's Moral Universe," 35: "Baldly stated, paradise must be destroyed because paradise threatens the *Enterprise*. . . . The series often raises interesting moral questions only to dodge them because one choice alone can save the ship."

15. Wagner and Lundeen, *Deep Space and Sacred Time,* 31.

16. Cf. Hark, "*Star Trek* and Television's Moral Universe," 35: "What it all boils down to is that Roddenberry believes work and progress are the tools to redeem the fallen world; he possesses the Faustian vision that continued striving leads to salvation and that to try to arrest the perfect moment or situation inevitably kills the soul"; Pearson, "From Thwarted Gods to Reclaimed Mystery?" 29: "From most religions' point of view, our capacity for spiritual growth (or moral perfection, if you will) is what defines us as humans."

17. On the other hand, the nobility of sacrificing the good of the individual for the good of the group—when it is willingly embraced by the individual and not forced on him or her—is the central theme of the second and third movies in the franchise: see J. Wagner, "Intimations of Immortality: Death/Life Mediations in *Star Trek,*" in Star Trek *and Sacred Ground: Explorations of* Star Trek, *Religion, and American Culture,* ed. J. E. Porter and D. L. McLaren (Albany: State University of New York Press, 2000), 119–37, esp. 125–29.

18. There is a reference to the translation in "Is There in Truth No Beauty?" and it is confirmed by the online Swahili-English dictionary at http://www.yale.edu/swahili/. It would fit with the idea that each show is a "morality play," for medieval morality plays were populated by characters named for abstractions such as "Beauty" or "Vice."

19. Cf. Lamp, "Biblical Interpretation in the *Star Trek* Universe," 194: "Throw in a 'half-breed' alien and an interracial kiss and one is left with a society that approximates Dr. Martin Luther King's 'I Have a Dream' speech."

20. Cf. Hark, "*Star Trek* and Television's Moral Universe," 32: "What exactly does *Star Trek* define as paradise? It is a place where security and happiness are given, not earned. Contentment becomes uniform, and diverse elements in need of harmony level off to a common denominator. Ultimately it qualifies as another form of excess."

21. Jane Elizabeth Ellington and Joseph W. Critelli, "Analysis of a Modern Myth: The *Star Trek* Series," *Extrapolation* 24 (1983), 241–50, quotation on 243, though they include Scott in the holistic group.

22. Karen Blair, *Meaning in* Star Trek (Chambersburg, PA: Anima Books, 1977), 41.

23. In addition to the works by Ellington, Critelli, and Blair cited in the previous two notes, analysis of the three main characters is treated in Richard Hanley, *The Metaphysics of* Star Trek (New York: Basic Books, 1997), 4–39; and Diana J. Schaub, "Captain Kirk and the Art of Rule," in *Faith, Reason, and Political Life,* ed. Peter Augustine Lawler and Dale McConkey (Lanham, MD: Lexington Books, 2001), 261–71.

24. Cf. Schaub, "Captain Kirk and the Art of Rule," 265: "Because *Star Trek* revives the tripartite Platonic soul and particularly its problematic third element, *thumos,* its account of the soul is fuller than the modern psychiatric account."

25. Cf. Hark, "*Star Trek* and Television's Moral Universe," 29: "Vulcans do not lack emotions; in their distant past they in fact suffered from an overabundance of aggression. To save themselves from destruction, they developed their logical powers to the extent that these emotions are always in constant control."

26. Cf. Schaub, "Captain Kirk and the Art of Rule," 266: "His [Spock's] mistakes all stem from his failure to share in, or at least understand, an outraged sense of justice, on the part of both the crew and the creatures."

27. The "sense of wonder" or awe at life and the universe is a fundamental quality of *Star Trek:* see Thomas Richards, *The Meaning of* Star Trek (New York: Doubleday, 1997), 149–85.

28. Spock's aesthetics are somewhat ambiguous, as he is repeatedly shown to be a virtuoso on the Vulcan harp (e.g., "Charlie X," "The Way to Eden") and even smiles while playing it.

29. Perhaps because of his more extensive experience with evil and subterfuge, Spock seems better equipped to combat it. His evaluation of it in "And the Children Shall Lead" is quite realistic: "Evil does seek to maintain power by suppressing the truth. . . . Without followers, evil cannot spread."

30. Cf. Richards, *Meaning of* Star Trek, 184: "*Star Trek* may at times seem to favor reason over revelation, but when it comes right down to it, the series does not trust reason too far. In the *Star Trek* universe reason always requires revelation as a stay against a lifeless rationality."

31. Thus Blair, *Meaning in* Star Trek, 35–40.

32. Ibid., 35.

33. Cf. Hark, "*Star Trek* and Television's Moral Universe," 32, 34: "The series contains a definite Puritan streak that looks unfavorably upon unmitigated happiness. . . . But just because Kirk lives by the work ethic, why must they?"

34. This is an important difference from the Platonic analysis of the soul: see Schaub, "Captain Kirk and the Art of Rule," 266: "Despite *Star Trek*'s debt to the ancient account of the soul, this is not Plato's *Republic.* Instead of spirited auxiliaries assisting a philosopher-king, here spiritedness rules in consultation with both reason and appetite."

35. See ibid., 267–68, who uses the more accurate labels "gentle" and "fierce" for the two Kirks.

36. Cf. ibid., 269: "*Star Trek* insists upon the dignity of those who meet the difficulties of the human condition with maturity and virtue. Its antileveling animus is most apparent in those episodes that deal with children ('Miri' and 'Charlie X') or overgrown children ('The Squire of Gothos,' and 'Elaan of Troyius'). There is none of the contemporary idealization of youth. Self-control and responsible action are presented as choiceworthy."

37. Cf. Lamp, "Biblical Interpretation in the *Star Trek* Universe," 194: "The vision has always been more than a vehicle to carry the storylines; it has also contained a strong element of proclamation. As such, it is a vision of aspiration, a vision for humanity's place in the scheme of things, at root a prescriptive vision for how a constructive future may and perhaps should look."

38. *Star Trek*'s evaluation of human limitations could be highly heuristic in current debates over our meddling in biological processes through abortion, cloning, genetic engineering, or euthanasia: we may well have the intelligence to manipulate such processes, but may never attain the wisdom to do so without causing awful, unforeseen, and irreparable harm.

39. Wagner and Lundeen, *Deep Space and Sacred Time,* 31.

40. It was Hark ("*Star Trek* and Television's Moral Universe," 23–24) who reminded us of this episode's importance and offered a trenchant analysis.

41. The episode deliberately accentuates the similarities between the two commanders, having the Klingon admiringly say to Kirk, "You are much like us," and giving him a name, Kor, that is strikingly similar to Kirk's. See Schaub, "Captain Kirk and the Art of Rule," 263: "The enemy commanders always admire Kirk. (Their names too usually begin with the same strong 'K,' witness the Klingon commanders Kor, Koloth, and Kang, as well as the superman Khan)."

42. Cf. Caprio, Star Trek*: Good News in Modern Images,* 77: "Our best heroes, just like David and Paul and many other Biblical heroes, have human weaknesses."

43. The identification of McCoy with the Samaritan is from Blair, *Meaning in* Star Trek, 34.

44. See the excellent analysis of Larry Kreitzer, "Suffering, Sacrifice and Redemption: Biblical Imagery in *Star Trek,*" in Star Trek *and Sacred Ground: Explorations of* Star Trek*, Religion, and American Culture,* ed. J. E. Porter and D. L. McLaren (Albany: State University of New York Press, 2000), 139–63, esp. 142: "'The Empath' strikes at the heart of the theological dimension of the faith, namely, the sacrificial death of Jesus Christ on behalf of others."

45. Also noted by ibid., 144: "The second image, much more graphic in its expression, is the fact that both Kirk and McCoy, each in his own turn, is tortured by the Vians by being suspended from chains in a typical crucifixion pose, with arms outstretched and (in the case of Kirk) the upper body exposed."

46. Gem therefore basically combines the powers of two of the X-Men: Rogue can transfer other superheroes' powers to herself, and Wolverine is capable of miraculous self-healing.

47. Schaub, "Captain Kirk and the Art of Rule," 261, 269.

48. Cf. Wagner and Lundeen, *Deep Space and Sacred Time,* 22–23, 33: "*Trek* explores this potentially divisive issue in a way that only myth can do, reframing it on a plane where it appears, however illusively, to lend itself to reconciliation—and what's more, a reconciliation that valorizes humanism while avoiding an overt confrontation with America's religious sensitivities and even, for some fans and commentators, expressing a serendipitous harmony with Judeo-Christian ideals. . . . Human self-determination is not, in American popular belief, incompatible with religion. The uplifting, empowering 'Wizard of Oz' moment echoes repeatedly in the *Star Trek* theme of the false-god-exposed; and although such a revelation can be read as antireligious, our culture allows us the latitude to read it in other ways—to have our humanism and our religion too, if we so choose."

49. Hark, "*Star Trek* and Television's Moral Universe," 37.

Chapter 3: Human Freedom

1. "The Prisoner," from the album *The Number of the Beast,* which begins with the opening narration from the show (EMI, 1982).

2. The commentaries consulted for this chapter are Steven Paul Davies, *The Prisoner Handbook* (London: Boxtree, 2002), and Matthew White and Jaffer Ali,

The Official Prisoner Companion (New York: Warner Books, 1988). The others are hard to obtain on this side of the Atlantic. On fan activities and publications, see Davies, *Prisoner Handbook,* 165–93.

3. On the possible film, see Davies, *Prisoner Handbook,* 220–26.

4. See ibid., 38; White and Ali, *Official Prisoner Companion,* 133–34. What claims to be a photo of the original Rover is now on one *Prisoner* website: http://www.retroweb.com/prisoner.html.

5. See White and Ali, *Official Prisoner Companion,* 33, for a discussion of this scene.

6. On how McGoohan got the idea for Rover's death, see Davies, *Prisoner Handbook,* 66–67.

7. Cf. Alex Cox, writing in the foreword in ibid., 12: "I cannot remember an episode in which Number Six was more than momentarily violent. . . . Because of the series' essential pacifism and surrealism, it isn't possible to eagerly await a big-budget Hollywood dose of soma."

8. See ibid., 12, 137; White and Ali, *Official Prisoner Companion,* 84–85, 147–48.

9. R. K. Prabhu and U. R. Rao, *The Mind of Mahatma Gandhi,* rev. ed. (Ahemadabad: Navajivan, 1967), ch. 28, "Between Cowardice and Violence," available online at http://www.mkgandhi.org/momgandhi/momindex.htm.

10. The interpretation and application of such difficult exhortations is, of course, a matter of some debate, but the inclusion of humor and sarcasm in Jesus's preaching is noticeable. On the difficult sayings on nonretaliation, see W. Wink, "Neither Passivity nor Violence: Jesus' Third Way (Matt. 5:38–42 par.)," in *The Love of Enemy and Nonretaliation in the New Testament,* ed. Willard M. Swartley (Louisville: Westminster John Knox Press, 1992), 102–25. On humor in Jesus's parables in general, see Kenneth E. Bailey, *Poet and Peasant* (Grand Rapids: Eerdmans, 1976), and idem, *Through Peasant Eyes* (Grand Rapids: Eerdmans, 1980). On humor in Luke's Gospel in particular, see Joseph A. Grassi, *God Makes Me Laugh: A New Approach to Luke* (Wilmington, DE: Michael Glazier, 1986).

11. All three of these episodes were written and directed by McGoohan himself: see Davies, *Prisoner Handbook,* 87–89, 142–52; White and Ali, *Official Prisoner Companion,* 28–34, 103–17.

12. According to White and Ali (*Official Prisoner Companion,* 33), the scene was not shown in the original broadcast in Great Britain, because of its violence.

13. Filmed shortly after *The Prisoner,* the final scene of *Beneath the Planet of the Apes* (1970) plays out in a similar setting with similarly bizarre, fanatical, robed figures.

14. White and Ali (*Official Prisoner Companion,* 113) interpret their chant as "Aye, aye, aye." The series is full of such homophones, such as the recurring music, which can be heard as either "For He's a Jolly Good Fellow" or "The Bear Went over the Mountain," both of which are appropriate to the series.

15. Cf. White and Ali (*Official Prisoner Companion,* 165), who set these two explanations in opposition, but this seems unnecessary. Cf. the interview with McGoohan given in Davies, *Prisoner Handbook,* 176: "It was about the most

evil human being, human essence, and that is ourselves. It is within each of us. That is the most dangerous thing on Earth, what is within us. So, therefore, that is what I made Number 1—oneself—an image of oneself which he was trying to beat."

16. Cf. the list of contemporary parallels to the *Prisoner*'s dehumanizing society in Davies, *Prisoner Handbook,* 153–63.

17. See White and Ali, *Official Prisoner Companion,* 171–73.

18. See Davies, *Prisoner Handbook,* 22, 214, 228; White and Ali, *Official Prisoner Companion,* 123, 177, 181.

19. See the list online at http://www.afi.com/tvevents/100years/handv.aspx.

20. Davies, *Prisoner Handbook,* 214.

Chapter 4: Sin and Grace

1. Marc Scott Zicree, *The Twilight Zone Companion,* 2nd ed. (Los Angeles: Silman-James Press, 1989).

2. Ibid., xii.

3. Augustine, *Confessions,* 1.7.11, translation by Kim Paffenroth.

4. Ibid., 3.7.12.

Chapter 5: The In-Breaking Bedazzlement of Truth

1. Eric Voegelin, *Order and History,* vol. 4, *The Ecumenic Age* (Baton Rouge: Louisiana State University Press, 1974), 251–52.

2. Quoted on the Redwolf *X Files* website, season 2, "End Game," http://www.redwolf.com.au/xviles/season02/2x17.html.

3. The word *apocalypse* is Greek; the word *revelation* is Latin, related to such English terms as *to reveal* or *to unveil*. The Greek word functions metaphorically, for a *calypton* is a humble kitchen item, the lid of a cooking pot; the prefix, *apo*, signifies removal, so that the root meaning of *apocalypse* is "to lift off the lid." The Greek word for truth, *aletheia,* is also a negation: translating literally, one would have to render it into English as "unforgetting," for *lethe* means forgetfulness while the *a* is a prefixative negation.

4. Edgar Allan Poe, edited by H. Beaver, *The Science Fiction of Edgar Allan Poe* (New York: Penguin, 1976), 306–7.

5. Ibid., 70–71.

6. E. R. Dodds, *Pagan and Christian in an Age of Anxiety: Some Aspects of Religious Experience form Marcus Aurelius to Constantine* (New York: Norton, 1970), 20, 19.

7. Voegelin, *Ecumenic Age*, 265, 256.

8. Ibid., 254, 256.

9. Robin Lane Fox, *Pagans and Christians* (New York: Harper and Row, 1986), 122.

10. Ibid.

11. Ibid., 123.

12. Jim Marrs, *Alien Agenda: Investigating the Extraterrestrial Presence among Us* (New York: Harper-Collins, 1997), 564.

13. Ted Edwards, X-Files *Confidential: The Unauthorized X-Philes Compendium* (New York: Little, Brown, 1996), 11.

14. John E. Mack, *Abduction* (New York: Charles Scribner's Sons, 1994), 418.

15. Quoted on the Redwolf *X Files* website, season 2, "Colony," http://www.redwolf.com.au/xfiles/season02/2x16.html.

16. Mack, *Abduction,* 418.

17. Ibid.

18. Quoted on http://www.ufoevidence.org/documents/doc839.htm.

19. Quoted on the Redwolf *X Files* website, season 1, "EBE," http://www.redwolf.com.au/xfiles/season01/1x16.html.

20. Quoted on the Redwolf *X Files* website, season 1, "Deep Throat," http://www.redwolf.com.au/xfiles/season01/1x01.html.

21. Ibid.

22. Ibid.

23. Ibid.

24. Quoted on the Redwolf *X Files* website, season 1, "Conduit," http://www.redwolf.com.au/xfiles/season01/1x03.html.

25. Ibid.

26. Quoted by Brian Lowry, *Trust No One: The Official Third Season Guide to the X Files* (New York: Harper Prism, 1996), 209.

27. Mack, *Abduction,* 324.

28. Ibid., 324–25.

29. Jacques Vallée, *Dimensions* (New York: Ballantine Books, 1988), 243.

30. Quoted on the Redwolf *X Files* website, season 2, "Little Green Men," http://www.redwolf.com.au/xfiles/season02/2x01.html.

31. Quoted on the Redwolf *X Files* website, season 3, "The Blessing Way," http://www.redwolf.com.au/xfiles/season03/3x01.html.

32. Quoted by Brian Lowry in *The Truth Is Out There: The Official Guide to the X Files* (New York: Harper Prism, 1995), 233.

33. Victor Klemper is a somewhat unfortunate choice of names, as it is a variant of Klemperer, a typically Jewish name; in fact, a Victor Klemperer, a Jewish-German resident of Dresden, wrote a series of diaries during World War II describing his experiences under the anti-Semitic regime. Is it a coincidence that these diaries appeared in English translation around the time of the *X Files* episode in question? Probably not, so the writers should have been more discerning.

34. Quoted from the third-season DVD set (Twentieth Century Fox, 2001).

35. Quoted on the Redwolf *X Files* website, season 3, "Talitha Cumi," http://www.redwolf.com.au/xfiles/season03/3x24.html.

36. Quoted on http://www.turning-pages.com/xf101/text/3x02.htm.

37. The name Richard Matheson is not random or coincidental. Richard Matheson was a writer of genre fiction in the 1940s, '50s, and '60s, specializing in science fiction, fantasy, and the macabre; he wrote many scripts for *The Twilight Zone*.

38. Quoted from the third-season DVD set (Twentieth Century Fox, 2001).

39. Quoted on the Redwolf *X Files* website, season 3, "Piper Maru," http://www.redwolf.com.au/xfiles/season03/3x15.html.

40. Voegelin, *Ecumenic Age*, 253–54.

41. Ibid., 261.

42. Quoted on the Redwolf *X Files* website, season 3, "Talitha Cumi," http://www.redwolf.com.au/xfiles/season03/3x24.html.

43. Quoted on the Redwolf *X Files* website, season 3, "Jose Chung's 'From Outer Space,'" http://www.redwolf.com.au/xfiles/season03/3x20.html.

44. Ibid.

Chapter 6: Preaching the Word

1. Eric L. Gans, *Science and Faith: The Anthropology of Revelation* (Baltimore: Rowman and Littlefield, 1990), 114.

2. Heraclitus, *Fragments*, trans. Brooks Haxton (New York: Penguin, 2001); quotations from 3, 63, 23, 3, 5.

3. Eric L. Gans, *Originary Thinking* (Stanford: Stanford University Press, 1992), 60.

4. Quoted in http://www.chronology.org/noframes/b-five/visions.html.

5. Quoted in http://www.mateengreenway.com/b5/b5.htm.

6. Heraclitus, *Fragments*, 61.

7. Gans, *Originary Thinking*, 48.

8. Quoted in the Science Fiction Timeline website, "Final Note of Season 3," http://www.chronology.org/b-five/.

9. Quoted in http://www.worldsofjms.com/usenet/post.oso13oa.htm.

10. Augustine, *Confessions*, trans. A. C. Outler (New York: Dover, 2002), 7.9.114.

11. Plotinus, *The Enneads*, trans. S. Mackenna, ed. J. Dillon (New York: Penguin, 1991), 233.

12. Ibid., 247.

13. Ibid.

14. Ibid., 545.

15. Plotinus, *Enneads*, 424.

16. Augustine, *Confessions*, 7.8.120–21.

17. As our introduction remarks, this sense of God's creation, as something beautiful and good, is the ultimate ground of science; because modern science likes to distinguish itself institutionally from religion, the commonality that affiliates them has become lost to contemporary people. One of the nice touches of *Babylon 5* is the way in which its producers blend the moral and scientific projects of their characters.

18. In *Early Christian Writings*, trans. by Maxwell Staniforth (New York: Penguin, 1987), 179.

19. Lucretius, *On the Nature of the Universe*, trans. R. E. Latham (New York: Penguin, 1994), 2.65.

20. William Olaf Stapledon, *Star Maker*, in *Two Science Fiction Novels by Olaf Stapledon* (New York: Dover, 1968), 317.

21. Ibid., 345.

22. Quoted in http://www.babylonsounds.com/en/staffel5_en.html.

23. Quoted in the online Lurker's Guide to *Babylon 5*, http://www.midwinter.com/lurk/guide/102.htm.

24. Heraclitus, *Fragments*, 27.

Toward a Conclusion

1. Mircea Eliade, "The Terror of History," in *The Myth of the Eternal Return* (Princeton, N.J.: Princeton University Press, 1974), 161.

2. Nicolas Berdyaev, *Truth and Revelation*, trans. R. M. French (London: Geoffrey Bless, 1953), 44.

3. In David Kyle, *The Illustrated Book of Science Fiction Ideas and Dreams* (New York: Hamlyn, 1977), 131.

4. Augustine, *Confessions*, trans. A. C. Outler (1955; repr. Mineola, NY: Dover, 2002), 13.

5. Ibid., 14.

6. Eliade, *Myth of the Eternal Return*, 152.

7. Gordon F. Sander, *Rod Serling: The Rise and Twilight of Television's Last Angry Man* (New York: Dutton, 1993), 69.

8. Ibid.

9. Ibid., 143.

10. In ibid., 148–49.

11. David J. Howe and Stephen James Walker, *The Unofficial and Unauthorised Guide to* Doctor Who (Tolworth, Surrey: Telos Books, 2003), 437.

12. Ibid., 337.

13. John Tulloch and Manuel Alvarado, *Doctor Who: The Unfolding Text* (New York: Saint Martin's Press, 1983), 151.

14. Ibid.

15. Ibid., 152.

16. Nicolas Berdyaev, *Slavery and Freedom*, trans. R. M. French (London: Centenary Press, 1944), 121.

17. Ibid., 151.

18. Ibid., 152.

19. Colin Wilson, *Science Fiction as Existentialism* (Hayes, Middlesex: Bran's Head, 1978), 2–3.

20. Ibid., 3–4.

21. Roger Scruton, *The Intelligent Person's Guide to Modern Culture* (South Bend, Ind.: Saint Augustine's Press, 2000), 60.

22. Ibid., 67.

23. Berdyaev, *Slavery and Freedom*, 241.

24. Ibid., 240.

25. Ibid., 243.

INDEX